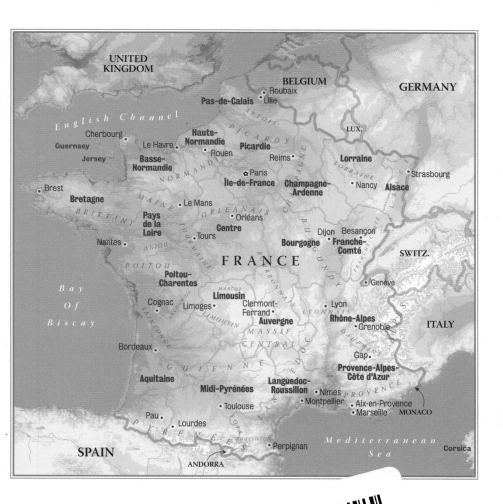

Luxury Hotels

Boutique Hotels of the World
www.greatsmallhotels.com

Five Star Alliance
www.fivestaralliance.com

Grandes Étapes Française
www.grandesetapes.fr

Great Hoi
www.ghotv

**Johansens L
and Spas**
www.johansen

Luxury Hotels of the World
www.lhw.com

...ith.com

& Châteaux
www.relaischateaux.com

**Small Luxury Hotels
of the World**
www.slh.com

GRAHAM WATSON'S

TOUR DE FRANCE
TRAVEL GUIDE

BOULDER, COLORADO

1830 55th Street
Boulder, Colorado 80301-2700 USA
303/440-0601 · Fax 303/444-6788 · E-mail velopress@competitorgroup.com

Distributed in the United States and Canada by Publishers Group West

Library of Congress Cataloging-in-Publication Data
Watson, Graham, 1956–
Graham Watson's Tour de France travel guide / Graham Watson.
     p.   cm.
   Includes index.
   ISBN 978-1-934030-38-7 (pbk.: alk. paper)
   1. Tour de France (Bicycle race)—Guidebooks.   I. Title.
II. Title: Tour de France travel guide.
GV1049.2.T68W39   2009
796.6—dc22   2009007407

For information on purchasing VeloPress books, please call 800/234-8356
or visit www.velopress.com.

Photographs by Graham Watson except those listed below.
Ted Costantino: pages 46, 71, 77 (both), 84, 179, 180, 181, 182 (bottom), 183
Casey B. Gibson: page 292
Hans-Alfred Roth: page 272
Presse-Sports: 264, 266 (both), 267, 268
Maps by Charles Chamberlin
Cover and interior design by Erin Johnson
Title font Archive Grotesque Shaded; body text typeset in Warnock Pro and
Bureau Grotesque

09 10 11 / 10 9 8 7 6 5 4 3 2 1

CONTENTS

ACKNOWLEDGMENTS

Travel writer or photographer? Or perhaps a bit of each. Who better than a photographer to write a book about traveling around France and seeing the Tour? After all, it is the photographer who sees everything as he works, sees how the cyclists race, sees the beauty of where they race and sometimes the drama when it all goes wrong. The photographer spots a snowy alpine peak many minutes before the Tour gets anywhere near it, and he glimpses a picturesque cascade that has escaped the attention of just about everyone else. The photographer uses his observational skills to record other things in his day-to-day life on Le Tour—a medieval village in Provence, villagers playing *boules* in Drôme, children dressed in the regional costumes of Brittany, and vacationers picnicking alongside the road in Languedoc.

The same photographer remembers a certain village inn five years after he stayed there, and the precise details of a succulent meal he savored in a remarkable restaurant one year earlier. The photographer sees, records, and remembers just about everything passing in front of his eyes, making him the perfect person to write this guide. Even so, photographic memory only works so well, and is not as consistent nor as profound as its possessor would wish; the passing of the years has left its toll on even my attentive brain.

Which is why this guide came about with the help of several people and enthusiastic use of the Internet. Through friends like Jacqueline and Jacky Koch, I've had my eyes opened to a Gallic world that is there only for those who know it's there—cuisine, culture, character, and traditions have all been laid bare before me. Similarly, Paul Sherwen, a seven-time competitor in the Tour and television commentator who is as fluent in French as any foreigner can decently be, shared his understanding of French life, which was a gold mine of information for this comparative heathen.

It is to the Internet that I have turned to fix any human failings, and in so doing have discovered an absolute almanac of information. Sites like www.memoire-du-cyclisme.net have become my stablemate for all things cycling and the Tour, while extensive dependence has been placed on *Wikipedia* for just about everything else, it seems, leaving me to wonder how on earth travel writers managed their research in pre-Internet days! As a great fan of travel and adventure, I've kept just about every map or atlas I ever bought, and have used them extensively to recall a route I once took or the name of some obscure road I once cycled on. Even so, interactive sites like www.viamichelin.com have covered more ground in far less time than a paper map ever could have, and I cannot recommend the virtues of this site more strongly, even if there are other, similar sites to work from.

My quest to recall hotel and restaurant names from years ago has led me through a myriad of helpful sites, and in doing so introduced me to establishments I plan to visit in the future. The Web site www.aftouch-cuisine.com repaired the many gaps in my culinary knowledge, most especially in the identification of regional dishes, while www.patriciawells.com took me deeper into the kitchen with some choice recipes and cooking phrases that further lifted the mystery that is French food. And speaking of food, I should also thank Lance Armstrong for winning the Tour seven times; without his successes, I'd still be a slave to roadside pizza vans and only rarely entertained in serious restaurants and hotels. Thank you one and all!

INTRODUCTION

It's not often anyone can claim that a single voyage changed his life, but in 1977 one such journey changed mine forever. That many summers ago, I traveled to Paris as part of an organized trip with fellow cycling fans to see the tail end of the Tour de France. It was my first sighting of the great race, and also my first experience of the French capital and all its magnificence.

If my young eyes were engrossed almost totally by the racers and the race, at least a small part of my attention was captured by the majesty of my surroundings, first by the eye-opener that was the Palais de Versailles and then, a day later, by the Arc de Triomphe and its famous avenue to the east, the Champs-Élysées.

I became smitten at once with Paris and the Tour, and returned in 1978 with far greater ambitions, choosing to leave behind the group and strike out alone, save for the company of a friend on certain days. We used a combination of car and bicycle to see the whole Tour. By 1979, we were using only our bikes to get from stage to stage, with the occasional help of a train for the longer transfers. A car replaced the bicycle in 1980, but I covered the Tours of '81 and '83 exclusively by bike before my burgeoning career as a cycling photographer forced me to get serious and switch transport loyalties once and for all.

In those early, carefree days, I found accommodation in youth hostels, campsites, and even on park benches, depending on how far I'd managed to ride and how close to the next day's stage I'd gotten by nightfall. It wasn't unusual for me to dismantle my tent at four in the morning and get a hundred kilometers in before stopping for brunch and rendezvousing with the Tour stage, especially if I'd gotten my calculations wrong the evening before or had encountered an annoying headwind that stopped me prematurely.

I ate where and when I could, and it took me many years to factor the dreaded French lunch break into my calculations, a break that was—and still is—rigidly held at three full hours in rural areas. Turn up in a village with an empty stomach at one minute past noon, and I'd find all the pâtisseries and grocery stores firmly closed. At that point, my options were to either ruin my budget and slow my progress by buying a restaurant meal or simply ride on for a few hours more. It was also back in those naive, adventurous days that I learned the hard way to anticipate what Bastille Day, July 14, means to the French, especially if the national holiday comes immediately before or after a weekend, which shutters the country for three or four days. With ATMs as yet not invented and the banks firmly closed, I'd often beg food off fellow campers in order to keep my tour on the road.

Of course, such hardships lessened when I began using motorized transport in the mid-1980s, and nearly disappeared when I got myself into the Tour on a motorcycle in 1987. I was now earning money from my chosen passion, and my experience of France and the Tour expanded accordingly. Enjoying the relative wealth that comes from such access, I discovered another France, a France in which one slept in a quaint Logis-de-France hotel, the kind that always seemed to have carpeting as wallpaper in the bedroom, and where the bed's design seemed distinctly similar to that of a *banane*. These were hotels where the bread served with dinner reappeared the next morning as dull, dry toast for breakfast. Mind you, that evening meal would have been the best I'd ever had, at least until I enjoyed the next day's meal at another idyllic country inn.

By the late 1980s, free of the discipline needed to stay in shape to ride a hundred miles each day, I was drinking less and less Perrier and more and more *vin du pays*. And then the greater wealth of the Lance Armstrong years a decade later corrupted my palate for good by exposing me to the great wines of Bordeaux, Bourgogne, and Côtes du Rhône. With the Armstrong era also came overnight halts in some of France's most exclusive château-hotels, where my fellow dining guests were quite likely to be suave, successful billionaires, not the grubby campers and hitchhikers of my youth. When I first experienced French life, I thought a *sommelier* was a churchbell ringer; I now know very differently!

I often think of those two distinct worlds as I speed around France today. It is impossible not to think of them, for although each July brings with it new adventures and experiences—and, yes, even hardships—it also sends me back in time to long-forgotten French summers when the thought of staying in a hotel or eating in a classy restaurant was as alien to me as flying in a commercial jet (a cross-channel ferry was the best I could hope for). These days, when I descend the Alpe d'Huez, I can't help but look to my left at La Cascade campground, noting the secure gates restricting access to "guests only." Back in 1981, I remember sneaking past the same entrance well after midnight to pitch my little tent, before slipping out, without payment, before dawn . . . just as I'd done in so many other campsites along the way. "*Auberge de Jeunesse*"—how many times do I now flash past those little yellow youth hostel signs while searching for my night's lodgings, remembering the days when a stale loaf of bread and a rickety cot were the norm, and any touch of luxury a rare exception in my travels.

These days, I spend many moments of each July envying the fans enjoying the Tour the way I once enjoyed it. I see the club cyclists—Dutch, Belgian, German, British, American, and French—mingling at the roadsides, content to get their one glimpse of the world's greatest bike race as it flies by before they engage their cleats with their bike pedals and take off on a breathtaking descent to a car, a tent, or a hotel somewhere far below. A great evening is in store for those guys, I just know it! As I cruise by at 50 kilometers per hour in the wake of an *échappée*, I catch other fans, those without bicycles, sunning themselves on a lush green mountainside or cooling off beneath the shade of a forested road in the Landes, a half-finished bottle of chilled chardonnay at their side. How covetous I am of the simplicity of their day in comparison with my work-loaded schedule, where the hope of finding a decent meal—any meal, in fact—becomes the big draw when it's already 10 P.M. and there's still another hour's work ahead. But I cannot truly complain.

To be honest, the real Graham Watson enjoys a France somewhere between the simplicity of the 1980s and the extravagance of the 2000s—the real France, I like to believe. I embrace a world in which the greatest delight comes from experiencing a little bit of everything that's good about France, and sometimes what's bad about it as well. Each July in France links me to previous summers there, be it through a treasured *bistro*, a much-loved country hotel, or a long-forgotten *départemental* road, the kind one only finds in deepest rural France. I may still be very much the quintessential Englishman who craves his fish 'n' chips or cottage pie, but I also love coming back each July to the whole range of French cuisine, from an elegant three-hour lunch to a *menu rapide* served up in some backstreet of Montpellier.

It was through the Tour that I discovered France, and through France that I discovered some of the most beautiful landscapes in Europe, if not the world. I took my first sips of real wine in France, and learned that there is more to cheese than a simple chunk of Camembert or Brie. I learned a form of politeness and courtesy that far exceeded anything I'd experienced in England, even if the rationale of French manners was sometimes impossible to fathom—and still is! I learned to kiss in France—not the "I love you" kind of kiss, but the socially correct peck on the cheek that secures a warm and genuine welcome into French households. The arcana of France's *gastronomie* are still largely a mystery to me, but that's the way I like it, for it keeps bringing me back to learn more.

Researching this book has taken me to France between Tours, when the country has dropped its summertime overcoat of tourism. I've seen a France much like the one I first saw in the late 1970s, one that is still largely unspoiled by the growth of population that seems to afflict its neighbors. Now, as I drive down quiet highways or cycle along deserted country lanes, I realize how much France can be loved if one has the time to relax and absorb the passing minutes of a day the way many French people do.

Reacquainting myself with France outside of the Tour was like a second honeymoon for me, one during which I could enjoy the quiet backwaters of the Dordogne, the sheep-dotted hillsides of the Pyrenees, the wide-open plains of the Vaucluse, and the great restaurants I had not seen for a decade. I rediscovered some of my favorite hotels, many of which had changed in name but, thankfully, had lost none of their charm.

And of course, I made peace with the French, with whom I have a true love-hate relationship when working most Tours. It is a peace based on enjoying decadent meals with no time constraints, selecting exactly the wines one wants with no fear of having to share them with colleagues or assistants. It is a peace that serves to remind me just how much I love this country and its people. And here, at last, is my chance to share my France with you. If France captures your soul as it has mine, you will be blessed with a love affair that lasts the rest of your life.

As you will soon discover, this is an intensely personal book. It is packed with the many useful things I've learned in more than thirty years of following the Tour, as well as the exciting things that I've seen along the way. My goal is to take you into the world of the Tour, to show you how it works, and to share with you the best ways I've found to follow it. At the same time, I hope to show you the France—the beautiful, congenial, welcoming, and sometimes confounding France—that I am still discovering after all these years.

Of course, it all started with the Tour for me, and the Tour is still the center. When I took my place behind the barriers on the Champs-Élysées to watch the end of the 1977 Tour, it was impossible for me to imagine that I'd one day be on the other side photographing cycling greats like Bernard Hinault, Laurent Fignon, Greg LeMond, Stephen Roche, Pedro Delgado, Miguel Induráin, Lance Armstrong, and Alberto Contador as they rode into Paris as the Kings of the Tour de France. My longevity in the Tour is partly due to having such a great and varied group of champions to photograph and appreciate, as well as the hundreds of their loyal teammates who have earned their relative stardom the hard way; I've had much pleasure photographing them all.

The Tour is a unique phenomenon, something that has no equal in our busy lives. It is an event we spend an entire year talking about, yet, sadly, only three weeks actually watching. While some people can only watch, others manage a career writing about the Tour or earn a living by photographing it. I like to think I have chosen the best option. And I like to think that in this book I have opened up options for you, so that you will have a richer experience, whether you choose to watch the Tour for just a few days and then explore France, or decide to follow the race for a week or more, or even try your hand as a photographer. Whatever you choose, I hope that this book convinces you that you can't go wrong. But beware—this experience could change your life.

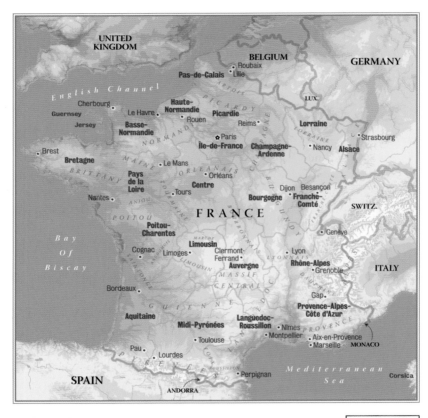

PLANNING YOUR TRIP

A BELLE FRANCE, A LAND OF MYSTERY AND INTRIGUE, OF CONTRASTS, OF cultures old and new. A land rich in beauty, where mountains and lakes and rivers traverse the landscape apparently at will, where rock pools form at the feet of deep gorges, where brightly colored flowers glow in glistening alpine meadows, and where long, sandy beaches stretch far beyond the scope of the eye.

France, with its endless tapestry of agricultural fields where wheat, barley, oats, and corn grow. Sunflowers and lavender drop bright colors into that summery mosaic, while huge forests add a contrasting hue to the general palette. Cities enhance rather than spoil this vision, the history and architecture hidden within them further complementing an already glowing portfolio.

This is a nation celebrated for its *gastronomie*—its art of good eating—and its fine wines and champagnes, all of which have their roots embedded in those rich pastures of a land surrounded on three sides by the sea. These bodies of water—dark gray and brooding to the north, deep blue and powerful to the west, turquoise, luminous, and irresistible to the south—surround the country like a giant moat, as if keeping foes at bay. No wonder France has so often been thought of as a woman, when she is so well endowed. No wonder her marriage with the Tour de France has been so celebrated.

This lyrical description may not match your first impressions of France if you happen to have just flown into Paris via the dreary gray Roissy–Charles de Gaulle airport or chugged into the crowded Gare du Nord by train. But as each day passes on your journey to see Le Tour, so will the unique characteristics of French life slowly permeate your soul, tempting you to stay longer.

Although Paris is the place you are most likely to visit first, it is the rest of France you need to see, to experience, in order to appreciate the finer aspects of life in this extraordinary country. Paris is to France as London is to England, New York to the United States, Rome to Italy, Capetown to South Africa, Sydney to Australia. Yes, by all means go to each of these places, but go with the realization that there's more to the country than the museums, cathedrals, and shopping streets of its most popular city.

Luckily, the excuse of having to follow the Tour de France gives cycling fans a huge advantage over other travelers; you'll get to see parts of France that most tourists never find. That's not just because of your natural spirit of adventure; it's because the Tour makes a point of visiting as many different parts of France as it can in three weeks. The Tour is also careful to rotate its itinerary each year, so that the whole country can claim to have seen the Tour pass through with some regularity.

The Tour visits large cities of a million people and tiny villages of just a few hundred. It goes to remote rural areas completely forgotten by the rest

CROWNED WITH CLIFFS   *The Tour de France passes along the Dordogne River at La Roque–Gageac in 2007.*

of the world and into bustling regions already overflowing with activity from tourism or industry. It goes to such places by way of narrow country lanes or along wide, flowing highways, passing ancient castles or skirting the sea atop towering cliffs. The Tour crosses bridges two, three, four, five times each day, traversing rivers and streams and lakes and canyons as it eats up long swathes of this vast and utterly diverse country.

It sometimes intrudes into such natural wonders as the Gorges du Verdon, a river canyon in the southeast, or the Gorges du Tarn, a similarly spectacular formation in the southwest. It may sweep through the indescribable wonder that is the Grotto of Mas-d'Azil in Ariège. It spends many a long hour squeezed between corridors of *platanes* (plane trees), entertaining picnickers comfortably seated in lush, grassy meadows.

The Tour enters the mountains of France with a great fanfare of expectation, with every meter of altitude gained noted by a watchful, sometimes nervous world. It leaves those same mountains to a chorus of cheers and a torrent of respect. If it races outside of France, it only does so for financial gain and to remind the world what France and French life are all about; the race then returns to an even greater reception from its citizens.

There's probably no sport that could have influenced and embraced French life the way the Tour has. A soccer team visits Lille; the Tour de France *arrives* there. A rugby team plays in Béziers; the Tour de France makes a *passage* through the city, a far greater affair.

PLANNING YOUR TOUR OF THE TOUR

Two of the most straightforward facts about the Tour de France are, one, that it takes place in July each year, almost always starting on the first Saturday of the month; and two, that it always ends up in Paris, three weeks and one day later. Another helpful tip: The popularity of the race in the last decade has meant that information about the starting point usually leaks out in the press even before the previous year's event has started, thus enabling the visitor to create an initial strategy a full year before making the trip.

THE COUNTRYSIDE   *Wines of Alsace, seen with an autumnal glow.*

VISA AND PASSPORT

Visas are not required for residents of the United States, Canada, Australia, or New Zealand for short stays of ninety days or less. You need only show your passport upon arrival and departure, though you'll also have to fill in a landing card on your inbound flight. Make sure that your passport is valid and will not expire within six months of your departure. If expiration is imminent, you may be refused entry.

TRAVEL TIP: Carry a few photocopies of the passport page that shows your photo and passport number. You can then leave your passport safely locked in your hotel room when you go out during the day or evening, or use the copy to get a new passport if your original is lost or stolen. Alternatively, you can scan the passport pages and then e-mail the scan to yourself, retrieving the scan to get a replacement. To get a new passport, you'll need to contact your country's embassy or consulate in Paris, or in a major city like Marseille, Bordeaux, or Nice, where experienced staff are always on duty for such occurrences.

The first thing is to ascertain the strength of your interest in the Tour. Do you want to see all of it or just some of it? Do you want to see just the Pyrenean stages or do you want to enjoy the Alps as well? Or is there more attraction to simply dropping in for a few days here and there between visits to parts of France blissfully unaffected by the colossus that is the Tour? Maybe a long weekend in Paris is all you want—a chance to see the Tour coming home while enjoying the sights and sounds of one of the world's most romantic cities. Or perhaps your chosen Tour is exclusively *sur le vélo* (on the bicycle), a hard but exhilarating three-week slog that will stand as one of your life's great achievements.

ORGANIZED TRIPS TO SEE THE TOUR

Whichever of these options you eventually choose, the easiest and least stressful way to travel is to book your time in France with an established tour operator, one that specializes in taking groups of people to see the Tour each summer. As recently as 2005, the Tour de France organizer, Amaury Sport Organisation (ASO), granted official rights to a limited number of companies to operate trips to the Tour, moderating what had become an absolute deluge of tourism in and around the great event. At the height of Lance Armstrong's popularity between 2001 and 2004, for example, there were literally dozens of tourist buses clogging the approach roads and parking areas around the Tour, a nuisance that led to the Tour's attempt to limit this fee-paying entourage of bike fans.

Logically, one of these official companies is the first port of call for anyone wanting to see the race with relative ease, although as the cost of being an official licensee is so high, most of the unofficial tour operators are still in business. A few of the unlicensed operators even offer some of the premium services that accompany official Tour status, such as five-star accommodation in a château, helicopter rides to mountaintop finishes, escorted bike rides, and attractive alternative trips for those not totally consumed by cycling and the Tour.

To combat this kind of competition, ASO now offers additional considerations that you will only get with an official licensee. These include a limited number of day passes for tourists wishing to have access to the media center, the *village du départ* (start village), and even one of the semi-exclusive VIP grandstands, or *tribunes*, at the finish. The chance to ride part of a stage, complete with gendarme escort, is another available attraction, as is the thrill of following a time trial (TT) stage in an official guest car.

The Tour has an amazingly secure cordon around it each day, and no one, but no one, gets near its starts, finishes, stars, or water carriers without an official badge or a much-sought-after guest pass, such as the one that comes with the official package deal. Official tour operators also offer some economical packages, so there are alternatives to those luxury trips aimed at the well-heeled among us.

The privileged access of an official tour is not to everyone's taste, and in any case is only available to premium-paying clients. Nevertheless, I would strongly recommend that a first-time Tour fan consider an organized trip of some kind—official or otherwise—especially if your time in France is limited to a week or less. The experience gained, albeit it at a price, can be put to good use in the future, for a longer, more adventurous self-guided trip.

CASH AND CREDIT CARDS

The currency in France is the Euro (€). You should avoid carrying a large quantity of cash with you, although of course you will need some for small purchases and possibly your taxi upon arrival.

Banks and ATMs are easy to find, and the easiest way to deal with the daily money chase is to carry a debit or credit card from your home bank that doubles as a Visa or MasterCard. That way, you can use it as a credit card in restaurants, hotels, and so on, and also use it to withdraw cash from nearly any ATM using your home PIN (as long as it has no more than four numbers; if it has more, contact your bank about changing it before you leave). ATM fees are generally between 1 and 2 percent, and most ATMs have a language button that will switch the screen to English.

American Express cards are welcomed across France but many smaller restaurants and hotels will not accept Amex; at that point, it is best to have a Visa or MasterCard in your wallet as a backup, rather than counting on finding an ATM that will let you withdraw enough cash with your Amex card to settle the bill.

If you lose your credit card, here are the numbers to call in France:
- American Express: 0800 900 888 or call collect 336 393 1111
- MasterCard/Eurocard: 0800 901 387
- Visa: 0800 901 179

If you don't travel overseas regularly, you should call your bank before heading to France to let them know. That way, your account won't be flagged for unusual activity and your credit unexpectedly cut off.

The Official Tour de Tour

There are just four official packaged-tour operators for the Tour in existence, but they accept bookings and inquiries from all over the world. In addition to their regular trips to see the great race, all four offer similar perks in the VIP package that gives finish-line viewing, access to TV and media areas, and access to the team parking areas at starts and finishes. Three of them offer a drive in an official car on time trial stages, plus the chance to ride part of one stage a few hours ahead of the *caravane publicitaire* (publicity caravan) and peloton and be photographed on the iconic Tour podium. They also offer a discount on merchandise at the official Tour boutiques and guarantee priority access to the spectator grandstands on the Champs-Élysées.

Custom Getaways (www.customgetaways.com) is the Florida-based North American operator currently endorsed by the Tour de France. Its offers include a self-guided Tour de France for those cyclists or drivers wishing to travel the whole way around France, using some of the same roads as the race and occasionally meeting up with the company's guided clients.

Ronan Pensec in the 1990 Tour de France time trial.

Ronan Pensec Travel (www.ronanpensec travel.com) is the operator selected for France. A Harley-Davidson fan and fluent English speaker, Pensec is an ex-Tour cyclist—a very special one, having worn the yellow jersey for a few days in 1990. Regrettably, Pensec's offerings are currently restricted to a behind-the-scenes look at stage starts and finishes, with no actual traveling. Nevertheless, Pensec would make a very interesting guide to your tour of the Tour, for his teammates in that 1990 race included the American winner Greg LeMond and Scotland's Robert Millar.

Australians and New Zealanders around the world can look to **Bikestyle Tours** (www.bikestyletours.com) for some Down Under–inspired fun in France, while British bike fans have for years sought the expertise of **Sporting Tours**, the oldest cycling-tour company in the world. One of the highlights of Sporting Tours' packages is that you are based for about one week in either the Alps or Pyrenees, letting the Tour come to you while you enjoy some leisure cycling. Sporting Tours was bought by a bigger company in 2007, and can be found at www.sportstoursinternational.com; the expertise and experience are still very much there, and I'd recommend this official operator ahead of all the others.

The Unofficial Tour de Tour

Based on feedback from the hundreds of cyclists I meet each July, here are the best of the unofficial operators.

At the top of the list, if only because of the audacity of its Web site name, www.tourdefrance.com.au, comes **The Adventure Travel Company** from Australia. While this company has a variety of trips to the Tour that resemble those from many other companies, The Adventure Travel Company is the *maillot jaune* of the unofficial operators because it offers Phil Anderson's daily expertise. Anderson was a Tour legend back in the 1980s, and he is an absolute fitness fanatic today. He'll still show you a clean pair of heels on your daily bike rides in France!

Steve Bauer, an esteemed teammate of Anderson when they both rode for the Motorola Cycling Team, offers his own company for your Tour de France experience (www.stevebauer.com). Bauer, like so many Canadians, is one of the most affable people you could meet. A keen photographer, he naturally drinks beer and wine like they're going out of fashion, but that's after a day's hard, yet sociable, bike riding on Le Tour. Both Anderson and Bauer offer a laid-back *haute qualité* kind of Tour experience—but from two-time wearers of the Tour's yellow jersey, you wouldn't expect anything else, would you?

One of the oldest operators in the United States is **VéloSport Vacations** (www.velovacations.com), run by the husband-and-wife team of Chris and Kathy Gutowski. This couple has been running cycle tours for almost twenty years, and actually had a group in France when LeMond won the 1990 Tour!

Phil Anderson, a stage winner of the 1991 Tour de France.

Steve Bauer celebrates his yellow jersey in the 1990 Tour de France.

Two notable casualties of the Tour's cleansing of unauthorized travel companies in 2005 were the low-budget **Breaking Away Bicycle Tours** (www.breakingaway.com) and the high-end **Trek Travel** (http://trektravel.com). Both have returned for 2009. Breaking Away is offering a brief, three-day look at the alpine stages. Trek Travel, however, never one to be shy, is offering weeklong luxury packages to see the Tour and witness Lance Armstrong's bid to win an eighth time.

Calling itself the Official Team Astana Tour Operator, with access to the team and its entourage, Trek Travel is looking to reclaim the top-dog status it enjoyed in the Lance years. Its use of helicopters for transport and accommodation in some of France's best château-hotels will help set its tours apart, albeit at a high price. But that price includes the use of Trek's iconic Madone bicycles and closer-than-anyone-else views of the Great Man himself. I'm personally pleased to see this operator return with the charismatic enthusiasts they brought to the Tour of old, and I'm looking forward to the chance to drink a finish-line glass of champagne with many of them after a hard day's shooting.

GOING SOLO

Still, there's nothing quite like going it alone, is there? If you're the do-it-yourself type, then the first step is to await the announcement of the entire route in late October. Watching this announcement is best done via live video on the Internet, eavesdropping on the glitzy, media-hyped presentation from the center of Paris at the Palais de Congrès. Log on to the Tour's official site, www.letour.fr, to get the lay of the land.

Once the route is known, the daring traveler can really start to plan, with a priority being given to choice of transport, which in turn dictates your choice of accommodation. The transport options are obvious: car, camper, train, bicycle —or, in excellent combination, car and bicycle, camper and bicycle, train and bicycle. A car allows one to camp out, stay in hotels, use youth hostels, or even sleep rough if need be. A camper acts as a sort of mobile *pied-à-terre*, saving you money on accommodation and allowing you to stop as and where you want to. The train offers many options, not least the chance to travel overnight if you are going a long way, or maybe wanting to get away from the Tour for a few days, or playing catch-up after some delay or unplanned diversion. The French railway

The launch of the new Tour route is held each October in Paris.

system, SNCF, also offers a service that allows you to rent a car or a modest bicycle upon arrival at your destination, adding even greater flexibility to your trip. Flying within France is an unnecessary chore—take the train instead!

By Bike

It is obvious that the noble bicycle holds the key to getting the very best out of your Tour watching, and that's the way it should be! Driving a car or a camper will get you close to the best places, but it is the two-wheeled beauty, that most elegant and brilliant of inventions, that can take you to the very heart of the Tour, be it on a crowd-packed mountainside or a deserted *route départementale* (secondary road) in Limousin.

If the logistics of bringing the bike begin to seem a bit of a chore as you get into the details of planning your trip, stop and consider the advantages it might bring. At the crowded, crazy Tour, those advantages are almost endless: closer access to the race, the chance to pedal up some of the climbs, the chance to stretch your legs for a few hours riding in the countryside, and simply a transport utility for getting you into or out of the nearest village for evening drinks or dinner, or for fetching a salad-filled baguette for lunch at some idyllic riverside halt. If you've arrived too late at a Tour roadblock and your car or camper isn't allowed to proceed by the gendarmes, your day on some famed ascent might just be saved by switching to the bicycle for the last few kilometers. The more adventurous cyclist can avoid the worst of the traffic jams altogether by pedaling from farther away, combining this ease of movement with a serious cross-country ride, and so making your visit to the Tour something of a touring or training holiday as well.

The Tour has grown in size tenfold since I last rode my bike all the way around France in the early 1980s, and I have no idea how many cyclists still make the effort to pedal their way around France today. All I know is that they're out there somewhere—I just can't see them through the mass of other humanity that follows the Tour in the twenty-first century.

All the same, planning a bicycle-only trip to the Tour is really no different from planning one with a car, plane, train, or camper. All that is additionally required is the mindset that comes with such an ambition, as well as the required level of fitness to deal with some long days in the saddle and the constitution to thwart any little illnesses along the way.

Accommodation is the most serious consideration, as it dictates the style of cycling you'll be doing—traveling light from hotel to hotel, or taking your lodgings along for the ride with a tent. Traveling light is a dream, but difficult to attain when you cannot be sure of getting to your hotel before it closes for the night, as most country hotels do around 10 P.M. in France. Unless you are lucky enough to have a friend, husband, or wife driving a car as an accessory to your cycling, someone who can rescue you late at night when you're still 40

An optimistic fan makes his case at the 2007 Tour de France.

kilometers from the hotel, without lights, and hungry, then camping or youth hosteling might be the best solution. Another alternative, of course, is to travel with a cycling tour operator that uses vans to pick up and drop off its clients; for that, see page 9.

Camping

Like hotels, campsites in France are now bookable on the Internet, making life quite easy if you have a reliable Web connection as you travel. On the other hand, the whole point of camping is the flexibility that comes with it: bedding down for the night as and when you want, without the pressure of arriving on time, and before someone else has taken your reserved spot at the campsite.

Cyclists in particular can get their day's riding in, eat along the way, then pitch their tent in the first convenient—and safe—place. You can camp almost anywhere in France—behind a thick hedge, in a farmer's field, on a grassy riverbank if you feel happy about it. The only precaution is never to pitch your tent in open view of a road; that might be asking for trouble from unwanted visitors—or intruders.

Carrying a tent on your bike will slow you down an awful lot, but it will afford you that extra degree of flexibility when you're looking to get a few hours of well-earned sleep. Cyclists are obliged to travel with the smallest and lightest tent available, and with the bare minimum of clothing, if they are to make sufficient progress each day. They also have to make the important choice of whether to bring a small cooking stove and the utensils with which to cook, or to travel lighter and depend on purchased food. I'd always recommend that each cyclist have full independence in equipment and clothing—especially separate tents—just in case something happens to turn a pair of cyclists into two separate entities along the way. Following the Tour can be rough on relationships when there's so much to contend with already.

While the freedom of pitching your tent wherever is appealing, I would still recommend booking ahead for those sought-after campsites where the hordes of fellow Tour followers will also be heading. Yes, you can wing it for three or four days a week, pitching up at the roadside or finding last-minute availability at recognized campsites along the way. But when the Tour arrives in bottleneck resorts like Bourg-d'Oisans or Morzine, it is vital to have booked ahead.

Unlike thirty years ago, it is not so easy now just to sneak into a campsite under cover of darkness and put up your little tent; your neighbors are bound to have you ejected, because they most certainly have reserved and paid for their spot. Many Dutch and Belgian families target areas of France where the Tour is scheduled to visit, particularly the Alps, spending a whole week in a campsite before dragging themselves and their picnic furniture up the mountain to watch the race for just one afternoon. The Dutch and Belgians are not the lords of camping and trailering for nothing, but they'll be the most welcoming and entertaining of neighbors if you play by the rules. Never mind if your little one-person tent and total lack of accessories make you feel utterly inadequate alongside their family-sized castles; before you know it, they'll be inviting you over for dinner and drinks, and regaling you with tales about cycling and the days when Eddy Merckx, Lucien van Impe, and Joop Zoetemelk ruled the Tour.

FINDING CAMPSITES

Campers have several Web sites to search through, but at first they need go no further than www.campingfrance.com, the official Web site of the **Fédération Française de Camping et de Caravaning** (FFCC). It's a very easy way to search for suitable campsites along your route in France if your French is good, although there is no online booking available; you have to call each camp to make your reservation. You can buy a PDF version of several camping guides, or the FFCC handbook if you prefer, but this can only be done from the FFCC itself at www.ffcc.fr. Be forewarned, though—it is all in French, the payment system and the guide itself.

For English-only speakers, try instead the **Camping and Caravanning Club of Great Britain**: www.campingandcaravanningclub.co.uk. You are encouraged to join the club for about seven pounds sterling, plus a yearly fee of thirty-five pounds, but nonmembers can book online after they've searched for each campsite they need. A link takes you to "camping abroad," so the site can be used by English-speaking people the world over.

FINDING HOSTELS

Anyone planning to go youth hosteling should first check out www.hihostels. com, the Web site for **Hostelling International**, from which you can make direct bookings. You have to book at least seventy-two hours in advance of your planned stay, but if you can go through this Web site, you will be spared from browsing through the French hosteling site www.fuaj.org, which in turn saves you from trying to pronounce the full name of the French hosteling organization: **Fédération Unie des Auberges de Jeunesse!** In fact, the French site is identical to the international version, and both offer online booking as well as booking by fax or post after you've downloaded and filled out a PDF file. Almost all questions can be answered online, so all you have to do is book and then show up at your chosen hostel. Another welcome feature is that you can see how far the hostel is from a village or town center, allowing you the chance to go camping or stay in a hotel if the hostel is too far off your route.

Hosteling

Youth hosteling is something most youngsters try at least once in their lives, but these days hosteling in France is open to all ages. Nor do you have to be a member of your national youth hostel association, as you did before; you just pay a small surcharge to stay in any one of the thousands of hostels around France. Hosteling suits the lone traveler, for it affords an opportunity to meet likeminded people seeing the Tour alone (you may even pick up a traveling companion for a day or two). Yet it is quite acceptable for a family of four to rock up in their Citroën and check in for the night as well.

Generally, you can find cheap hotel rooms for about the same price as a youth hostel, but when the Tour is in the region, you may find the *Auberge de Jeunesse* is all that's available. As with camping, it is the long-distance cyclist who can get the most out of hosteling, for just a few creature comforts, such as a fresh shower with soap and a reasonably firm bed for the night, can go a long way to rejuvenating your morale after days of sweating it out on the open road. There are a few drawbacks to hosteling, such as the occasional unavailability of cooked food and the difficulty in finding the more remote hostels. But the company you'll enjoy when you find such a remote place—along with a good chance that you'll be able to beg some food off your new companions—more than makes up for this.

By Train

Logically, Paris will be most people's point of entry into and departure from France, even allowing for those exceptional years when the race is starting in another country—as it did in Dublin in 1998 and London in 2007 and will do in Monaco in 2009. My favorite form of transport in France is the TGV, the hub of which is, naturally, in the capital city. The *Train à Grande Vitesse* (high-speed train) is a mind-boggling yet relaxing experience that allows one to enjoy some of the very, very best of the spectacular scenery of France while traversing the country at speeds of up to 350 kilometers per hour (km/h)! Paris to Marseille in four hours, Paris to Bordeaux in about three hours, Paris to Strasbourg in just over two hours—it is an incredible thing to experience.

Sadly, bicycles are not allowed on these trains, so cyclists wanting to use the train as their favored transport will need to book themselves on the slower but still reliable long-distance SNCF trains that crisscross France.

The TGV can best be used by those basing themselves in Paris for a few days or a week, day-commuting to see a stage start or finish in a major city like Rennes, Tours, Lyon, or Lille, before returning to the capital for dinner at some *rive gauche* (Left Bank) eatery. TGVs also run between other major cities—Nice to Bordeaux, Lyon to Toulouse, Lille to Montpellier and Perpignan, Strasbourg to Marseille, for example—making a visit to one of France's great provincial cities an experience in itself, one that surely deserves an overnight stay.

Note, too, that TGVs now leave directly from beneath Roissy–Charles de Gaulle airport, enabling the arriving air passenger to avoid Paris altogether and head straight for the provinces.

On no account should one visit France and not take a TGV ride—it is an experience almost as uniquely French as the Tour, for no other country in Europe has a train system equal to France's. When Belgium and Great Britain

The TGV connects France's main cities with speed and efficiency.

joined with France to form the original Eurostar high-speed train system in 1994, it was a French-designed train they used as well as the special rails needed for such high speeds.

Prices are quite reasonable, with a round-trip from Paris to Marseille in first class for around €120, or a Paris-Bordeaux round-trip for €110. First-class travel is a great treat to enjoy, and it is typically just 20 percent more than second-class travel, a difference soon forgotten in the quieter-than-a-church tranquility of the air-conditioned carriage. Mind you, this added privacy, in slightly bigger seats, is the sum of what first-class travel in France offers; you'll still need to go to a dedicated buffet car like everyone else to buy your sandwiches and drinks.

Reservations are obligatory for all TGV travel, and are highly recommended for normal trains too, particularly if you are traveling overnight to the Alps or Pyrenees and want to sleep in a *couchette*, a four- or six-berth compartment that might see you spending the night with complete strangers—another delight of rail travel in France!

Whether you've opted for an all-train itinerary, a series of day trips, or train travel with bikes, you can do a lot of planning by searching the Internet before you depart for France. **Rail Europe** (www.raileurope.com) is where most searches end for English-language travelers, and its site offers rail travel throughout Europe as well. This site, like the one linked to the SNCF French rail system (www.sncf.com), is not much fun to work through, and the French one in particular suffers from an overdose of Gallic "creativity" that will confuse the visitor.

You might find simplified joy by going directly to www.tgv.com if you can understand a little French and only want to travel by TGV. But as soon as you click on the little Union Jack flag or the U.S. flag for English, you get sent back to RailEurope.com. Therefore, it is best to know beforehand that online tickets can only be purchased on some of the routes offered, and only then if you book at least one week before so your tickets can be sent out by mail. In other words, I suggest that you only use the sites and their timetables as a guide, and not as the be-all and end-all of your rail-travel ambitions; otherwise, you'll get very frustrated.

Luckily, rail tickets can be bought quickly at all major French railway stations, either in person or by using one of the automated machines. There used to be two types of machines: blue ones that sold tickets only for the region the station is in—Île de France (Paris) or Côte d'Azur (Nice/Cannes), for example—and purple machines that offered longer-distance travel and TGV bookings. Most stations in France have now switched to new all-purpose machines, which are painted yellow to avoid confusion, though a few of the older machines still exist. This all sounds very organized and thoughtful, until you navigate your way through the menu (there's an English-language flag you can click on), only to discover that your machine is one of the older ones that doesn't accept non-French credit cards! So give yourself the time to visit the *salle d'accueil* in bigger stations, and get your tickets there if need be; it'll be right next to the ticket machines, be they yellow, blue, or purple.

Most railway clerks in the major cities speak English, so don't be shy; you'll find many of them charming and interested in your inquiry. You may struggle at some of the smaller *gares* (stations) in the provinces, but by the time you have got that far, you'll have been in France long enough to at least be able to say *bonjour* and *merci*, and that's usually enough to get the help you need.

By Car or Camper

For those who lack the motivation and stamina to cycle around France to watch the Tour, as well as for the greater number who are not

---

TRAIN TALK

Aller simple: one-way
Aller-retour: round-trip
Billet plein tarif: full-fare ticket*
1ère: first class
2ème: second class
Tarif enfant: child's ticket
Côté couloir: aisle seat
Côté fenêtre: window seat
Correspondance: connection or transfer
Quai or **voie:** platform
En semaine: Monday through Saturday
Dimanche: Sunday schedule
Jours fériés: holidays
Annulé: canceled
En retard or retardé: delayed
Consigne des bagages: stored baggage**

* Full fare is generally the only choice for tourists; you must be a resident with a subscription card—*carte d'abonnement*—to take advantage of reduced-fare prices.

** Stored luggage areas used to be common in French railway stations, but many have been closed with the onset of counterterrorism measures since 9/11. Some still exist in regional stations, but don't expect always to be able to store your backpack, bicycle, or suitcase for the afternoon while you watch the Tour.

TO THE MOUNTAINS *Campers and cars line the climb of the Col du Galibier.*

wealthy enough to hire a helicopter each and every day (indeed, any day . . .), the more obvious choice is a car, one with space enough to throw a bike or two in the back, as bike racks are rarely available for rental. There is also the even more enticing option of a camper to take yourself, the family, and a few bikes around France. Both forms of transport have their advantages. The car yields easier access to the minor roads used by the Tour and allows you to see every stage if you so desire. The camper, on the other hand, is a great asset when it comes to settling down for the night, as and where you like, without the need to look for accommodation.

Anyone following the Tour seriously is bound to head for the mountains at least once during the trip, a choice that virtually forces travelers to sleep on, or near, the mountain where they've chosen to watch the race. A camper affords a greater degree of luxury than a car, although many Tour followers are quite happy to pitch a small tent for the night before driving off in their rented car

DRIVING PERMIT

If you plan to rent a car, motorcycle, or camper, a credit card and your driver's license will probably be sufficient if you are an EU citizen or a citizen of Canada, the United States, Australia, New Zealand, or South Africa. To avoid any possible problems, however, especially in smaller villages, it won't hurt for non-EEC citizens to get an International Driving Permit (IDP) in advance. The cost is low—$15 in the United States—and the application process is painless. You will need two passport-size photos and a valid local license. Permits are available from your local automobile association; in the United States, information is available on the AAA Web site, which administers IDPs in the United States: www.aaa.com/vacation/idpf.html. In Canada, see the Canadian Automobile Association Web site: www.caa.ca.

early next day. Campers can be rented all over France, but the best choice in terms of variety and price in France is to be found in and around Paris. For an even better deal, however, you can rent your camper from a Dutch, German, or Belgian company and save even more money; see the next page for details.

Car Rental

It is as easy to book a car rental in France as it is at home, and all the popular companies operate out of Roissy–Charles de Gaulle airport northeast of Paris, your most likely arrival point. However, note that if you are coming from North America, you will nearly always get a better rate if you book in advance from home rather than waiting until you get to Europe. You can also consider leasing a car, if it is for a minimum period of one month, which saves you sales tax as well.

It is always best to go for a big-name firm, as any breakdowns or damage to your car while on the move can be rectified far more quickly than with cut-price rental companies. Recommended companies include the Paris-based

Europcar (www.europcar.com), **Sixt** (www.sixt.com), **Avis** (www.avis.com), **Budget** (www.budget.com), and **Hertz** (www.hertz.com).

Renting a car in France means you can drive it into any other European Economic Community (EEC) country at no extra cost. Note, however, that a one-way drop-off charge can be expensive if you rent in France and leave the car in, say, Italy or Spain.

Most companies charge a fee per day for having an extra driver on the paperwork, but it's a vital necessity for insurance, so don't tempt fate by trying to bypass this requirement—it can get expensive if your uninsured driver has even a small accident. Also note that if you require an automatic transmission, you will probably be forced to rent a bigger model, as anything less than a mid-size car is likely to be only available with a stick shift.

When booking your rental car, consider the option of dropping off the car at a convenient stage-finish town a few days before Paris and then taking the train—yes, the TGV!—into the city. It's a less stressful way to enter Paris, and you can easily take a taxi or the *métro* to your hotel before going to watch the race on the Champs-Élysées. There is an Avis office close to virtually every railway station in France, and an office adjacent to, or even inside, the biggest stations. Avis's main rival, Hertz, is never too far away, either, whereas the other major companies generally have their depots as near to the station as possible but rent their space from car service stations. All of France's regional airports have the major renters on-site, giving a further extension to your journey options if you choose to fly to a city other than Paris.

Camper Rental

Camper rental is less easy, for it appears that only a handful of operators control these kinds of vehicles in Europe. But at least that makes your research easier! Most companies require a minimum fourteen-day rental period in July, and many are closed on Saturdays and Sundays. Prices seem to start at about €180 per day for a seven-day rental, and go slowly down to €136 per day for a full month. That's based on a four-berth camper that supposedly accommodates two or three adults and one child. Personally, having seen the inside of these vehicles, I would definitely rent this size for an adult couple, with or without a child.

Motorhomes Worldwide (www.motorhomesworldwide.com) seems to be the most popular company. Its site is fairly easy to navigate, offering different categories of vehicles and many pickup and drop-off locations around France, and it only takes a few minutes to get a quote.

UK and Europe Travel (www.ukandeuropetravel.com) is a company based in Melbourne, Australia, but with a good network of campers in France. UK and Europe offers one-way rentals as well for a €200 fee, making it an interesting company with which to start your search if you want to follow the Tour for a week or so and then leave the vehicle in, for example, Toulouse.

Both Motorhomes Worldwide and UK and Europe Travel work in association with Avis, though Avis itself has its own camper outlet in **Avis Car-Away** (www.aviscaraway.com). Avis is the only car-rental company that appears to be involved in renting campers; even the Hertz Web site links you to Motorhomes Worldwide via Avis Car-Away.

Two other companies of note are South Africa–based **Ashtons** (www.ashtonsgroup.com) and **RV Motorhome Hire** (www.rv-network.co.uk). Ashtons highlights the chance to rent from a variety of countries—not only France—meaning you can get a wider choice of vehicle in, say, Holland and a price that is considerably lower than an equivalent vehicle in France. It'll mean flying in and out of Amsterdam instead of Paris, but the huge savings more than make up for the extra day's drive to reach your Tour starting point in France. And don't forget the 2010 Tour actually starts in the Netherlands! Ashtons' Dutch stock of vehicles seems to be more diverse than those typically available in France, including an adapted Volkswagen California twelve-seater van with an elevating roof and dinette.

RV Motorhome Hire offers conventional camper rentals, but also specializes in arranging fixed-itinerary rentals to coincide with major events such as the Tour de France. Renters get the option of picking up in one city and dropping off in another, and they get a well-researched guide to the Tour along the route they choose to follow.

No matter whom you choose to rent from, accessories can be booked as well, such as picnic tables and chairs, bedding, and bike racks. Bedding is best handled by bringing your own sleeping bag with you, a far simpler arrangement in a tight space than sheets and a blanket.

A bike rack can be useful if there are many bicycles involved, but otherwise there should be enough space to leave one or two bikes inside when you are driving. On no account leave any bikes outside at night or even when parked on the roadsides of the Tour; each July, travelers wake to find their precious bikes have been stolen off the camper and the racks have been taken as well! If you are really pushed for space, padlock the bikes to the roof of your camper; that way you'll thwart any would-be thief, who knows he'll wake you up. But don't try driving with bikes strapped to the roof; it is dangerous, and illegal, in all European countries.

Booking Hotels

The main reason for getting early details of the Tour route is to get a jump on booking the hotels that even camper users may want from time to time. For this task, a lot of patience and planning are required; the Tour is so huge that the organizers block-book just about every decent hotel room in the region—and they do it the previous August, even before the new route is announced!

Fortunately, the Internet has made the task of finding accommodation a lot simpler than in years gone by. Dozens of local and regional Web sites help alleviate at least some of the headaches of finding rooms, whether you're searching one year before your stay or just a day before.

As a rule, the Tour organizers first take all rooms belonging to hotel chains like Ibis, Novotel, Mercure, and Sofitel. They next spread their net wider to include the Campanile, Etap Hotel, and Première Classe chains, the priority being to book the hotels that provide in-house dining for the cyclists and officials. Best Western hotels also fall into ASO's clutches, as do some of the grander Logis-de-France addresses.

This relentless room grabbing wouldn't appear to leave a stick of furniture for anyone else, but in France there are thousands upon thousands of small, independent hotels whose booking procedures are too archaic for the Tour to get involved with. This is where the aforementioned Web sites work on your behalf, automatically spreading their geographical searches to a wider area, until a suitable room has been found.

Any group of more than two people needs to reserve accommodation well in advance, leaving only the odd night or two to be found, ad hoc, when you arrive at your destination. It's just too difficult to find multiple rooms, or even rooms with more than two beds, at the last minute. But lone travelers or pairs can take the risk of finding rooms along the way, for there is always a room to be found somewhere. Tricks of this trade include doing a second sweep of the Internet sites in mid-June, and again in early July, as this is when the Tour organization starts to give back rooms it has decided it no longer requires.

The seriously adept traveler will use other skills in his search, like waiting for a sick or injured Tour cyclist to abandon a stage before calling that team's hotel to try to secure the stricken rider's vacant room for the following day. Whole hotels became available in 2007 following the withdrawal of two teams from the Tour due to drug-related disqualifications. Normally, however, shrewd tactics can involve calling a team hotel and pretending you are a sponsor's guest, or impersonating a guest whose name you can see on the room list but who has yet to check in. Fact is, almost every hotel holds back a room or two to allow for overbooking, and once you've got in and made use of the bathroom or minibar, it's very rare to be ejected. It takes a bit of nerve, but fortune favors the brave!

All the same, be prepared to travel far and wide, especially in the mountains and in remote areas like the Massif Central and the Vosges. Creativity is also required wherever your fellow tourist, the non-Tour breed, is likely to be vacationing. The British, Belgians, Dutch, and Scandinavians migrate south across France in July, swamping the Loire Valley and most of Burgundy as they stop overnight after some wine tasting on their way down to Provence, the Dordogne, or even Spain and Italy. Fortunately, the Tour almost never goes to these areas, or to the beach resorts of Aquitaine or the Côte d'Azur, where its size and disturbance levels are unwanted, given the holidaying thousands who have booked a full two-week stay. Ironically, the Tour will visit the Côte d'Azur in 2009, for the first time in almost thirty years, after its start from Monaco; it remains to be seen how much of an impact this will have on local tourism.

The Tour does find a decent welcome near the beaches of cycling-mad Brittany and Normandy, as well as the sleepier coastal towns of Languedoc-Roussillon, where purpose-built hotels away from the beaches are more accommodating.

The Alps are also a popular destination for French and foreign tourists in the summer; you'll find it quite hard to book a single night's accommodation in July, as many hoteliers rent out rooms by the week only.

The Pyrenees are far more remote than the Alps, and the small ski resorts there—of which there are few anyway—find it hard to cater to overnight halts. The Tour might finish atop the Pla d'Adet, Plateau de Beille, or at Hautacam, but it usually leaves immediately, preferring to sleep in towns like Pau, Tarbes, or Foix, after a complicated evacuation on tiny roads, which must be shared with hundreds of thousands of tourists heading for the same town. This situation is not altogether bad for the independent-minded, however, for while the Tour takes every available room in the cities, the tourist can find a most

TIPPING

Bars and restaurants automatically include a service charge of 15 percent; you'll see it spelled out on your receipt (*service compris*, or service included). It's required by law, and no further tip is necessary. If you are paying with cash, it's customary to leave the small change behind (up to a euro) unless you are dissatisfied with the meal or service. If you are paying with a credit card, you need add nothing extra.

No tip is required for taxis, and if your fare shows €16.75 for a trip, you can expect the driver to give you €3.25 in change. It is illegal for taxi drivers to solicit a tip, though some travelers feel they are obliged to tip, and they may do so if they wish.

The porter who carries the bags to your room and the bell captain who hails your cab are doing jobs they are paid for; they are not allowed to ask for tips, and few Europeans give one. It is a personal choice; do not feel obliged. If you want to leave the housekeeping staff some cash, by all means do so, but if a different person cleans your room each day, the one you tip may not be sharing the cash with his or her colleagues. Do not leave a tip for housekeeping on your final bill when you check out; most hotel managers never pass on tips paid by departing guests. Best to give cash on a face-to-face basis, though no one really expects a tip in this day and age.

hospitable welcome among the hundreds of tiny villages that make up the Ariège, Bigorre, and Béarn—the three subtly different regions of the Pyrenees. Campsites, youth hostels, and family-run hotels adorn these areas, making the Pyrenees a most desirable region to visit and stay. There are more Logis-de-France hotels in this region than anywhere else in France, and you'll find restaurants where the choice and quality of cuisine are at least as good as anything gastronomy-mad Provence has to offer. Sadly, many unwary tourists end up in Lourdes, a town of huge convenience with hundreds of hotels, but with a horrible, stifling, hypocritical exploitation of religion. Be warned, Lourdes is not for the fainthearted traveler!

Accommodation-Booking Tips

I've often used the following Web sites to search for my hotel accommodation in France: www.booking.com, http://hotel.fr, www.hrs.com, www.venere.com, www.planigo.com. I try to avoid the bigger, "global" sites that restrict your search to cities, don't offer an English-language version, or seem to have exclusive arrangements with hotel chains like Campanile or Balladins.

My favorite is Booking.com, which claims to be the most popular hotel-booking site in the world. It deserves this title. Not to be confused with Bookings.com, Booking.com is a Dutch-based company that offers a wide variety of hotels with a search option that easily lets you prioritize quality, price, location, or hotel facilities. It also allows you to book a full year ahead of your arrival, an important factor if you start booking your July hotels before the grande Tour presentation in October. Booking.com also allows you to cancel your reservation up until 18:00 (6:00 p.m.) on the day of your arrival, a vitally important freedom if you're booked into a hotel a hundred kilometers away, but then find a better choice one kilometer from your stage-town arrival point.

Both Venere.com and Planigo.com are almost as good as Booking.com, and have the delightful asset of letting you click on an "active" map of France and then the town of your choice to help you locate a hotel. Hotel.fr finds those cheaper, local hotels better than most, while the German-based Hotel Reservation Service (www.hrs.com) guides clients toward the better-quality hotels and châteaux.

Finding Luxury Hotels

For those of you who demand the very best in luxury accommodation and who do not mind missing the Tour for a few days—I know I wouldn't mind, if it meant staying in some of France's most luxurious hotels—skip all the aforementioned sites and go straight to one of these: www.lhw.com (Luxury Hotels of the World), www.fivestaralliance.com (Five Star Alliance), www.slh. com (Small Luxury Hotels of the World), www.ghotw.com (Great Hotels of the World), www.greatsmallhotels.com (Boutique Hotels of the World), www. grandesetapes.fr (Grandes Étapes Française), www.relaischateaux.com (Relais

& Châteaux), www.johansens.com (Johansens Luxury Hotels and Spas), and www.mrandmrssmith.com (Mr & Mrs Smith).

Some of France's truly great hotels appear on several of these sites, but each site seems to have its own specialty or favorite resort. Try the **Grand Hôtel Barrière** with Luxury Hotels of the World, a "Second Empire–style" delight overlooking the English Channel at Dinard, or the **Abbaye de Talloires** with Great Hotels of the World, a gorgeous stopover of unspeakable decadence on the Lac d'Annecy in the French Alps—though it might be a challenge getting in there in July! Further extravagance can be found with Small Luxury Hotels of the World at the **Auberge de Cassagne**, near Avignon, a useful base for a view of the Tour on Mont Ventoux if it is going there (though you'll be sluggish after eating in the Michelin-starred restaurant the night before).

Five Star Alliance is not a well-known hotel group, but in fact it includes the iconic **Hôtel du Palais** in Biarritz—former residence of Napoleon III—among its seventy-three offerings in France. Great Small Hotels of the World is my favorite top-end Web site, for it mixes château addresses with boutique-style accommodation, and has such offerings as **La Lucarne aux Chouettes** in northern Burgundy and **Château de la Couronne**, near Angoulême in the southwest. Johansens, part of the Condé Nast group, is another favorite, with exotic-looking hotels all over the country. Take a peek at the **Manoir de La Roseraie**, a pearl surrounded by rose gardens in the Rhône Valley between Valence and Avignon. The long-established, and quite austere, Relais & Châteaux is another gem to enjoy. It too mixes château accommodation with other divine properties, and none more so than the **Domaine de Rochevilaine**, in Morbihan in Brittany.

Mr & Mrs Smith was around long before the Angelina Jolie/Brad Pitt film of the same name in 2005, but has benefited enormously from its association with it. The British company offers romantic accommodation in boutique-style hotels, houses, and châteaux, with fewer than one hundred exclusive addresses in France. I could spend the rest of my life staying in their accommodations, but if I only had one night—which is often the case—I'd choose **Pershing Hall** in Paris, a five-minute walk from the Champs Élysées.

Through no fault of my own, I've stumbled upon many other superb hotels during the course of the Lance Armstrong years. Top of the list is the **Hôtel Villa Augusta** in Saint-Paul-Trois-Châteaux. Armstrong and his U.S. Postal/

Discovery teams stayed in this Provençal village many times at the height of their powers; luckily for me, they stayed in the splendid **Hôtel L'Esplan**, leaving me and my entourage of two to enjoy the more modern luxury of the Augusta and its excellent cuisine. (Though I did have lunch at L'Esplan once—highly recommended!)

In 2002, I stayed in what is probably the most expensive hotel in the Logis-de-France network (see next section), the **Auberge du Choucas**, after a stage to Briançon. This converted seventeenth-century farmhouse, halfway up the Col du Lautaret, just has to be visited once in your life. Its antique, timber-beamed bedrooms are not particularly luxurious in themselves, but add on the exquisite cuisine to be enjoyed in its caved restaurant and you'll remember this delight for many years to come.

The Tour of 2000 allowed me to cash in on Lance's growing value in my camera viewfinder and stay at the **Hôtel des Neiges** in Courchevel, one of the most superb hotels in the Alps, with views across the mountains and far down into the Tarentaise Valley. This hotel was where the race organizers took their special guests, either to luxuriate in the large spa pool, sunbathe on the wooden deck while awaiting the stage finish, or indulge themselves in a highly gastronomic meal. Never mind that Lance lost that stage to Marco Pantani; the meal and atmosphere were unparalleled!

DRESS WEAR

The French are wonderfully relaxed people, especially at the dinner table, and they are most forgiving when a foreigner shows up in a plush establishment wearing shorts and sandals. They figure that visitors are all uncivilized anyway, so you can get away with this if you must. Still, it is a sensible idea to pack at least one set of smart, informal clothes if you are planning on eating expensively in a major city. You'll get a better response from the waiter if you are well dressed, and it is a courtesy your fellow diners will appreciate.

< OPPOSITE   *The Auberge du Choucas in Monetier-les-Bains.*

Logis-de-France: Charm, Adventure, Exceptional Food

All the best hotel chains, such as Relais & Châteaux and Small Luxury Hotels of the World, have guidebooks that complement the information on their Web sites. Logis-de-France (www.logisdefrance.com), on the other hand, desperately depends upon its printed handbook to compensate for its archaic Web site of the same name. You'll find the handbook free at any Logis-de-France hotel, and you should grab one the moment you spot its green cover. The Web site is great to look at, with over 3,200 French hotels to muse over. But try making a booking online and you'll wait three to five days for an automated response, which is likely to be in the negative for July. Best to use the site for guidance only, and telephone each hotel you select using the number on the site or in the handbook. Even with the help of an online map, it's a long-winded operation.

Once you've reached your destination, however, you'll be delighted with the hotel itself. It's rare to find a bad Logis-de-France address, even if it takes the home-cooked meal to lighten your mood after a day's traveling. Searching for a small Logis-de-France hotel in the deep countryside is like making a voyage of discovery, a step into the unknown. Unlike a chain hotel, which can usually be tracked down by a motorway exit, a major junction on a roundabout, a shopping center complex, or even by proximity to a soccer stadium, finding a Logis-de-France hotel often requires map-reading skills of the highest order, a good sense of direction, and the courage to ask locals when you get lost. Even

---

LE TRAVERSANE

One of the quainter delights found in French hotels in general and Logis-de-France hotels in particular is a long, thin pillow they call *Le Traversane*. No one knows where this pillow originated, and certainly very few of us travelers can ever figure out how to remake the bed and place the *Traversane* among the bedsheets correctly. Nevertheless, it acts as a very nice sleeping aid, and it can also be used as a wedge between your legs if you sleep on your side and don't want to get hip or knee trouble.

TOUR VILLAGE *An artist at work in the* village du depart—*the start village set up each day for the race—in 2008.*

a GPS system may not be much use! But when you do find your chosen hotel, it becomes an experience to remember. Logis hotels are found mainly in villages or small towns, which means you'll be able to experience a bit of local atmosphere before moving on.

Planning Longer Stops

With so many challenges involved in traveling with the Tour, one of the most enjoyable alternatives might be to take a weeklong vacation in an area due to be visited by the great race—the Alps, for example. Or, as you wade through the logistics of following your chosen itinerary, you may see the appeal in branching off for a few days, cooling off on a beach, or taking a nap on the banks of the Lot River near Cahors. Another idea might be to drive a few days ahead of the race, set yourself up in the area you've chosen, and wait for the Tour to get to you.

ELECTRICITY

Voltage in France is 220 at 50 cycles, and wall plugs are of the standard European type with two round pins. If you're arriving from North America, where the voltage is 120 at 60 cycles, your computer charger, cell phone charger, and the chargers for accessories like iPhones and camera batteries have built-in flexibility and will work fine; you will only need a plug adapter for the French outlets. For other items, however, such as electric irons, hair curlers and dryers, electric razors, and so on, you will probably need a converter to bring the current down to the right level unless the device is marked "110/220." You can find small and portable travel converters, as well as plug adapters, at Radio Shack, in department stores that have large luggage sections, and at most major airports.

TRAVEL TIP: Buy your adapter(s) before you leave home, as it is almost impossible to buy an adapter for non-French plugs once you arrive, although some airports do stock a multinational adapter. I recommend purchasing a Swiss Travel Adaptor if you can find one; it is a brilliant invention that has no geographical preference, allowing you to adapt any appliance on any continent of the world. You can also use it at home if you happen to have bought a hair-dryer or other gadget while away.

When studying that route unveiled in October, be sure to research the areas near where the Tour is slated to pass. Even if it doesn't actually roll through, for example, the Gorges du Verdon in the south or the battlefields of the world wars in the north, you might still have the potential for some non-Tour sightseeing there, the kind that is either for your own entertainment or the sanity of your traveling companions. A day, a weekend, or a week away from the race might be just the thing to broaden the interest of the trip, as well as to heal wounds inflicted by the manic nature of chasing the Tour around France.

Spending time in one place adds another option to your accommodation choices. France has a massive network of *gîtes* and *chambres d'hôtes*; you'll see the signs for these types of places nearly everywhere, but most especially in the countryside. A *gîte* is basically a rented holiday home, where you are most likely to be cooking for yourself or popping into the nearby village for your meals and provisions. A *gîte* is often to be found in part of a farmhouse, or in an outbuilding on some huge country estate. The *gîte* is where many French families go for their summer getaway from the cities, so you'll need to book far, far ahead to get such a place—although as most French families don't start their holidays until the first weekend of August, you may get lucky. Even so, a *gîte* is often only available for bookings of one week or more—though that can make it an ideal base for watching the Tour.

The *chambre d'hôte* is a form of bed-and-breakfast within a large house or even château, and that may make it even more suitable to Tour followers. You'll find *chambres d'hôtes* easier to rent for a day or two, or a week, and you may also

A popular sign for inexpensive, welcoming accommodation in rural France.

be offered the chance to eat with the family whose property you are on.

To broaden the appeal of these lodging alternatives, and to avoid confusion, there's a growing trend to mix the characteristics of a *gîte* and a *chambre d'hôte* into a new hybrid. You may find that breakfast is included with your *gîte*, for example, or that it is available for a shorter minimum stay.

Both *chambres d'hôtes* and *gîtes* cost a lot less than conventional hotels, but you are expected to keep your room clean and tidy and change the linen yourself. Don't come home after a long day at the Tour and expect to see your pillows fluffed and a bottle of ice-cold champagne waiting in the fridge.

FINDING GÎTES AND CHAMBRES D'HÔTES

Gîtes de France (www.gites-de-france.com) controls both *gîtes* and *chambres d'hôtes* in France, but you can also get information and a brochure about this type of accommodation through the French National Tourist Office in your home country. Visitors passing through London on their way to France can find a mountain of information at the Maison de la France in Piccadilly, and that includes the *Gîtes de France* guide that you will also be able to get at any tourist information office in France.

If you've any energy left, then go to one more Web site, www.us.france guide.com. This comprehensive site is educational and entertaining at the same time, and from it you can research and reserve almost anything. I loved the link to "Lost in Francelation," a video blog that takes a tongue-in-cheek look at the tourist in France. (And here you always thought it was us making fun of the French!) Finally, anyone in desperate need of accommodation can contact the local tourist office where they're stuck. Look for the **Bureau du Tourism** or **Syndic d'Initiative**. Both offices keep up-to-date lists of hotels with available rooms as a way to promote local businesses.

ON TO PARIS

As the Tour reaches its dramatic peak in the Alps or the Pyrenees—it tends to alternate between the two from year to year—you'll realize that Paris is just a few days away, and that everyone's thoughts have turned to getting there as quickly and safely as possible. The Tour's cyclists usually have two or three stages between the last mountains and Paris, including one that will almost certainly be a time trial somewhere in south-central France. Or at least that was the pattern until 2009 when, unexpectedly, Mont Ventoux became the Tour's penultimate stage.

No one can say for certain what the race organization will dream up in the future, but whether you are planning to end your stay in Paris at the conclusion of the Tour or simply want to see the last stage on the Champs-Élysées, you'll have to have your travel plans and accommodation well thought out in advance. Those brave touring cyclists following the route will want to pedal all the way if they can. For most other people, a choice has to be made to see the next-to-last stage and drive up to Paris immediately, or to skip it and get to Paris a few days early. If you are in one of these two groups, hotel reservations need to be made early, for tens of thousands of weekend fans and tourists flood into the city to watch the *grande finale* played out. And if you've yet to try the TGV, now is the time to do so; just make sure to book well ahead.

COMPUTER AND PHONE

Okay, you've booked your flights, chosen your transport, booked 75 percent of your accommodation, mapped your itinerary, taken out full travel insurance, and managed to arrange for a neighbor back home to come in and feed the cat once a day. What else is there to plan for on your first trip to see Le Tour?

Are you bringing a laptop computer with you? It's a handy tool to have if you plan on checking e-mails or surfing the Internet for hotel rooms or information about trains or the Tour itself. France is pretty well covered for wireless Internet except in really remote areas, where good ol' dial-up may have to suffice. But if weight or size is a problem, most decent hotels in France have Internet-linked computers you can use, though it can be frustrating to have to wait to use them.

How about a cell phone? It's the best way of staying in touch with folks back home, calling ahead to confirm reservations, and trying to find your travel companions in a busy city packed with Tour watchers. Just make sure your phone is at least dual-band, if not triple; otherwise it may not work in France. And make sure you've subscribed to a cheap international pricing deal; if you don't, incoming calls will cost you a lot of money. If your phone is not blocked, so that it can be used on any network anywhere in the world and not just the ones twinned with your domestic provider, consider buying a SIM card when you arrive in France. You can get one at such main-street stores as Orange, Vodafone, or Bouygues, and the French number you get with the card means it is the caller who pays to speak to you, not vice versa.

The only thing that remains is to consider learning a bit of French in the months leading to July. Go on, give it a try!

LEGENDS OF THE MODERN TOUR

If a fleeting glance were enough to know a legend by, then either Eddy Merckx or Bernard Thévenet should head the list of great champions I've photographed in the Tour de France. But my first glimpse of them both was just about the last, since 1977 was Merckx's final Tour and Thévenet was a shadow of his former self in the succeeding years. Instead, I prefer to think of that 1977 Tour finish in Paris as a chance to say *au revoir* to Merckx and Thévenet, two men who flicked across my radar screen all too quickly and belatedly. Instead, it is the name Bernard Hinault that kicks off my list of all-time great Tour legends, for in his case first impressions were only the beginning.

BERNARD HINAULT

I'd never seen Hinault race before the 1978 Tour, so his head-on arrival in my viewfinder at Super-Besse, in the center of a small group of race favorites, created something of a stir in my head. "So this is Hinault," I remember saying to myself, hardly believing that I was about to take a picture of the French star. I was to see a lot of the man over the coming weeks, for Hinault was always at the front of the race, his gritty, determined features made all the more debonair by the French champion's jersey he was proudly wearing in competition for the first time.

That blue, white, and red *tricolore* was still on Hinault's broad shoulders with one day of the Tour to go, and I remember chancing my luck to grab a defining shot of him in the penultimate day's time trial. Imagine, I'm at the end of a two-week-long trip, and have failed to get a decent individual shot of race-favorite Hinault, the man slated to win the 1978 Tour *pour la France*. It had been a great fortnight nevertheless, with an introduction to the Tour and France that I could never have imagined before making the trip. It was a fortnight when Hinault became the dominating influence in my day-to-day existence. The man was everywhere I looked—on TV every evening, and in the French newspapers that I tried so hard to read each morning.

He was in my camera sights most days as well, yet the crystal-clear, tightly cropped action shot I so desperately wanted just would not materialize, no matter how much I ignored the other cyclists racing with him. It was a time trial that finally decided the '78 Tour, and it salvaged my burgeoning career.

After a long day on a rolling forested road, somewhere between Metz and Nancy, Hinault raced into view, preceded by two gendarmerie motos. As soon as the motos passed, I jumped out to get my treasured shot. There was the man— France's absolute idol that July—pedaling right at me, eyes focused on the road, legs pumping like pistons, shoulders rock-steady. His expression was one of raw determination and outright contempt.

Bernard Hinault time trials to victory at Saint-Priest in 1982.

The image I got, thankfully pin-sharp and correctly exposed, was one that I took again and again over the following eight years; Hinault literally grew on me. Just as with Lance Armstrong in his seven-Tour reign, I spent every working minute of the Hinault years with my eyes on the lookout for his distinctive features. With the exception of that rookie year in '78, Hinault was in yellow for most of the winning Tours that followed, meaning he was an easy target for people like me who wanted a pristine image of the *maillot jaune* in action.

Hinault would always lead the way on climbs, or be at the head of a daylong escape designed to ruin his rivals' chances. Not that Hinault had any rivals back then. With Hinault—as with Armstrong over a decade later—you could plan your day's photography with the utmost accuracy, knowing he'd be in front at a certain point in the day. You'd also have a good idea of who'd still be with him if he hadn't managed to shed all his challengers by then.

As his earlier Tours were won and passed into history, I became more engrossed in the legend that was building in front of my eyes. A shot of him at Alpe d'Huez in 1979, a descending beauty on the Col de Soulor in 1982, a corker of a time trial shot in 1985—these were all magical images I knew would accompany Hinault into the setting sun of his career, as well as accompanying the emerging dawn of my own career.

Yet it was the shots I didn't get that cemented Hinault's greatness for me. Back in those days, I was still a few years away from the opportunity that propelled me into the front row of Tour photographers with motorcycle access, and for every decent shot I got of the man, my colleagues were getting a hundred a day. Many of these were quite explicit, capturing the raging fury of Hinault's pride both on and off the bike, and almost all of them ended up in the pages of *L'Équipe*. It was there that I saw what I was missing: iconic pictures of Hinault jostling with rivals like Michel Pollentier or Hennie Kuiper on the mountains around Grenoble, or joking with a Renault-Elf teammate like Yvon Bertin early on in a stage.

Hinault races to Morzine-Avoriaz with Luis Herrera in 1985.

A rare, sought-after shot was of Hinault talking shop with Laurent Fignon in the 1984 Tour—yes, they did manage to get along, it seems. Occasionally, you'd see a published image of Hinault with all his anger on show, castigating a Colombian cyclist who'd got in his way, or chewing out a race official who wouldn't let a teammate bring him fresh water. One fiery incident showed him remonstrating with Phil Anderson, the day after a stage-ending crash had almost taken Hinault out of the 1985 Tour. The Frenchman needed someone to blame; best it be a foreigner as opposed to one of his own!

Hinault took great care to embrace and nurture his popularity in France, and one element of this campaign was to intimidate any foreigners who might get in his way. He also showed great contempt for most of the foreign media, something that endeared him even more to his loyal supporters. Hinault was clearly a man who spoke his mind and then backed it up with a potent physicality that photographers and fans loved, regardless of their nationalities. He bullied his rivals into submission by either attacking them when he knew it would hurt the most or taunting them with "or else" warnings if he thought that would help him get his way with them.

Some older Belgian journalists still believe Hinault had a hand in getting Pollentier expelled from that 1978 Tour. The Belgian was caught cheating in a drug test with someone else's urine, a trick, Pollentier says, that everyone was exploiting in those days. Their suspicion may even be justified—any number of French officials could have been swayed by Hinault to remove the risk of Pollentier actually winning the Tour and ruining a huge industry waiting in the wings for a Hinault victory.

Today, more than twenty years after his last Tour victory in 1985, you can still see Hinault at stage starts, or as a front-seat passenger in one of the Tour's two royal-blue Skoda cars, the ones reserved for the most special VIPs. Hinault looks charming enough, sure he does. But the man is as arrogant, as contemptuous, as aloof as he was thirty years ago. So don't expect him to say *bonjour* to you right away, even though he still makes a great target for your camera!

PHIL ANDERSON

He never placed higher than fifth in a Tour de France, but Australia's Phil Anderson is one of just three non-winning cyclists in my list of favorites because of the competitive way he raced the Tour. When the 23-year-old attacked on the Pla d'Adet in 1981, an act of daring that pushed him into the yellow jersey, he was only doing what he thought he should do: attack. That he attacked Hinault, of all people, at a time in France when such an act was tantamount to committing a crime, only endeared Anderson more to the foreign media and fans on the Tour.

Anderson may have let his enthusiasm go too far by ignoring his duties to his team leader, Jean-René Bernaudeau, earlier in the day. It was a naive act that led to Bernaudeau losing over four minutes, and it also led to Anderson's career being peppered with accusations that he always raced for himself. But his audacious debut guaranteed the Aussie lifelong popularity with the English-speaking world, which believed it had found an alternative to the dominance and arrogance shown by Hinault and his disciples in the French press.

Anderson's leadership of the Tour lifted the morale of English-speaking race followers to the highest point since 1962, when Tom Simpson of Great Britain had taken the yellow jersey before eventually finishing sixth overall. Although Anderson lost over twenty minutes during the alpine stages in 1981, he returned to the Tour year after year with renewed determination to win.

From a visual perspective, Anderson was superior even to Hinault. His body language on the bike was younger and sharper—a sign of determination—than the Frenchman's. Even at his most aggressive, the best Hinault could manage was a growl from between clenched teeth—a fearsome expression, but nothing on the scale of his rival's. With Anderson, that growl became a massive roar that erupted from a cavernous mouth with shark-like teeth, as he sought to stay in contact with Hinault. Even standing at the roadside with my camera in hand, it was impossible to miss the Aussie in a group of riders, for if it wasn't his ferocity you saw coming, then it was the way his stocky legs pedaled the bicycle, or how his crouched-cat shoulder angle exposed the effort he was making.

Whether in a sprint, a time trial, a brutal mountain ascent, or a terrifying descent in the Alps, Anderson took pole position in my daily search for action shots in 1981, and his physicality was so eye-catching that it mattered little that the yellow jersey had only been on his back for a day. His team-issue Peugeot jersey with its distinctive black-and-white checkered flag design was as singular as the broad ribcage it covered. Nevertheless, I was a very happy man one year later, for Anderson won a stage of the 1982 Tour and stayed in the *maillot jaune* for ten whole days, making him an even greater subject for the camera.

Anderson had come along just at the right time for me in 1981, for his emergence as a Tour contender pried open a market for my images that had not existed before. I knew I could easily sell a few images of Hinault as Tour winner, but the explosion of media interest when Anderson took the *maillot jaune* was unprecedented, and I've felt indebted to the man ever since!

Anderson's natural intensity and his burning ambition to succeed meant that he was not often a fellow you'd engage in finish-line small talk, especially if his day had been even one degree less than satisfactory. It took me a few years to finally say a few words to him, and only then because a journalist had set up a photo shoot and interview in a dingy hotel room in the Pyrenees. When not changing positions to get a better shooting angle in the

A typically determined Phil Anderson in the yellow jersey at Pau in the 1981 Tour de France.

fading light, I listened in on the interview, mesmerized by the moody yet forceful nature of Anderson's character as he gave his side of the story of how he had become a true champion of the "Foreign Legion," as the non-French on the Tour were called. By this time, 1986, others had followed in his footsteps—Australians, Americans, British, Irish, Kiwis, and South Africans—and were building careers for themselves. All of them turned to Anderson for advice, which he was more than happy to give. He still harbored big ambitions for himself in the Tour, yet I sensed he also enjoyed being a sort of captain on the road for younger cyclists to refer to.

I got to know Anderson much better in the years when he raced for Motorola, where he was a big player alongside the likes of Steve Bauer, Sean Yates, Dag-Otto Lauritzen, Andy Hampsten, and, of course, Lance Armstrong. By then, Anderson had ridden the Tour several times with Panasonic and TVM, two very different Dutch teams where his talents were either stifled by infighting between climbing specialist Robert Millar and sprinting legends like Eric Vanderaerden, Eddy Planckaert, and Olaf Ludwig, or ruined by poor team management (in the case of TVM).

The experience Anderson brought to Motorola was one of the core reasons that team succeeded. In typical Anderson style, he won a stage of the 1991 Tour at Quimper to establish himself as team captain before anyone else got the chance. Yet by then he was mature enough to see the value in sharing his experience and strength with his teammates.

Anderson was one of just two riders Armstrong looked up to—Sean Yates being the other—when Armstrong joined Motorola in 1992. Although Anderson's somewhat premature retirement in 1993 robbed the team and Armstrong of a powerful asset, the Australian's tough, no-nonsense attitude to racing and training had already been adopted in full by the precocious Texan. At least a small piece of Phil Anderson would have been inside Armstrong when he started his seven-year winning sequence at the Tour, and that's the kind of legacy Anderson would have liked to pass on, from one champion to another.

FOLLOWING THE TOUR

ONCE YOU'VE DETERMINED THE METHOD YOU'LL USE TO FOLLOW THE Tour, the next question is, how do you find it? In the run-up to the event itself, the Tour is seemingly everywhere—in the news, on the Web, plastered across magazines and newspapers on every continent. But of course the actual Tour itself is a traveling circus, putting up its tents in a new town almost

The peloton finds some welcome shade in Languedoc in 2008.

every night. For the Tour follower, tracking it down and planning a series of strategic interceptions is the next order of business.

First things first: Before you leave home, buy a copy of the *Official Guide to the Tour de France*. It is published in English, French, Spanish, and German (*VeloNews* publishes the North American edition, *Procycling* has the license in the UK, and *Ride Cycling Review* takes care of the edition for Australia and New Zealand), and it contains all the information you will ever need to follow the race. The contents include a map of the Tour route, detailed maps of each stage, and profiles of the more significant stages, as well as a near-exact itinerary for each stage, so you'll know where to be and when to be there. There are also great articles to read on Tour history, former winners, the top contenders, and the likely lineup of each team racing the Tour.

Newspaper kiosks, where you'll find L'Équipe *and the Tour guide, are common throughout France.*

Statistics abound in this glossy magazine, so it is a must to get a copy as soon as you can when it appears in May. If you fail to get a copy before you land in France, both the English and French versions are usually available in all good *Presse* in France (as newsstands are called) and at the Relay chain of newspaper and magazine stores in airports and major railway stations. You can also purchase these guides at one of the mobile Boutique du Tour shops that you'll see at the race starts and finishes each day. You'll then be given a free list of Tour starters, the definitive one that was not available when you bought the official program back home. Study this guide thoroughly, and don't lend it to anyone—it will become your best friend for all of July.

The guide is best used in conjunction with a good map. The standard and perhaps most useful reference is the traditional folded-paper Michelin map of France, although IGN (Institut Géographique National) makes maps that are more inspiring and easier to navigate through, if you can find them. IGN

TOUR CHEER   *Two young fans celebrate the 2004 race.*

also makes a series of fold-out maps that show where the wines, cheeses, food products, and national monuments are in France, making a nice distraction from your formal map reading.

Whether the reliable Michelin or the hard-to-find IGN, a big map of France is the clearest and most portable way to get the overall lay of the land and to calculate time and distance. Depending on how you are traveling, however, and how much of the Tour you plan to see, you could instead buy a heavy, spiral-bound atlas of France, or simply purchase large-scale individual maps of only the region (or regions) where you plan to see the Tour. Most spiral-bound atlases include a series of city maps as well, so you can navigate your way into a large metropolis as well as down tiny country lanes.

The best bet is to buy all these maps once you arrive in France, to save dragging them with you in your already overweight luggage. You can find them in French airport or railway station shops, as well as town-center *Presse* stores. But if you want to really plan ahead, visit Stanfords in London, Barnes and Noble in the United States, or buy them online once the Tour route has been

HORS DE FRANCE   *The Tour passes the site of the battle of Waterloo in Belgium in 2004.*

announced in October. The Tour's Web site, www.letour.fr, generally puts the full itinerary up on its site as early as April, allowing the race follower to really plan ahead.

Using a combination of the maps, the Tour's Web site, and the official guide, you can start planning your race watching immediately. Try highlighting the Tour route in one color on your map, and then highlighting your planned route in another color; where the colors meet represents your chosen viewing point of the day. Study the map and the guide together to select points of interest along the Tour route, such as a bridge over a major river, a Provençal village, a famous château, and so on. The Tour sticks to smaller *routes départementales* (secondary, "D" roads) as much as it can, allowing race followers to use the bigger *routes nationales* (major, "N" roads) or other D roads to bypass the Tour route.

The golden rule of daily Tour planning is to keep things simple. Don't try to see the Tour twice a day, for example. Don't try to see the start and then scoot around the race route; it just won't work. Target one location per day, and give

PRE-RACE *A giant Crédit Lyonnais lion greets the crowd from the publicity caravan that precedes the race.*

yourself enough time to get there, preferably by breakfast time or at the latest by mid-morning. Factor in such things as the time it might take to walk to see the race if you have to park well away from the route, and allow for delays at *autoroute* ("A" road) tollbooths—*péages*—if you are making a long diversion. There are a lot of travelers in France in July, and not all of them are watching the Tour; these misguided souls tend to travel more slowly, so allow time to get around them.

All access roads to the Tour's route are guarded from dawn and then closed at least four hours before the race convoy is due to pass, so there's your cutoff time. Your estimations must be based on the passing of the *caravane publicitaire* (publicity caravan), not the race itself. No one is allowed to drive against the race route once the *caravane* has left its starting point, even if that is 200 kilometers away.

MOUNTAIN STAGES

Mountain passes on the Tour route are usually closed all day, so anyone driving to see the Tour in the mountains should get there the day before, or plan on arriving during the night. As these are the most important stages to see, prioritize everything that will ensure that you get to your preferred location in time to see the Tour climb high. You are advised to miss the previous stage if it helps guarantee you a good place on the mountain (and the same often goes for seeing a time trial stage of the Tour as well).

You'll have to plan even farther ahead if you are trying to see back-to-back mountain stages. For this, you can expect to arrive in the dead of night if you already saw the Tour flow over a *col* (pass) earlier that same day.

If you plan to see an uphill finish of the Tour, don't expect to get down for many hours afterward, unless you've cycled or walked up. If you have, and you are moving on to another mountain stage after a stage that had an uphill finish—Alpe d'Huez for example—plan ahead and leave your four-wheeled transport on the road you plan to take once you've gotten down off the mountain. And leave it well along that road, several kilometers if you can, to give yourself a fighting chance to drive away faster than if you'd left your car nearer to the foot of the mountain. As you can see, the bicycle gives you a distinct advantage in such situations.

DRIVING TIPS

Once the Tour has gone by, you will have to wait ten or fifteen minutes before being allowed onto the route by car or bicycle. This delay is held to secure the road closure long enough to make sure there are no last-minute surprises, such as a team car racing to catch up to the race after a breakdown, or an official's motorcycle that's made a pit stop for gas in a nearby village. If you've parked your car some distance away, however, you can use this delay to make it back to your car and burn off some nervous energy along the way.

In a matter of days, you'll become accustomed to which roads to use to reach the Tour, or to get around it, and by keeping your ambitions modest, you

ROADSIDE *French fans cheer the peloton in the 100th anniversary Tour in 2003.*

won't make too many mistakes, such as arriving just as the peloton whizzes past. As you make your way along the roads that parallel the Tour route, you'll often see bright orange Tour signs indicating the way; these are used to guide official cars to the finish by a route other than the race route. If you find yourself on one of these roads and see some of the Tour vehicles ahead or behind you, you are more or less going in the right direction!

One thing foreign drivers must be aware of in France is a growing difficulty in finding places to fill up with gas. In many areas, particularly those close to cities and larger towns, unmanned gas stations, or *automatiques,* are becoming popular, both for economic reasons and to thwart robbers. The problem for the foreigner is that some prepay machines in these stations only accept French-based credit cards—an illogical situation, seeing as how France is the most visited country in the world for tourists! The likelihood of your foreign card working in an *automatique* is fifty-fifty, so make it a practice to fill up whenever you get a chance, especially on *autoroutes,* or in the country. Don't just assume you'll happen upon a "normal" gas station; they are disappearing fast.

You should also know that if you have rented a car in France, the license plate on it will end with a 60, indicating the car is registered in the *département* of Oise, to the northeast of Paris, regardless of where you've actually picked up the vehicle. This is done for administrative and financial reasons; local taxes for registering cars in that *département* are far lower than in all other parts of France. The problem with having the number 60 on the license plate is that it advertises the fact that the car is rented, and that the driver is almost certainly a tourist, making it a potential target for a thief looking for valuables to steal. So store valuables in the trunk, and make sure you never leave anything in the car, even if you think it is hidden from view; the curiosity of a thief can be awakened by even the most innocuous personal belongings left on a seat.

WATCHING THE RACE DEVELOP

A good traveler quickly learns to be adaptable, and flexibility in one's plans is a key attribute that every Tour spectator should embrace. One of the best ways to stay abreast of the race's daily developments is to follow the Tour in the pages of *L'Équipe,* the daily sports newspaper. You can find it each morning in your local *Presse* shop, and scouring its pages will let you modify your plans

CAR TALK

Cédez le passage/cédez la priorité: Yield, give way

Priorité à droite: Right-of-way to cars entering on the right

Vous n'avez pas la priorité: You do not have the right-of-way

Rappel: Obey signs

Vitesse limitée: Speed limit

Doublage interdit: No passing

Par temps de pluie: When raining

Rue piétonne: Pedestrian street

Sauf riverains: Local traffic only

Stationnement interdit/parking interdit: No parking

Parking payant: Parking fee

Parc de stationnement: Parking lot

Garage couvert: Covered parking garage

Sens interdit/entrée interdit: No entry

Voie sans issue: No exit

Sens unique/voie unique: One-way

Route fermée: Road closed

Déviation: Detour

Allumez vos feux: Turn on your lights

Entrée: Entrance

Sortie: Exit

Sortie des camions: Truck exit

Station de service: Gas station

Aire/Aire de repos: Rest stop (on *autoroutes*)*

Péage: Tollbooth

Télépéage: Automatic tollbooth reserved for Télépéage subscribers (though some allow use of normal credit cards as well)

Cartes bancaires: Tollbooth reserved for credit card users

continued >

CAR TALK *continued*

Manual: Tollbooth for cash users (often signaled by a neon-lit figure wearing a cap)

Toutes directions: To all directions (unless your destination is indicated on a separate road sign)

Autres directions: To other directions (if your chosen destination is not listed; it will be eventually)

* There are two types of rest areas on *autoroutes*: simple ones with picnic tables and sometimes a toilet, and fully equipped service areas with gas, food, lodging, and car accessories. If you're tired of driving and need a nap, the simpler areas are a lot quieter. But avoid nighttime halts in them; you are safer sleeping in your car in a well-lit service area, with other travelers nearby.

---

to suit any race developments that may bring you closer to your ideal Tour. For example, perhaps an American, a Brit, or an Aussie has become the new *maillot jaune*; in that case, a visit to a stage start is a good place to see this happy chappy in his yellow jersey, much better than trying to glimpse him for an instant in the middle of a fast-moving peloton. Likewise, your favored cyclist might be on the verge of taking the *maillot vert*, or green points jersey, making a visit to the next day's finish a tempting prospect to watch the sprinters arrive. You might even want to visit that rider's team hotel before or after a stage.

A waiting fan scans the horizon for a sighting of the Tour.

TOUR SALUTE   *French patriotism on a stage of the 2007 Tour, near Dunkirk.*

L'Équipe publishes about twelve pages of news and pictures of the Tour each morning, so it is a valuable source even if you cannot understand everything in it. Having a laptop computer and access to the Internet can be a good alternative, and of course you can find content there in English to boot, another reason to consider taking one along if you have space in your carry-on luggage.

GETTING AROUND

Driving in France can be quite a pleasure, even in summertime. But when following such a mass of humanity as the Tour de France, it constitutes a much more serious challenge. About four years ago, the French government created a lower rank of gendarme, especially to police local events like the Tour. These cadets might look inexperienced, but they have the same training as a real gendarme, they all carry handguns, and they are quite able to act in whatever way is needed to solve a problem. You'll find these young specimens spaced every 500 meters along the Tour's route, leaving their superiors to police the major junctions that run parallel to the race route.

Well-wishers await the 2004 Tour. Paris is a mere 3,016 kilometers away.

Always obey a gendarme's orders, for they are the absolute law in France, and you cannot win an argument or a debate, so don't even bother trying. Many of them—both the cadets and the real ones—speak English as a matter of course, so they are also there to help you out if you have a problem.

The gendarmes are extremely rigid on enforcing traffic laws, particularly speeding. The old days of whizzing through the French countryside without a care in the world have long since gone. Drive through a village at 10 kilometers above the speed limit (usually 50 km/h), or do the same on a normal road (where the limit is 90 km/h), and you are likely to be stopped and fined on the spot. More serious offenders are often taken to the local gendarmerie, or police station, where their driver's license is confiscated and mailed back to a local police station in their country of residence, effectively ending the trip by car, unless someone else can drive.

AT THE ROADSIDE

With so many logistics and challenges to face up to, you have got to really want to watch the Tour. Once installed at the roadside of your choice, therefore, it is important to assume the responsibilities of a true fan and cheer loudly at everything that passes by. Luckily, the Tour's famous *caravane publicitaire* acts as a great warm-up for the roadside spectators: It's a five-mile-long convoy of out-

MOON SHOT   *Youthful French fans offer their own salute to the 2004 Tour.*

landish cars, motorcycles, and trucks that precedes the arrival of the race by an hour or more, and it makes for an entertaining diversion before the main event arrives. You can get water-sprayed by a malicious fireman, watch professional dancers jive their day away (how do they keep that act up for a whole three weeks?), and have an endless stream of small gifts and trinkets thrown at you, such as key rings, whistles, rattles, and sun hats. Sun cream comes flying out of the sky as well, care of the Tour's medical supplier.

Half the fun is watching the other spectators enjoying themselves; their fun creates a wonderfully unique atmosphere that you'll want to experience time and time again. Mind you, you don't have to take your clothes off and moon the cyclists, as some French fans do, nor do you have to dress up as a chicken or a cowboy or a devil, or parade inside a giant egg, as some others do. But see what your conventionally attired fellow fan is doing, and then do it louder and more forcefully than that. If you are ever bored, you can even cheer the motorcycle photographers—we appreciate all the support we can get!

LEGENDS OF THE MODERN TOUR

LAURENT FIGNON

With his shaggy blond hair, wire-rimmed Cartier spectacles, and saucer-shaped blue eyes, Laurent Fignon did not look like a typical Tour de France cyclist. Indeed, he didn't look like a cyclist at all. Yet the elegant Parisian won the Tour in 1983 and 1984 and became something of a pinup boy in a France totally switched on to the Tour because of the successes of Bernard Hinault in the previous five years.

Fignon had it easy in the 1983 Tour, for Hinault was out injured, and another cyclist, Pascal Simon, had to quit the race with a damaged shoulder while still wearing the *maillot jaune*. All Fignon had to do was follow the right moves in the mountains and wait for Simon to pull out, which he did at Alpe d'Huez. Fignon then won his only stage of that Tour, in the penultimate day's TT, to secure a narrow overall victory over Spain's Angel Arroyo.

The next year was altogether different, and all of France watched excitedly as Fignon took five stages to win the 1984 Tour by over ten minutes from a still-convalescing Hinault. It would be an exaggeration to say the country was split down the middle, half supporting city-slicker Fignon, half country-boy Hinault, but their duel was certainly captivating. No one knew it then, but France would never have such a hard choice again. Around the corner awaited an American-Irish-Spanish-Danish-German-Italian-American-Spanish series of winners. If only Fignon had done better, some might say.

Fignon tried to win more, but injuries and a host of personal problems sent his career into free fall when he should have been in the prime of his life. He was dogged by the stardom that comes with two Tour wins, and the press never let Fignon out of its sights when things went wrong. It didn't help that Fignon was fast losing his hair at the relatively young age of 24, making him an even greater attraction for the paparazzi photographers, who zeroed in on his clumsy hair transplant around 1987.

Laurent Fignon was devastated to lose the 1989 Tour in Paris by eight seconds.

By the time Fignon re-emerged in 1989, an avant-garde ponytail was part of his new image, and by then he seemed to be coping better with the media attention. He'd won the season-opening Milan–San Remo one-day classic, and then scorched the Giro d'Italia with great aplomb. Tragically for Fignon, he came up against a phenomenally strong Greg LeMond in the Tour, ultimately losing the race on the very last day with that famous time trial between Versailles and Paris. Fignon had started the day with a fifty-second lead; he finished the time trial with an eight-second loss, the smallest margin in Tour history.

I remember finding myself inches from Fignon in the first moments of his desolation on the Champs-Élysées, his head in his hands, tears pouring from his eyes. I shot a series of images of a man I considered to be almost suicidal at that point. Thankfully, Fignon showed remarkable fortitude, recovering his pride and dignity and continuing to race. He even became quite matey with LeMond a few short years later.

A character like Fignon comes along rarely in one's career as a photographer. Often we are drawn to such people by their emotions or by a sense of their mystique, more than by their stardom. Fignon displayed all the characteristics of a turbulent and troubled young man. He may have been a great cyclist, but it was the frailty that we sensed within him that made Fignon such an attraction. Colorful, contentious, opinionated, cranky, driven, and often demented, Fignon had camera lenses pointed in his direction every minute of every day on the Tour, and I am pleased to report it was not at me that he once threw a full *bidon* (water bottle) in mid-stage. Nor was it me he once spat at; that particular venom was directed at some Paris-based photographers Fignon despised for their in-his-face tactics.

My favorite memories of Fignon are almost all athletic, from the time when he dominated that 1984 Tour and gave this roadside photographer oodles of wonderful picture opportunities. Fignon then strove to win back some respect in the bad years that followed. To have witnessed Fignon soloing to his last Tour stage win over the Ballon d'Alsace in 1992 remains a thrilling moment in my career—awesome stuff!

And it truly wouldn't have bothered me if it had been Fignon who'd won that 1989 Tour, for I felt he had genuinely earned it, even if LeMond had, too. They should have declared the contest a tie!

STEPHEN ROCHE

A single image sums up Stephen Roche's Tour de France win in 1987. The Irish star is lying poleaxed on the ground at La Plagne, an oxygen mask pressed against his mouth. There's a glazed, faint look in Roche's eyes, and without the benefit of hindsight, one might assume his bid for Tour victory had just ended. A desperate chase of race leader Pedro Delgado on the fifteen-kilometer climb had pushed Roche into oxygen debt. In fact, however, Roche virtually won the Tour that day, overturning a one-minute time gap to finish just four seconds behind the Spaniard at the line.

La Plagne was episode seven of a nine-frame saga that had begun on stage 10 when Roche put 2:29 into Delgado. It would end three days later with another TT victory for Roche and with it, the final *maillot jaune*. What lay between was a tumultuous duel that thrilled millions of roadside fans—many of them French and looking to Laurent Fignon for a French victory—with Delgado gaining back time on most of the ascents, yet losing time on the descents and in the TTs.

It's certain that if Roche had not had the courage to dig so deep at La Plagne, there never would have been an Irish winner of the Tour de France. For my money, it still rates as one of the most riveting Tours I've seen.

Stephen Roche on the attack to Alpe d'Huez in 1987, his triple-crown year.

Almost every image from that epic Tour shows Roche seeking, striving, searching for the extra seconds he needed to keep Delgado close for that final TT. He wasn't always a pretty sight in his titanic struggle against the Spaniard, but Roche had intelligence so far above his rivals that he was able to read a race to perfection and save his energy while others wasted theirs.

He also had the physical capacity to deliver ice-cold statements with his legs, and a beguiling charm that made finding friends among his few enemies a simple task. He formed easy friendships with the media as well, who saw in him a unique source for their stories. It helped that Roche was an extremely tough athlete who always had something interesting to say.

I knew how cunning he was too, having watched his controversial Giro d'Italia win in 1987, when he'd ridden against his Italian team leader, Roberto Visentini, and then had the balls to face off with him over supper at the Carrera team table. A few days later, the Italian crashed and went home, disgusted with it all. Roche, meanwhile, spent many a Giro evening locked in his own room, his meals prepared and served by a faithful *soigneur* (trainer) who knew which side his bread was buttered on. Roche didn't trust many of his teammates, or the hotel cooks, who might spike his food with a harmful or even prohibited medicine. This caution paid off, and a suitably toughened Roche came to France with his Giro victory acting as a hard-earned trophy envied by all those around him. That year, he was simply unbeatable.

Roche was the absolute boss of the peloton at the end of 1987, after adding the world championship to his remarkable summer on the run. Yet he was never again the same man, and struggled to find even a hint of the Tour form that had put him on top of the world.

He was a nonstarter in 1988, a nonfinisher in 1989, and a lowly finisher in forty-fourth place in the 1990 Tour; Roche's career had spectacularly fallen away from him. Worse was to come in 1991, when his team started the stage 2 team time trial while Roche was apparently still in the bathroom coping with a last-minute stomach complaint! Forced to ride the 36-kilometer course alone, Roche lost fourteen minutes and his place in that year's Tour. Surely his career was at an end? Not so. But Roche clearly wanted out of the sport, the trappings of fame and wealth in 1987 having suffocated his ability to train and race properly.

The next year, 1992, was to be Roche's farewell, and to achieve a sufficiently respectful end, the Irishman rejoined the Carrera team, with whom he'd won that Triple Crown in 1987. Stage 16 of the Tour was his target, and stage 16 was the stage he won, alone and in the mountains of the Massif Central.

Roche halted his career a month after finishing the Tour in ninth place, his reputation almost intact. I was one of a handful of friends Roche took to the Criterium of Château-Chinon, where he said a last goodbye to the peloton. He won that race too, though I suspect it was gifted to him by the friends he was leaving behind, most of whom, incredibly, were Italians.

THE FLAVOR OF FRANCE

WHETHER YOU HAVE TIME FOR ONLY A QUICK LOOK AT A FEW STAGES of the race or plan to make a long holiday of your trip, you can't separate the Tour de France from the country of France. The passions of one are informed by the personality of the other, and the character, the spectacle, the precise regularity, and the occasional fickleness of the race arise in large

An accordionist serenades the Tour in the Hautes-Pyrénées in 2007.

part from the character of the French people who have nurtured the Tour's development for over one hundred years. In any case, a visit to the Tour is a prime opportunity to absorb the nature of the land and people who created it. The wise traveler will seize the opportunity and make the most of his or her time in France, watching not only the race but also a culture that truly is like no other, anywhere in the world.

THE PEOPLE

A simple way to prepare for a visit to France is to look at a map of Europe and see how the country has been influenced by its geopolitical position, specifically by the fact that its 210,000 square miles of landmass sits centrally between northern and southern Europe, as well as hard against the Atlantic, like no other country on the continent. As a result, not only does France have a variety of temperatures to complement its land position, it also has a vast range of cultures, some influenced by its cold neighbors to the north and northeast, others by its hotter, more volatile kin to the south and southeast.

France embraces one of the most complex and least understood populations in the Western world, a result of the uneasy mix of its colonial influx of North and West African, Caribbean, and Indochinese immigrants with an unmoving, chauvinistic homegrown population. It's hardly surprising that the French are always at odds with one another over social and political issues, yet the mélange of old and new cultures is another great attraction to French life as we know it today. While the world around them changes beyond recognition and leaves the older French looking, and sometimes feeling, decidedly isolated in their arrogance, it is the younger French people who respond by exporting a new image to the outside world. It's not for nothing that France is also a world leader in banking, electronics, and aviation.

Such detail about French life might seem superfluous for the visitor and Tour follower, but one clear way to make the most of your trip is to understand and appreciate how the locals think, as well as how they carry themselves through life. Certainly, it is sufficient to be able to mutter a few words of French in a café or restaurant, and to treat oneself to a tasty *chausson aux pommes*—a miraculous little apple turnover in a flaky, tasty shell—in a village pâtisserie somewhere in France. But to understand why it takes a barman twenty minutes

TOUR DANCE   *Two brightly dressed women salute the Tour on a stage to Alpe d'Huez in 2008.*

to serve you—even though you've managed to wedge yourself right against the bar, between imbibing locals—requires a certain knowledge of how that same barman is thinking. (He's almost certainly letting the locals see how brazenly he is ignoring a foreigner.) There's not a more polite person in France than the little lady behind the counter in that pâtisserie. But you need to know why she is deliberately serving the next person, and the next person, in line behind you first. (Quite simply, she knows you won't be back, whereas her regulars come in twice a day for their baguettes.) Most of all, you need to know why it takes a waiter forty minutes to bring you the bill (*l'addition*), despite the fact the same person has just served you a three-course meal with great rapidity and sincere grace. Really, there is no explanation, other than that the French hate to rush their food and that some waiters are completely arrogant.

Other things can annoy or amuse you in equal proportion, and the fact that little or no logic can be discerned only serves to remind you how remarkable the French really are. At some stage you are certain to ask a French person for directions, or to seek help and assistance if something has gone wrong. The French take great pride in helping the traveler out, so you'll be well taken care of—as long as you understand the subtlety in the precious words uttered back to you.

Well, that's if you actually get words. Most questions, at least in rural areas, get a shrug of the shoulders as a first response; this is quite normal. But you mustn't take this at face value—body language for *Non!*—for you've probably directed your question at an innocent soul who is simply trying to give himself the time to consider a fuller response.

That weathered farmer who has wandered up to you at some gateway in Beaujolais because your car has broken down, the one with a beret on the top of his wrinkled forehead and a stained Gauloise cigarette hanging near to death from the corner of his mouth? He might look unhelpful—he might even look beyond help—but he could be the angel who's about to wrestle open your car's hood and fix the problem in a jiffy, and for nothing more than to see a smile appear across your face and to know he's proved you wrong.

Body language can be the most difficult language to grasp, and if it happens to be a French person doing the gesticulating, pouting, or shoulder shrugging, your task is going to be challenging. It doesn't help that we English speakers tend to talk with a barely audible lilt, or simply a nod of the head, and often have our hands stuck firmly in our pockets—that's a stance guaranteed to stir the blood of a true Frenchman!

The French, naturally rebellious at the best of times, love to stretch out a point, to turn a discussion into an hourlong debate, to frustrate their foe by whatever means if it gives them the upper hand along the way, so don't be surprised if your simple question about the arrival of today's stage is met with some astonishing theatrics. They're only playing with you! Either that or they simply hate the Tour and the upheaval it has brought to their part of the world for a day.

A vintage Citroën Tour de France car on the roadside of the 2006 Tour de   OPPOSITE >
France (top), and villagers in Normandy awaiting the race in 2002 (bottom).

The Tour races through Limousin in 2004.

The French are experts at trying to make you hate them. All the same, it's not that they want to be hated; it's a defensive mechanism set against a world that they feel less and less a part of. Whenever I'm faced with an awkward situation, I tell myself to respect the fact that 40 percent of the English language is made up of French vocabulary, and that, were I French, I too would be pretty frustrated that English is considered the foremost language in the Western world!

THE LANGUAGE

For anyone who has learned a bit of French prior to the trip, as well as for those who bring an expanded fluidity back to France each year, it is a horrifying experience to discover that upon arrival you cannot seem to understand a word being said to you. It's not because the French haven't understood you (despite what you may think when the person you are addressing gives a perfect Gallic shrug of the shoulders and overdoes the raised eyebrows trick, designed to unsettle you). It is simply because most French people adopt a jargon that does not exist in your English-French phrase book, nor does it appear in the hours and hours of recorded vocabulary for which you overpaid in the winter.

Proper French is indeed spoken like the French you so carefully learned—but that's the French of business, school, diplomacy, and department stores. For everyday conversation, French becomes a riot of slang. Nouns are replaced by jargon; sometimes lazily abbreviated local expressions are sprinkled about generously, dialect is applied, and before you know it, your efforts to speak French correctly seem worthless. This applies less to the service industry that gladly lives off your hard-earned currency, from whom you will get an almost exemplary response to questions and demands, than to the locals you try to engage in conversation—especially those you might need to send you in the right direction from time to time.

Everyday French slang is called argot, and is different from, say, the Cockney slang of Dickensian London, in that people from all social levels in French life

TRUE FRANCE   *The Tour at Le Lude in the Loire Valley, as French as one can get in France.*

LANGUAGE VARIATIONS

TRAVEL TIPS: When asking for directions or distances, you'll often hear the word *borne* (pronounced "bonne") in the response. Not strictly slang, *borne* is the name of the yellow/white stone post that marks each kilometer of French roads. Hence, a distance may be given as *cent bornes* (100 kilometers), *vingt-cinq bornes* (25 kilometers), and so on.

In the same way, many questions about money receive an answer using *balles* instead of Euros. *Balle* (pronounced "barl") is the old slang for the French franc, but is still used to say *cent balles* (100 euros), *vingt-cinq balles* (25 euros), and so on.

An anxious question to a French person—you are lost, hungry, out of fuel, out of money—will often receive an *"Ah bon?"* response that is baffling to most foreigners. It sounds as if the person is laughing at your predicament—"Oh good!"—when in fact he is saying "Oh, really?" So expect to hear this from time to time and don't be too upset when you do!

speak it as a matter of course, from presidents to street cleaners. There is actually an argot dictionary available; of course, it is only available in French!

Out of every negative must come a positive, and if you learn some of that slang, doors that have been firmly closed in your face might just start to open. You might even be able to work your way to the bar and order a drink on a par with the locals. Fancy a glass of red wine, do we—a *verre du vin rouge*? Try asking instead for a *pinard*; that's what the locals do. The French have a unique obsession with dogs, and big, burly men seem to display little shame that their dog, their *chien*, is a tiny Pekingese all of five inches tall. Before you engage the owner in polite conversation, try referring to his cute mutt as a *klebarb* instead—it helps!

You have a problem with your car, your *voiture*? Try using the universal term of *bagnole* instead. Okay, you've had a few glasses of pastis with your hotelier; you start to discuss life in general and your views of the opposite sex in particular. A woman—*une femme*? Best to use the term *gonzesse*, or even *meuf*, or *nana*; that'll get you noticed. A man—*un homme*? Try the slang forms—*un mec, un julot*—if you really want to impress.

Country bumpkins are found all over the world, but in France, a bumpkin is called a *plouc*, though it is best not to address such a person directly in this way. Even your job, *ton travail*, has its own descriptive: a *boulot*. Your close friend, *ton ami*? Try calling him *mon pote* instead. Most importantly, your bicycle—*ton vélo*—has its own slang too: *bécane*, or *spade*.

FOOD AND DRINK

Of all the idiosyncrasies you'll experience in France, nothing is more distinctive than the ordering and consumption of a square meal. For many visitors, food is something regarded as a necessity rather than a pastime, and this can apply, in the twenty-first century at least, to some city-based French citizens as well. It is in the country that the humble *repas* (meal) takes on an altogether different status, for in these rural areas the famous three-hour lunch is still rigidly respected and maintained.

LES CRUSTACÉS *Fresh shellfish on display at a poissonnerie in Paris.*

It is not just a simple question of selecting your dishes; it is all about how you eat, how long you take to eat, and most importantly, which wines you select to accompany your meal. I quite happily drink red wine when eating fish, but the French consider this an insult to the fish and the work that went into cooking that fish. They'll also consider me an ignoramus, but as long as I can drink red wine with my fish, I don't really care.

The French are certain that only they know best when it comes to cooking, serving, and eating food—and who are we to disagree with them? Nevertheless, some of their time-honored traditions need a bit of give now and then, which is why, on occasion, I play subtle games with the wine waiter, or sommelier. I always like a refreshing beer before dinner, and by having one just as the waiter arrives with a complimentary *apéritif de la maison,* I just know I'm going to wind him up.

The French serve cheese before dessert, the opposite way from most English-speaking countries. They do so in the belief that *fromage* cleanses the palate of tastes from the main course, allowing the diner to enjoy dessert all the more. It also allows the waiter to offer you a sweet dessert wine with your last course, with a glass of cognac or Armagnac coming at the very end. This is when the French consider your well-balanced meal to be finished—but they are wrong! They take no thought for wine-loving foreigners who plan on having more than a single bottle of wine—red, of course—between them, and who want to avoid

WATER

If you want a glass of plain water with your meal, ask for *un verre d'eau, s'il vous plaît.* A jug of water for the table is *une carafe d'eau.* Generally there's no charge for either of those, and the water is fine to drink. Bottled water, for which you'll pay extra, comes plain—*eau minérale*—or with bubbles: *eau gazeuse.* If you have a preference in bottled water, ask for it by name: Badoit and Perrier are popular fizzy waters; Évian and Volvic are still waters available almost everywhere.

LANGUEDOC   *The Tour in Languedoc, one of France's most food-conscious regions.*

eating that dessert altogether, or at least delay its arrival, because it will ruin the taste of the wine. I sometimes like to completely revolt the waiter by asking for some cheese *après* the dessert, if I've been foolish enough to succumb to the demands of my sweet tooth.

The French clearly value food over wine, even if the wine itself is considered to be a sacred accompaniment. Seeing as I regard the wine as more important than the food—especially as I tend to consume greater quantities of wine than quantities of food—I nearly always order the wine first, which confuses them even more. I have to eat, but I love wine; it's simple as that.

One of my all-time pet hates is when I've ordered a particularly nice wine— usually when I'm eating alone—which the sommelier then keeps out of arm's reach on a side table, along with other people's wines. It's another sign of the French telling the rest of the world they know best, except that this theory evaporates, along with your wine, when the sommelier doesn't bother to refill your empty glass. I once grew overly impatient in a Parisian restaurant and got up to pour the wine myself, at which point a vise-like grip took hold of my wrist, while the man's other hand took the bottle away. The glass got refilled, but the ordeal wasn't without its moments of tension, and the fellow made me wait just as long before pouring my next glass. The French can be so annoying at times, for you cannot make them see that by pouring wine more often, they may encourage the customer to order another bottle, maybe two more . . . and therefore the restaurant will make more money!

Still, we can learn a lot by watching how the French act at the dinner table. Some of them lay out the cutlery in opposing ways to the rest of the world—fork on the right, knife on the left, prongs of the fork pointed down, sharp edge of the knife pointing inward—and rarely offer butter with the bread that is delivered after they've taken your order because they believe the salt in the butter will spoil the taste of the food.

They also serve their salt from a five-holed pepper shaker, with the pepper coming out of a single-holed salt cellar, so be careful when you grab one to season your dish!

Classier restaurants may ask you to keep the same knife and fork throughout the evening—including the cheese course—and provide you with a *pose couteau*,

a tiny ceramic prop to stop your used knife from touching the tablecloth and picking up breadcrumbs. It's interesting to note the French hardly ever use a curved cheese knife, something we always assumed emanated from France.

More surprising is the almost total absence of a decanter for the wine, a regular attraction in the rest of the world whenever a customer orders that extra-special bottle. You do see a decanter used in some Parisian restaurants, if it helps entertain a set of tourists who've spent €50 on a bottle of wine, but no French sommelier worth his salt would produce the showy glass vessel for wines that are considered anything less than vintage. A twenty-year-old Bordeaux or Burgundy might—might—merit one, but certainly not a mere fifteen-year-old Côtes du Rhône. At least there is one rule we can easily (and regularly) adhere to: Eat simply or eat gastronomically, but eat well.

To the Tour follower in a hurry, my advice is to start the day with a visit to a decent *pâtisserie-boulangerie* (a pastry shop that also sells bread) and select from the array of delicacies that in modern times have made the local bread shop an Aladdin's cave of food treats. Unlike thirty years ago, the pâtisserie now stays open almost all day long, only closing for a few hours mid-afternoon after residents, visitors, and restaurateurs have got all the supplies they need. The shop then reopens around 17:00 (5:00 P.M.), in time to offer fresh bread and tempting cakes to accompany the evening meal. If, like me, you aren't exactly turned on by the average *petit déjeuner* (breakfast), try browsing your pâtisserie window before ordering such delights as *beignet de fraises* (strawberry fritter), *gâteau Suisse* (cheesecake), or a *pain aux raisins* (raisin brioche).

It is still permissible in France to order a *café au lait* in a bar and then sit down and eat the *pain au chocolat* you brought in with you—as long as the bar doesn't serve the same food. *Pain au chocolat* is a delicious variation on the standard croissant, rectangular in shape and filled with strips of chocolate and sometimes bits of hazelnut; it's called a *chocolatine* in southern France. If it is a small lunch you are after, try one of many quiches (baked eggs and cream in a pastry shell). These days, there's more to this style of cuisine than merely quiche lorraine, the original form of quiche, which adds ham or bacon to its base. Spinach, asparagus, leek, and even mushroom form a selection of quiches to enjoy.

< OPPOSITE   *Seafood is the most popular dish in Breton villages such as Le Roche Bernard.*

IN THE ALPS *Savoie and the Tour means regional dishes such as fondue*
or charcuterie Savoyard.

Most *boulangeries* (bakeries) offer freshly made sandwiches as well, allowing one to speed on one's journey with a minimum of delay; soft drinks and
bottled water are always available, too. If you really want to immerse yourself
into the French way of life, buy your baguette in the *boulangerie*, your pâté in
the local *charcuterie* (delicatessen), and your tomatoes, salad, and pickles in an
alimentation générale or *épicerie* (grocery store). Your *fromage* (cheese) should
of course be bought in a *fromagerie*.

Of course, the real way to eat in France is as the French do, and that means
taking the time each day to sit down in your chosen bistro and relax while
the waiter does his job. Some of the better lunch places are actually brasseries, establishments that are a combination of an upscale bar and a restaurant,
where the emphasis is on good food served quickly and with less expense than
a more formal restaurant. You'll find plenty of brasseries near railway stations,
or in village centers opposite the *boulodrome*, that dusty patch of land used by
the local men when they want to kill a few hours playing a round of *boules*, a

game similar to lawn bowling or the Italian boccie.

A French waiter is quick to spot new clients at his tables, and before you know it he (or she, although table waiting is still very much a male-dominated affair) will be cleaning the tabletop, removing the debris from the previous tenant, and replacing the silverware. You'll find this is done quite efficiently, and that's because waiting tables in France is a serious profession—what the French call a *métier*—not a part-time job peopled by college kids earning just enough to keep themselves in cigarettes and beer.

Of course, you will have taken care to select a restaurant frequented by other people, ideally some locals, for in France that still assures one of a very decent meal. An empty restaurant is a tempting prospect for someone who wants a quicker meal, or who has had a slow service experience else-

TOP *Poultry, cheese, and bread at an outdoor delicatessen on a Paris street.* BOTTOM *Crowded tables are a sign of good service and superb food.*

where. But that old adage of eating only where the locals go still stands today; break the tradition at your peril! Don't be surprised if your chosen table still has used *serviettes* (napkins) and cutlery on it; those are evidence of a popular eatery, and one that doesn't overcharge for its services.

Next step is to make friends with the waiter, who is immediately more appreciative of the latest client when his offer of an aperitif is accepted. The French hate to rush their food intake, so a good rule is to sit back and relax, let them see you're relaxed, and let them see you plan on eating and drinking your way through a few hours of the afternoon, just as they would if they were not working. You'll be so occupied enjoying that glass of *Ricard* (an anise-based drink) or white wine mixed with *crème de cassis* (a red, sweet, blackcurrant-flavored liqueur, also used in the aperitif *kir*) that you won't have noticed the menus that have been slipped onto your table.

Again, do what the locals often do: Consider the *plat du jour* (daily special) before burying yourself in the contents of the menu. A good restaurant only serves good food, but the plate of the day is a personal choice of the chef, and unless he's having a particularly bad time of it at home, the plate he recommends carries with it just a wee bit more thought and consideration than the regular dishes on the menu. *Plats du jour* tend to be less expensive as well.

In any case, one great way to learn more about France and its *gastronomie* is to throw caution to the winds and let your host call the shots, despite that habitual craving you have for *steak au poivre et pommes frites* (pepper steak

LE MENU OR LA CARTE?

Meals can be ordered two ways in French restaurants: You can order from *le menu*, or you can order from *la carte*. A *menu* is not a list of dishes; that's a *carte*, or what we call a menu in English. The *menu* is a fixed-price meal (also called a *formule*), from start to finish, and if you like everything on it (there are usually a few choices for each course), it's the economical way to go. If you want to choose each dish separately, or just want one simple course, order *à la carte* and have what you like. Wines will most likely be listed separately on the *carte des vins*, but there is no reason not to opt for the *vin de maison*—the house wine—as it will be less expensive but usually just as nice as a specially selected wine.

Pastry shops in France are not to be missed.

and french fries). The same applies with the wine; the waiter knows far more than you about which wine to drink with which course, so ask him for recommendations. He'll almost always suggest a local wine, often out of a *pichet* (pitcher), so unless you are eating in the extreme north of the country, go with his choice and learn. Up north they make beer, and they might offer you a glass of English wine as a way of making sure you drink their beer!

The ideal way to enjoy a day in France is to have a three-hour lunch break followed by a walk and a *sieste* (nap), and then stir yourself early evening for another round of eating and drinking. In reality, most of us are only capable of eating one major meal each day, so a choice has to be made between a full lunch and a feisty three- or four-course meal in the evening.

My days on the Tour offer me no such choice. I eat a *chausson aux pommes*, that puff pastry with an apple and cinnamon filling I mentioned earlier, just before the stage begins, and then try to hang on for dinner late in the evening, with the hope that I will be able to get a sandwich along the way during the day, or that the *salle de presse*—press room, that is—will have a mini-buffet of local meats and cheeses available. That's if the journalists have left anything for the likes of us photographers to enjoy.

Almost everyone else can make the choice of when to enjoy the big meal of the day, and by and large most traveling Tour fans are likely to opt for some evening extravagance, since they are on the move all day and therefore in more need of sustenance come nighttime. French meals in the evening are no different from French meals at lunchtime, except that sometimes the *plat du jour* might be a heavier version of its midday offspring. I do find, though, that the service is decidedly better in the afternoons than it is in the evenings. Turn up at a decent restaurant around 9:30 P.M. and you might be refused a table, as it is deemed too late to keep the kitchen open—either the chef is too lazy to cook for you or the owner doesn't want to pay him overtime.

Every region of France has its revered specialty—*spécialité de la région*—and for utmost authenticity, it is recommended that you select your specialty while in the place of origin. However, when you have chosen and enjoyed a *bouillabaisse* (fish soup) in its birthplace, Marseille, who's to tell you it cannot be reordered and enjoyed with even greater passion one week later in Nice? After all, one can order a *salade niçoise* almost anywhere in France.

Of all the complexities the traveler in France has to cope with, it is the choice of food that commands the most debate. Typically, you can eat the finest foie gras in the Béarn region of the Pyrenees, the tastiest sausage (*saucisson*) in Toulouse—also the home of the celebrated beef and bean stew, *cassoulet*—and the finest beef in the Lyon/Dijon area, where it forms part of the popular *boeuf bourguignon* stew.

You'd think that because fish can swim wherever they want, and because France has three distinct coastlines, no one region could lay claim to having the best seafood; everything is available everywhere. In fact, however, a general guide is to eat your mussels (*moules*) from the English Channel coast, your oysters (*huîtres*) from Arcachon or Oléron, your shellfish (*crustacés*) from the Brittany area, your sardines (*sardines*) from the Mediterranean, and your cod (*cabillaud*) from the Bay of Biscay. Freshwater fish like trout (*truite*), salmon (*saumon*), and perch (*perche*) are, of course, found wherever there is fresh water, but they are said to be especially tasty if they come from the Ardennes or Picardie.

VEGETARIAN FARE

Vegetarians have for years been considered aliens in this meat-loving, *charcuterie-*eating country, and even today you can struggle to convince a waiter that *végétarianisme* means just that—no meat, no fish, and even, for vegans, no dairy products. You should not be surprised, therefore, when the pasta you've ordered with only pesto sauce arrives with tiny shellfish for added flavoring. Salade niçoise has anchovies, which is why you ordered a *salade composée* (mixed salad), only to see tiny prawns hiding among the lettuce and the onions. Experienced vegetarians know the best thing is to cast such intruders to the side of the plate and carry on eating the rest, if only to avoid angering the waiter who doesn't understand your requirements.

It is not unheard of, however, for a considerate chef to come out of his kitchen to see exactly what you want, before suggesting some quite mouthwatering dishes—perhaps a simple *plat de légumes*, a vegetable plate embellished with the local olive oil and fresh spices. Or a *salade de crudités*—chopped raw cauliflower, broccoli, carrot, cucumber, and so on—with a layer of thin spaghetti placed on top. More often than not, though, I see vegetarians having to accept an omelet as part of their meal, maybe one tarted up with tomatoes, onions, spinach, asparagus, or mushrooms, depending on how amenable the chef actually is.

The situation is less dire in cities, especially after the health scares of the 1990s when British beef was found to be contaminated with mad cow disease. The French are even suspicious of their own beef, meaning there are now a few more veggie places sprouting in France.

Good resources for finding vegetarian fare are unfortunately thin on the ground, but the VegDining.com Web site is worth a try. Click your way to "Europe" and then "France," and you'll find a list of restaurants by city. In smaller villages, though, you may be on your own. For lunch you'll find that nearly every *boulangerie* offers some sandwiches filled solely with fresh, tasty vegetables. For dinner you will likely have to throw yourself upon the mercy of your waiter and the chef. With luck it'll be a delicious repast you'll want to write home about!

It's just when you've spent a few decades enjoying and learning these little nuances and have settled into a comfortable familiarity with their idiosyncrasies that someone tells you there's worse to come: the identification and selection of cheese.

Some French believe it is the humble cheese that carries the flag of regional pride when it comes to food. You can buy fresh *moules* when in Lyon because a plane, a car, or a truck brought them in overnight, just as you can order locally produced foie gras in a Marseille restaurant serving seafood; it's just a question of what you want to believe.

Cheese, however, carries a distinction all its own, and that is partly because there's so much of it available that its origin carries even more importance than meat or fish or *charcuterie* (cured meats from the deli). Also, cheese producers tend to be small outfits that can't easily export their products outside of the area of origin, meaning you'll have to go to Béarn to taste its wonderful

COFFEE AND TEA

The universal coffee in France is *café*, which is espresso: ground coffee brought to life with pressurized steam. If you want a large one, ask for *un café grand*. Other forms are:

café crème: espresso with steamed milk
grand crème: a large milky coffee
café au lait: hot milk with a little coffee
noisette: espresso with a touch of milk
café décaféiné: decaf espresso
Black tea (*thé* or *thé nature*) is available almost everywhere. Other forms are:
thé au lait: tea with milk
thé citron: tea with lemon
une infusion: herbal tea
Sugar for your tea or coffee is *sucre*.

DEEP FRANCE *Rural France presents a plethora of natural produce for visitors to enjoy.*

Saint-Lizier cheese. Blue cheese has fifteen known sources, from which fifteen distinct cheeses take their names—including Bleu d'Auvergne, Bleu de Gex, Bleu de Corse, and Bleu de Sassenage—as does *tomme*, a kind of cheese that comes mainly from Provence and the Alps.

In total there are about 365 recognized cheeses in France, with regions specializing in certain types: Bethmale from the Pyrenees, Broccio from Corsica, Echourgnac from the southwest, and Mimolette from the north around Lille (in the city itself, it is known as Boule de Lille). Most cheeses are named after their villages of origin, like wines, and just like wines they all carry a label of origin and appellation—it's a serious *affaire*!

What this all tells you is that the French know a fair bit about food and wine, and it is not a place for the foreigner to have any input, other than eating and drinking in copious quantities and trying to memorize a certain dish or menu for when you get home to your own kitchen. Thoughts of eating and drinking occupy the minds of most French people for 365 days a year; work is merely a means to earn the money needed to enjoy such a level of indulgence.

LE FROMAGE   *With about 365 recognized cheeses in France, shops are well stocked.*

Even though France has slowly and reluctantly integrated itself into a more modern world, it clings to its traditions when it comes to food, and it bases its reputation on making the simplest ingredients taste heavenly. Even before you've got that first bite in your mouth, you just know your meal has been cooked spontaneously, based on experience passed down over the years rather than a recipe gleaned from a rival restaurateur.

As you might guess from Chapter 1, I try to stay as often as possible in Logis-de-France hotels, and one of the main reasons is that the cooking is usually done by the proprietor or a close friend of the family. Whenever I taste something particularly special, I make a note of the dish so that I can try to order it again when I'm in another, similar, establishment—only to fail because the exquisite recipe was exclusive to the first address. So take the plunge, live for the moment, and always consider the exotic dishes on the menu!

LEGENDS OF THE MODERN TOUR

PEDRO DELGADO

If I live to be 100 years old—or, at the bare minimum, remain a Tour photographer until my sixties—I do not believe I will encounter a Tour de France winner as serene as Pedro Delgado. The Spanish climber was a runaway winner of the 1988 Tour, taking the race lead with over ten days to go and defending his position with ease. Yet he had to race the last week against an uproar of accusations that he'd taken banned substances. In fact he had taken some medications, but they weren't on the IOC banned list, so he'd broken no rules.

Delgado had almost won the Tour the year before, in 1987, and I remember feeling desperately sorry for the man who had come up against such an in-form and super-intelligent champion as Stephen Roche. I'd seen Delgado win the 1985 Tour of Spain, and knew what he was capable of if things went his way.

Things really did go his way in 1988, and by the time the Tour reached Alpe d'Huez, Delgado was in yellow, having attacked all day long to distance as many of his climbing rivals as he could. When he then buried his time-trialing ghosts by winning the following day's TT to Villard-de-Lans, Delgado seemed to have the Tour in the bag, with the Pyrenees and Massif Central still to come. At this point, Delgado was rarely out of my camera's sights, his mousy brown hair and matching eyes so appealing to this northern European, who was more accustomed to the cold-eyed stares and glazed features of my near neighbors in France, Belgium, and Holland.

Delgado looked absolutely radiant in his *maillot jaune*, and clearly wore it with pride, allowing a fellow Spaniard, Laudelino Cubino, to race away to a great stage win at Luz Ardiden, the challenging climb in the Pyrenees. Delgado bided his time before attacking close challenger Steven Rooks on the climb, a performance he repeated on the Puy-de-Dôme a few days later—except it was Danish rider Johnny Weltz with the Spanish team

Fagor who won, and the Dutch rider Gert-Jan Theunisse whom Delgado then attacked and demolished.

Both Rooks and Theunisse were from PDM, the team Delgado had left in 1987 to join Reynolds. The three had been teammates in that '87 Tour, and the two Dutchmen were now failing to fulfill their team manager's desire to ensure Delgado lost the 1988 Tour. As Delgado's race continued, the accusations against him grew in force, yet the Spaniard coolly pedaled his way toward Paris. A few days before the finish, the officials announced no rules had been broken, and, as a final flourish, Delgado clocked an amazing time trial on the penultimate day to secure his overall win.

Another Spaniard, Juan Martínez Oliver, took the stage that day, adding to my understanding of the unique patriotism of Spanish cyclists. Regardless of the teams they are on, Spanish cyclists often ride together as a unit, knowing the importance a Spanish victory will have for their fans and the media back home. Delgado's brush with the authorities had angered his Spanish colleagues, who felt that the allegations were a slur on their entire nation. Collectively, they left an indelible mark on that 1988 Tour.

Delgado should have built on that first win, for no Tour winner wants to settle for a single success, especially one that, in his case, was also slightly tainted. Tragically, in 1989, some sloppy team management had Delgado still warming up on his bike when the time came to begin his prologue ride in Luxembourg. He lost almost three minutes right away! Further trouble came the next day when a stressed Delgado dropped off the back in the team time trial, forcing his mates to wait for him; four more minutes were lost!

It all seemed over after just two days, yet Delgado launched into the rest of the Tour with a vengeful streak, almost beating Greg LeMond in the long, 73-kilometer TT on stage 5 before gaining a token thirty seconds at Cauterets as his teammate Miguel Induráin took the stage. Delgado then went ballistic the next day, gaining over three minutes against Fignon and LeMond at Superbagnères while Millar pinched the stage. Having started the Tour in such a disastrous way, Delgado was now less than three minutes off the race lead, and planning to do more in the Alps. In the uphill test at Orcières-Merlette, Delgado gained ten seconds on LeMond and almost a full minute on Fignon. He then raced into third place overall at L'Alpe d'Huez, after putting almost one minute into LeMond.

There was something of a party atmosphere when the top four riders overall raced away from the Alps to Aix-les-Bains, so superior to the rest of the peloton that they could literally amuse themselves on the climbs and descents before the final time trial. Delgado knew he was assured of third place overall, and knew too that he could have been the winner but for that stupid beginning. Still, he'd made a comeback on a scale not seen in a modern Tour, and had that '89 race not seen an equally tense battle for the yellow jersey, I do believe Delgado would have won. Yes, he was almost a three-time winner of the Tour.

I still see a lot of Delgado. He's a highly popular TV presenter whose unique input draws thousands of noncycling fans to the TV each day, especially the women! He also carries out reconnaissance on some of the mountain climbs for television previews of the key stages, giving the Spanish world a chance to enjoy his poetic riding style again. I love to hear him talk of that 1988 Tour, as well as his battles with Roche in 1987 and with Fignon and LeMond in 1989.

Delgado doesn't like to talk about his start in that '89 Tour. He is more forthcoming in his affection for Miguel Induráin, the Spaniard who helped Delgado so much in '88, '89, and '90, and whom Delgado then helped win the Tours of '91, '92, and '93. You sometimes see Delgado and Induráin sharing time on Spanish TV these days, their harmony proof of a genuine friendship that will last for the rest of their lives.

Pedro Delgado and Miguel Induráin after the 1990 Tour de France.

These two vastly different characters captivated a nation of sports enthusiasts for over a decade, making cycling the second most popular sport in Spain, after soccer. One such enthusiast may well have been Alberto Contador, winner of the Tour in 2007, who would have been less than 6 years old when Delgado won his Tour de France, and just 9 years old when Induráin won his first Tour. If, as expected, Contador becomes the next Spanish great at the Tour, there will be no one happier than Delgado himself.

SEAN KELLY

Sean Kelly was racing the Tour de France many years before the influx of Anglo-Saxons who threatened the chain of command in continental Europe. But because the Irish fellow was initially perceived as just an out-and-out sprinter, it took many years for him to share in the acclaim being enjoyed by all-rounders such as Robert Millar and Phil

Anderson. Kelly won a stage of the 1978 Tour, two stages in 1980, and one in 1981. But it was only when he took another stage in 1982, and with it the famed green points jersey, that people started to view him as a different and developing talent.

In 1983, having already won his second Paris-Nice a few months earlier, Kelly used his sprinting skills to take the race lead, but he was a highly disappointed man when he lost it to Pascal Simon in the Pyrenees just one day later. Kelly wanted more out of the Tour than mere stages or the green jersey, and he set about developing his skills across the whole range of disciplines. He'd use his new time-trialing and climbing skills to win the next five editions of Paris-Nice—still a record today—but a similar placing in the Tour proved to be beyond him. He got close to overall victory by taking seventh, fifth, and fourth overall in the Tours of 1983 to 1985, but Sean Kelly's place in Tour history is cemented as a four-time winner of the green jersey.

It took me a few years as well to see Kelly as anything more than a pure sprinter, but certainly his attempt to become a Tour contender meant I got more images of the man than if he'd stayed hidden in the group each day. It is quite impossible to capture close-up shots of a sprinter in a sprint, and Kelly was too serious an athlete to let his hair down and fool around with the other sprinters in the mountain stages as they rode their leisurely way to the finish in their own group.

Under normal circumstances, shooting decent action images of the green jersey wearer is a chore, for it entails letting the business end of the race disappear over the *cols* for half an hour or more while you wait for the Tour's top sprinter to arrive. The knowledge that you are missing the all-important battles up front is hard to cope with, which is why Kelly was such a dream for photographers: Here was a sprinter trying to climb with the climbers! Today I might wait thirty minutes or more to get a descending shot of sprinter extraordinaire Tom Boonen in the mountains, but with Kelly it would never have been more than a few short minutes. On some occasions, he'd be one of the first over a climb, on his way to a stage win at Saint-Étienne or Thonon-les-Bains, or seeking bonus points in some upcoming sprint in the valley below.

Still, Kelly was a complete mystery to me from day one, for his reserved, quite timid character seemed at odds with his physical brilliance. With such a mystique, Kelly was a fantastic subject to capture on film, and I was constantly seeking to photograph some of his quirky habits, such as licking his lips when considering a journalist's questions, or rubbing his chin between thumb and finger if an answer was not going to be forthcoming. His Irish eyes were suspicious of the outside world, yet twinkling with mischief too.

He'd always perch his KAS team racing cap on the very top of his graying head, the peak pointing backward, as he held court while sitting on the hood of his team car each morning, another delightful mannerism my camera lens homed in on.

Kelly's growing stature caught the attention of the Irish media, and this half-dozen-strong merry band of charismatic journalists sought Kelly's opinions and reflections on a twice-daily basis, at stage starts and finishes. Surprisingly for such a shy man, Kelly seemed to enjoy his morning chats with the press. He certainly knew how to intimidate his interviewers with long moments of silence, something an expectant journalist absolutely hates! If Kelly was reserved about giving them anything of interest to write about, the reporters at least managed to win status as unforgettable

A vintage Sean Kelly in a time trial during the 1985 Tour de France.

features of those Tours—and it wasn't just because, to a man, they all seemed to wear gray shorts and woolly black socks in the middle of a French summer! Almost every one of them went on to distinguished careers after Kelly retired, and it is said that "yer man," as they called him, actually comes along to their annual reunion in a Dublin pub each winter.

Kelly started fourteen Tours de France between 1978 and 1992, and was very much a senior statesman of the peloton by the time fellow Irishman Stephen Roche won in 1987. Kelly had dealt very well with the emergence of Roche as a Tour contender. Indeed, with so much attention on someone else, Kelly was able to concentrate more on his racing, a factor that helped him take those high overall placings in '83, '84, and '85.

Since he missed the 1986 Tour due to illness, 1987 should have been Kelly's best opportunity to make it to the final podium in Paris. Sure, by stage 11, Kelly was already five minutes down on Roche, who'd stormed to a brilliant time trial victory the previous day. But Kelly was deliberately avoiding the sprint finishes to make sure he was in the best condition when the mountains began; the TT was always going to be a bad day. Sadly, the Irish legend never made it to the Pyrenees; he crashed and broke his collarbone on the way south to Bordeaux.

That was the first year I had motorcycle access in the Tour, and although Kelly's was not the first Tour crash I saw, it was nevertheless a huge blow to see him suffer so much. Imagine a man who was one of my idols, crying in agony on the ground as he struggled to get up and ride his bike again. Kelly was still crying when he did remount, and cried again when doctors insisted he climb into the race ambulance a few kilometers later.

It took that crash for me to realize Kelly was human after all, which pushed me to take more pictures of him in the coming years, for I knew Kelly would not be around forever. He never won another Tour stage—in fact, he hadn't won one since 1982, the year he had stopped sprinting and tried to become an overall contender—but his efforts to keep racing with men much younger than he was gave me some memorable imagery.

Two years later, 1989 was a vintage Tour for Kelly, and therefore for me too, as I came away from France with a dozen strong images of him racing in the green jersey. I remember taking a few static shots on one of the final corners of the Col d'Izoard—shots of the overall favorites, such as LeMond, Fignon, and Delgado. I'd barely had time to wind on the medium-format film in my camera before Kelly pedaled by, every sinew in his arms, legs, and neck straining with the effort to keep pace with the leaders and maybe steal a few bonus seconds at the finish. I then recall trying to keep pace with Kelly on the long and very sinuous descent, until my nervous driver decided that Irish cyclists are best left alone at such times!

Until a car thief stole most of my Kelly images in 1990, the Irishman had accounted for the biggest portion of my expanding archive, and I was therefore extremely grateful to Kelly when he continued racing, year after year, allowing me to rebuild that library. Finally, Father Time called a halt in 1994. A decent-sized chunk of me stopped with Kelly that year, for the man had been central to my work enjoyment for almost fifteen years. I knew the world of cycling would never again experience someone as special as Kelly, and I felt honored to have experienced the very best of those years—the Sean Kelly years, I like to call them.

CHAPTER

THE REGIONS OF FRANCE

ONCE YOU'VE ESTABLISHED THE BASIC PLAN OF YOUR TRIP, THE NEXT step is to plot a course that will enable you to enjoy the full flavor of France. Of course, you can't really do that unless you make time to explore more than the route of the Tour. You may not be able to see every delightful corner of this magnificently varied country, but I can at least give you some idea of the opportunities that await the intrepid adventurer. As for the mountains, they demand a chapter to themselves, so while I've covered a bit of the Alps and Pyrenees here, look for more detail about all of the mountain regions, and the ways to enjoy them, in Chapter 5.

Officially, mainland France is divided into twenty-one *régions*, and then into almost one hundred *départements*. (The island of Corsica and four other overseas areas bring the full total of France's regions to twenty-six, but we'll ignore those outliers.) I believe this is a malicious trick to fool the innocent visitor, and I think it is why many writers prefer to categorize France into fifteen distinct regions, on a geographical basis rather than a historical or political one. But there's a structure to the country that gets confusing if you don't stick to the rules, so twenty-one regions it is!

All but a few deserve a weeklong visit at minimum, and Provence, the most captivating region of all, begs you to stay forever—which, to the distress of the locals, an increasing number of people actually do! This might just be a bit difficult for Tour followers to achieve; instead, the best bet is to plan ahead

to determine which areas of France the Tour will pass through in the year you choose to follow the race. By studying the route and placing it in relationship to known places of interest, the traveler can build a multicultural visit to France. It will be time well spent.

BRITTANY

Brittany is the most independent region in the country, and therefore an appropriate place for likeminded travelers to begin their planning. The Tour passes through almost every year, for Brittany is considered a heartland of French cycling, a region that has produced Tour winners such as Lucien Petit-Breton, Jean Robic, Louison Bobet, and Bernard Hinault, cycling greats who collectively won eleven Tours between 1907 and 1985.

When the Tour is playing elsewhere, Brittany reverts to its natural tranquility, with a windy northern coastline that conceals tiny beaches known only to the locals and a few wizened outsiders, and a western edge that experiences even more wind along its jagged and very spectacular sea cliffs. Because of its extreme position on a peninsula that juts well out into the Atlantic Ocean, Brittany is best visited when the Tour is there, so that the visitor has something to enjoy when the weather turns nasty, which it does on a regular basis.

I personally like Brittany for its long and rugged coastline—especially the Pointe du Raz, near Plogoff, very nearly the westernmost point of France—and most of all for the beguiling fishing villages that had an importance all their own when this region enjoyed total autonomy from France, as recently as the sixteenth century. One such place is Concarneau, a busy port sheltered within the Baie de la Forêt. There's actually a walled town built on a tiny island in the harbor, and a Musée de la Pêche (Fishing Museum) established in the ancient army barracks. Douarnenez sits sheltered from the Atlantic in the bay from which it takes its name, and is something of a regatta haven.

Bernard Hinault in a prologue time trial in Plumelec, Brittany, in 1985.

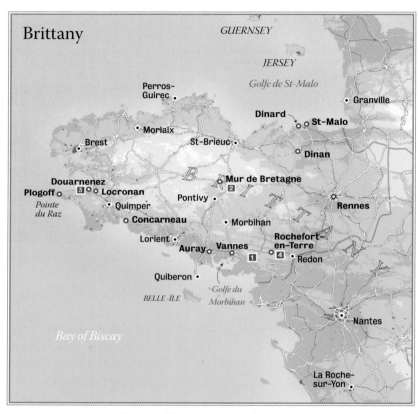

Brittany

GUERNSEY

JERSEY

Golfe de St-Malo

Granville

Perros-Guirec

Dinard

St-Malo

Morlaix

St-Brieuc

Dinan

Brest

B R I T

Mur de Bretagne

Douarnenez

Locronan

Plogoff

Pontivy

Rennes

Pointe du Raz

Quimper

Concarneau

Morbihan

Lorient

Rochefort-en-Terre

Auray

Vannes

Redon

Quiberon

BELLE-ÎLE

Golfe du Morbihan

Nantes

Bay of Biscay

La Roche-sur-Yon

RECOMMENDATIONS ⬛ LODGING ⬛ LODGING and FOOD ⬤ FOOD

1 Auberge Armor Vilaine

2 Auberge Grand Maison

3 Auberge de Kervéoc'h

4 Hôtel Château de Talhouët

LEGEND ROAD RAIL ⊙ CITY MENTIONED IN TEXT ⊡ POINT OF INTEREST 25km

BRITTANY   *The fishing village of Douarnenez.*

it's also popular for its proximity to nearby Locronan, one of France's most beautiful villages.

Brittany has hundreds of such places, varying in size and character, all the way from medieval Dinan in the east to the far west and south of the Gulf of Morbihan. Just 25 kilometers north of Dinan is the coastal village of Dinard, from where Greg LeMond launched the onslaught that won him the 1989 Tour, winning the long stage 5 time trial to Rennes and taking the *maillot jaune* with it. Rennes, the capital of Brittany, continues to be a place well worth a visit today.

Morbihan has one of the quietest stretches of Brittany coastline, with the Gulf of Morbihan tucked away inside an inlet famous for its tiny islands and expansive oyster beds. Morbihan numbers as one of its fishing villages Auray, from which a stage of the 2008 Tour began. Its waterfront buildings now contain many art galleries, along with small boutiques that proudly display the town's rich history of war and commerce.

The Tour is far too big to get into most of Brittany's fishing villages, so a diversion by the race follower is required to appreciate such delightful places as these. On a larger scale, the cities of Saint-Malo, Rennes, and Vannes are

BRITTANY   *Breton pipers play to the Tour in 2004.*

all worth visiting as well, particularly Rennes, the capital of Brittany, with its famous half-timbered medieval city center where you can sit and enjoy a rendition of Breton bagpipe music, *biniou*, a soulful sound made all the more pleasant if you are sitting at an outdoor café drinking a glass of locally made *cidre* and maybe eating a tasty *galette*, a thin, crusty wrap that is the great specialty of Brittany, despite all its wonderful seafood.

I Recommend

Auberge Armor Vilaine (no Web site; telephone 02 97 42 91 03) in Péaule (*département* 56), a typical Breton hotel-restaurant in the middle of a quiet village, just a few miles inland from the sea at Vannes. Modest in every way, yet with excellent cooking, especially if you order the seafood dishes. A Logis-de-France hotel.

   Auberge Grand Maison (www.auberge-grand-maison.com) in Mur-de-Bretagne (*département* 22). Renowned cuisine in an old-fashioned hotel, right at the foot of the Mur-de-Bretagne climb, in central Brittany.

Auberge de Kervéoc'h (www.auberge-kerveoch.com) in Douarnenez (*département* 29). You'll remember this establishment, a converted farmhouse with thirteen simple rooms, for its tranquility and tasteful cooking.

Hôtel Château de Talhouët (www.chateaudetalhouet.com) in Rochefort-en-Terre (*département* 56). There are just eight very regal rooms in this seventeenth-century manor, set amid quiet countryside near the Gulf of Morbihan, yet the prices are surprisingly reasonable. The restaurant is very much fit for royalty—definitely worth a short stay at least!

Regional Specialties: Brittany

Homard à l'armoricaine: Lobster served with a sauce of white wine, cognac, tomatoes, and butter.

Andouille de Guémené, oignons caramélisés: Slices of Breton pork sausage (smoked and aged, rolled pig intestines wrapped in a beef skin), served with caramelized onions and apples.

PAYS DE LA LOIRE

The city of Nantes, once the disputed capital of Brittany but now firmly established as the major metropolis of the Pays de la Loire, is where the river Loire flows through on its way out to the ocean, making the city a virtual gatekeeper of the revered Loire Valley. No trip to France is complete without a visit to one of the magnificent châteaux of this region, particularly one of its great Renaissance buildings at Brissac-Quincé, Plessis-Bourré, or Saumur.

The Tour rarely intrudes into this touristy area, though one stage followed the Loire all day in 2004, giving us glimpses of such gems as the châteaux of Le Lude and Montgeoffroy on its way into Angers. I'm sure journalists remembered the day more for the chance to sample this region's highly renowned wines—*vins de pays de la Loire*—while they waited for the stage to finish.

In the Vendée area to the south is the Puy du Fou, a popular theme park at the site of a major battlefield where the English and French fought each other during the Hundred Years' War (*Guerre de Cent Ans*). Of more interest to cycling fans is that this was where the 1993 Tour kicked off, and where Lance Armstrong began his seven-year reign as a Tour winner in 1999. Armstrong returned to the region to start what was supposed to be his final Tour in 2005,

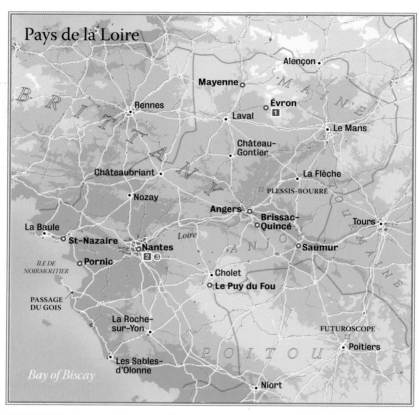

Pays de la Loire

Alençon

Mayenne

Évron **1**

Rennes

Laval

Le Mans

BRITTANY

Château-Gontier

Châteaubriant

La Flèche

PLESSIS-BOURRÉ

Nozay

Angers

Brissac-Quincé

Tours

La Baule

St-Nazaire

Nantes **2** **3**

Loire

ANJO

Saumur

TOURAINE

ÎLE DE NOIRMOUTIER

Pornic

Cholet

Le Puy du Fou

PASSAGE DU GOIS

La Roche-sur-Yon

FUTUROSCOPE

Poitiers

Bay of Biscay

Les Sables-d'Olonne

POITOU

Niort

RECOMMENDATIONS ■ LODGING ■ LODGING and FOOD ● FOOD

1 Relais du Gué de Selle

2 Hôtel de France

3 Le Pressoir

LEGEND   〰〰 ROAD   ── RAIL   ○ CITY MENTIONED IN TEXT   ⬚ POINT OF INTEREST | 25km |

PAYS DE LA LOIRE *The Château de Montgeoffroy in 2004.*

in a time trial won by David Zabriskie on the windswept road to the Île de Noirmoutier. In this same area, one can go and see the extraordinary Passage du Gois, the original connecting road to Noirmoutier, only usable during low tide and included in the route of the 1999 Tour.

In that Tour, the organizers got their calculations wrong, and the sea was still lingering on the causeway as the race sped toward it from the west. While Armstrong and his teammates were enjoying their second day as *patrons* of the peloton, a fleet of vehicles fitted with giant brushes on rollers drove up and down the causeway, sweeping

David Zabriskie tackles the time trial to the Île de Noirmoutier in 2005.

the sea away. The last-minute cleanup didn't quite do the trick, for a few cyclists skidded and crashed on the slippery surface, with some of them actually falling onto the wet sands just below the road.

Forewarned and already on the rampage in gusty side winds, Armstrong's U.S. Postal team got to the causeway first, moving their leader away from the pack and putting him out of danger, while adding to the carnage behind them as the speed forced irreparable splits in the peloton. Some of Armstrong's main rivals—particularly Alex Zülle, Ivan Gotti, and Michael Boogerd—lost all hope of winning the Tour that day. For some, the Passage du Gois had made a mockery of the stage, and that probably guaranteed that the Tour will never use the road again. But the way the Americans handled it had also been a first sign of the U.S. Postal team's tactical wisdom, an essential part of their weaponry for the next seven years. From this selfish photographer's viewpoint, they can go back there and run the same stage every year, maybe even run laps of the causeway for good measure—the pictures were that good!

The Tour, especially because of Armstrong, has brought great fame to the region. The American clinched his first Tour success at nearby Futuroscope in 1999, making his winning start at Puy du Fou all the more significant. He then led his Postal team to near victory in a team time trial in 2000. This was a stage dominated by the windblown ascent of the Pont de Saint-Nazaire, a cable-stayed bridge that connects Saint-Nazaire and Saint-Brévin-les-Pins. Gale-force winds forced Armstrong to wait for some of his weaker teammates, costing him victory that day. Though not as spectacular as something like the Golden Gate Bridge, the Pont de Saint-Nazaire is nevertheless worth a visit, if only to enjoy the remarkable views of the Loire river from the 200-foot-high span. The Tour first used the bridge in 1996 to celebrate the withdrawal of toll fees for car drivers. They should have charged the race photographers to go up there, for the results were quite impressive, even if the massive Tour peloton looked like a swarm of ants as it made its southerly traverse.

Saint-Nazaire has other claims to fame, too. Many of the world's ocean liners have been built in its shipyards, including the *Queen Mary 2*. And airplane-maker Airbus has a huge factory there, open for visitor tours.

Just south of the bridge lies the fishing port of Pornic, and it was from here that Lance Armstrong began his ultimate duel with Jan Ullrich in the 2003 Tour. The villagers probably forgot about Armstrong and the Tour quite soon after, but not the owners of the town's principal fishing-supplies store. This was where, under a really awful deluge of rain and wind, the actor Robin Williams went shopping for a sturdy umbrella while waiting for Armstrong to begin his ride, startling the shopkeeper as much by his presence there as by his ability to crack some of his better jokes in fluent French.

I Recommend

Relais du Gué de Selle (www.relais-du-gue-de-selle.com) near Évron (*département* 53*). A modern hotel and restaurant in the style of a traditional stone cottage, this roadside establishment has a natural lake and long walking path as one of its nearby attractions. The cooking is superb, offering typical Mayenne dishes from the sea, the lake, and the land. It is between LeMans and Mayenne.

< OPPOSITE *The Tour traverses the Pont de Saint-Nazaire in 1996.*

Hôtel de France, in the center of Nantes (*département* 44). An eighteenth-century classic, this hotel offers luxury and comfort without too much expense. Its **L'Opéra** restaurant is so good that you'll feel little need to wander the streets of the city for anything else, but be sure to check out **Le Pressoir**, one of Nantes' most popular restaurants, which offers *ris de veau* (veal sweetbreads) braised in *morille* (morel) sauce as one of its specialties.

Regional Specialties: Pays de la Loire

Brochet de beurre blanc: Poached pike, served with a white butter sauce.

Pigeonneau les Charmilles façon bécasse, toast d'abats, pomme tapée: Squab served with toasted giblets and potatoes.

HAUTE-NORMANDIE, BASSE-NORMANDIE

Like Brittany and the Vendée, the region of Normandy boasts a wealth of cycling heritage, most notably with the residence of five-time Tour winner Jacques Anquetil. Other famous Norman cyclists include Gérard Saint and Thierry Marie, as well as former technical director of the Tour Albert Bouvet. Normandy is also the home of Daniel Mangeas, the official announcer of the Tour you'll hear so distinctively at starts and finishes, if you've managed to get close enough.

Thierry Marie wins a stage of the Tour in Normandy, in Le Havre, 1991.

Normandy is a land most famous for the beach invasions by American, Canadian, and British soldiers during the last months of World War II, and a visit to those beaches north of Caen is an indispensable requirement for anyone within an hour's drive of the area. You'll quickly discover those same beaches were used by hostile Vikings back in the first century, Normans departing to invade England in 1066 (led by William the Conqueror), and the invading English in the fourteenth and fifteenth centuries.

Haute-Normandie
Basse-Normandie

English Channel

Amiens

Dieppe

Cherbourg-
Octeville

Baie de la Seine

Le Havre   Honfleur   Rouen
D-DAY BEACHES   Deauville
Bayeux   Creully   Lisieux
St-Lô   Caen

NORMANDY

Seine

MONT
ST-MICHEL   Granville   Fiers   Argentan   Dreux

St-Malo   Avranches   Bagnoles-de-l'Orne
Domfront   Chartres

Alençon

MAINE   Mayenne   Nogent-
le-Rotrou

Rennes

Laval   Le Mans

RECOMMENDATIONS ■ LODGING ■ LODGING and FOOD ● FOOD

1 Hostellerie Saint Martin
2 Le Clos Joli
3 Le Cheval Blanc
4 Chez Laurette
5 Côté Port
6 Entre Terre et Mer

LEGEND   ROAD   RAIL   ○ CITY MENTIONED IN TEXT   ⊡ POINT OF INTEREST   25km

HAUTE-NORMANDIE   *Normandy welcomes a stage of the Tour in 1995.*

Given such a checkered history, Normandy is naturally a unique area of France, with a distinctive architecture influenced by its succession of invaders. Although Le Havre, Caen, and Rouen were all but destroyed in World War II, most of the region's stunning towns remained intact, namely Bayeux, Deauville, and Honfleur. You must visit Honfleur, a fishing port at the mouth of the river Seine. The pretty town deserves its pretty name—it will take your breath away, with narrow, half-timbered houses seemingly holding each other up around the Quai Sainte-Catherine.

At the opposite end of the region is Mont-Saint-Michel, a tidal island that is another must-visit site for the traveler in Normandy. The rocky outcrop of land was first built upon in the eighth century, gaining enormous stature in the religious world because that first building was a monastery. Subsequent wars in that area only served to make Mont-Saint-Michel a bastion of power and influence, and it is hardly surprising to find this unique place high on the list of UNESCO world heritage sites.

Mont-Saint-Michel's biggest attraction is its exposure to the sea, and although a causeway now links the island to the mainland, people often use the original, and sometimes precarious, route to go across, walking over the sandbanks when the tide is out. Johan Museeuw, the Lion of Flanders, won a stage of the Tour that ended there in 1990, so there is a link to cycling even at such a religious shrine. The stage finished at the end of the causeway, right below the tiny walled city, where, sadly, the streets were far too narrow and twisty to contemplate an uphill finish of the race.

With quiet coastal roads and a wealth of river valleys, Normandy is a haven for touring and racing cyclists alike. It can get windy there, be warned, but a day spent pedaling in the deserted Normandy countryside is a treat like no other. Be sure to visit an area they call Suisse normande, a little bit of Switzerland in Normandy between Caen and Alençon; it's hilly, very pretty, and very peaceful.

I Recommend

Hostellerie Saint Martin (www.hostelleriesaintmartin.com) in Creully (*département* 14). Just northwest of Caen and near the D-day beaches, this establishment, like most in the Logis-de-France chain, wins a special mention because of the originality of its restaurant. The Saint Martin menus, of which there are five, include such delights as homemade duck foie gras flavored by a bit of Beaumes-de-Venise liqueur, or hot Crottin de Chavignol goat's cheese served on a plate of lettuce. The chef uses all the natural products of Normandy for his main meals—chicken, beef, duck, lamb, and, of course, a vast range of seafood.

Le Clos Joli, in Bagnoles-de-l'Orne (*département* 61). Set among woodland, approximately halfway between Alençon and Domfront, this pristine hotel is very much in the traditional Normandy style, with half-timbered façades all around and a hearty fare on offer in the classy restaurant. Ideal for a visit to Mont-Saint-Michel or a longer journey into Brittany; a great place to relax!

Le Cheval Blanc, in the center of Honfleur (*département* 14). Part of the Best Western chain, this is about the closest hotel to the *vieux bassin* (old port), where you can spend many an hour strolling between cafés and restaurants or watching the fishing boats come and go. Try eating at **Chez Laurette**, where the proprietor boasts of his seafood dishes cooked with spices and herbs. **Côté Port** is actually on the Quai Sainte-Catherine, and offers specialties such as *confit de canard* (preserved duck) served with forest apples, or a succulent *porc rôti* (roast pork) served with boiled potatoes and herbs. **Entre Terre et Mer** is one of Honfleur's *gastronomique* (gourmet) restaurants, with specialties such as sea bass (*bar*) served with ginger and chive butter, or lobster (*homard*) in a ginger and coriander *bouillon* (broth).

Regional Specialties: Normandy

Filet mignon de porc normande: Pork tenderloin cooked with apples, onions, and cider, and served with caramelized apple rings.

Filet de lieu à la normande: Black cod cooked in apple cider, served with a covering of creamy mushroom sauce.

Moules à la normande: Mussels in cream and white wine sauce.

PAS-DE-CALAIS, PICARDIE, CHAMPAGNE, LORRAINE

It has to be said that no matter how tempting it is to visit every region of the country, most tourists virtually ignore the northern reaches of France in order to find their pot of gold in the south or center. I could try to persuade them otherwise, tell them of the Côte d'Opale up there on the English Channel coast, with its wild, windblown beaches and sandbanked estuaries where few visitors ever go—but I won't. I could tell them of the beautiful city of Arras, its exquisite Place des Héros, and the labyrinth of underground tunnels under that same square that helped to fool the Germans in World War I and protected civilians in World War II—but I won't.

Farther south, I could describe the tranquility and peaceful ambience of the Picardie forests, particularly Compiègne and Chantilly, which house two of France's greatest châteaux. I could try to persuade the traveler to visit the valley of the Somme, not for the horrible history of war but for its gentle, meandering streams and rivers, where anglers spend endless hours in leisurely play, and where ornithologists trek to watch over three hundred species of birds in the Parc du Marquenterre—but I won't.

On the other hand, there probably doesn't exist a tourist in France who has not visited the Champagne region, based around the cities of Reims and Troyes, a land that has the hilly and forested Ardennes at its northern edge and the spectacular walled city of Langres to the south. East of Champagne

RECOMMENDATIONS ■ LODGING ■ LODGING and FOOD ● FOOD

1 Hôtel du Nord

2 Hôtel de la Plage

PdC
P

LEGEND ROAD RAIL ○ CITY MENTIONED IN TEXT ▢ POINT OF INTEREST 25km

ABOVE *L'Osserie memorial above the World War I graves near Verdun.*
RIGHT *The peloton in Champagne country in 2003.*

is Lorraine, where the cities of Metz and Nancy compete for importance in a region bordered by the Vosges mountains and dissected by no less than four important rivers, the Moselle, Meuse, Rhine, and Meurthe.

I Recommend

Hôtel du Nord in Compiègne (*département* 60). Simple rooms, no amenities beyond the basics, but an à la carte menu that will satisfy all but the most critical connoisseurs, especially lovers of *crustacés* (shellfish) or foie gras *chaud* (hot).

RECOMMENDATIONS ■ LODGING ■ LODGING and FOOD ● FOOD

1 La Hulotte au Lion d'Or

2 Hostellerie du Coq Hardi

LEGEND   ROAD   RAIL   ○ CITY MENTIONED IN TEXT   ⊡ POINT OF INTEREST   25km

Hôtel de la Plage (www.hotelplage-wissant.com) in Wissant (*département* 62). Charles de Gaulle used to holiday in this quaint, windswept village on the Côte d'Opale, although it's not known if he stayed in this nineteenth-century inn. This is an ancient hotel, with a décor and atmosphere that are distinctly set in the past. The rooms are quite simple, but thoughtfully spacious as in the old days. The restaurant is a classical room to behold, with the seafood cuisine still fit for a French president to enjoy. I loved this place for the access to long, sandy, deserted beaches, from which you can stroll out at low tide and enjoy the views of the surrounding *caps* (capes) of Gris-Nez and Blanc-Nez.

La Hulotte au Lion d'Or (www.lahulotte-auliondor.fr) in Signy-le-Petit (*département* 08). A country inn in a tiny village, 30 kilometers northwest of Charleville-Mézières. There's not a lot else in this little town, so enjoy a night or two in the cozy comfort of this Logis-de-France gem and explore the quiet *champenois* (Champagne region) countryside nearby. This is a "three-chimney" address, which means the rooms are above the normal Logis standard, and the food is extraordinary, using local produce as much as possible; flowers, herbs, and mushrooms accompany the locally fished trout and the locally bred pork.

Hostellerie du Coq Hardi (www.coq-hardi.com) in the center of Verdun (*département* 55). A truly classical hotel-restaurant that has been in existence since the mid–nineteenth century—so be forgiving when the floors creak beneath your feet! Views of the town of Verdun from across the river Meuse, as well as proximity to war-torn lands—as well as lakes, streams, and countryside walks—make this a great place to base oneself in Lorraine. The restaurant is as good as one can get, though a little pricey if you go for the full-course menu. There's also a bistro to the side of the hotel, and many other great eateries.

Regional Specialties: Pas-de-Calais, Picardie, Champagne, Lorraine

Waterzooi: Flemish soup, with eggs and vegetables to make the broth. It can be made with chicken (*waterzooi de poulet*) or fish (*waterzooi de poissons*). Variations include cooking in beer or wine. The name is actually Dutch, and literally means "watery mess."

Andouillette de Troyes: Sausage made from the stomach and large intestines of a pig. The mixture is marinated in onions, salt, and pepper and slowly cooked for five hours to produce a distinctive flavor.

Papillotes de hareng à la boulonnaise: Filets of herring with herring eggs, shallots, and butter, baked in foil with garlic, lemon juice, and butter.

ALSACE

For my money, the Tour de France doesn't venture often enough to the region of Alsace, a little slice of Germany currently part of France and likely to stay that way forever. The region is already doing well enough for tourism, with fine wines, exquisite architecture, towering castles, and Strasbourg, the official home of the European Parliament. Fact is, it does not really need the Tour.

When the Tour does visit, however, we get to see the vast, undulating vineyards that produce such fine white wines as Riesling, Gewürztraminer, and Pinot Gris. We become exposed to enchanting centers like Colmar and Mulhouse, and typical Alsatian villages like Betschdorf, Riquewihr, and its neighbor, the oh-so-pristine Ribeauville.

When the Tour started from Strasbourg in 2006, I felt I was one of the few members of the press who'd remember the *grand départ* for its *passage* along-

ALSACE   *The Tour departs from Strasbourg in 2006.*

Metz
Karlsruhe
Betschdorf
Haguenau
Sarrebourg
Saverne
Molsheim
Strasbourg
Nancy
Obernai
CHÂTEAU DU HAUT KOENIGSBOURG
GERMANY
Sélestat
St-Dié-des-Vosges
Ribeauville
Riquewihr
Villigen
Épinal
Colmar
Freiburg
Murbach
Guebwiller
Mulhouse
Basel
Zurich
Alsace
Belfort
SWITZ.

LORRAINE
Moselle
Rhine
BADEN

RECOMMENDATIONS ■ LODGING ■ LODGING and FOOD ● FOOD

1 Hôtel la Diligence
2 Domaine Langmatt
3 Hostellerie Le Maréchal

LEGEND ROAD RAIL ○ CITY MENTIONED IN TEXT ☐ POINT OF INTEREST 25km

side the outer canal of the enchanting inner city rather than the drug scandal that had begun a few days earlier. I know I'll remember stage 2 more for the crooked, half-timbered architecture in the start town of Obernai and the gentle ascent into the forested Massif d'Obernai than for the long, boring highway it then took to get the race into Luxembourg.

Alsace is an area of France made for tourism, on foot, in a car, and especially on a bicycle. You needn't stay long, for this is France's smallest region. One of the best ways to determine its attractiveness is to flick through a copy of the Logis-de-France hotel guide to discover the large number of lodges and inns established in the vicinity. Walkers can base themselves in any one of these little hotels and explore the hills of the Ballons, while cyclists can be more adventurous and travel down the entire length of the Route des Vins in a couple of short days (or one long one if they don't drink wine and are in a hurry).

The Tour has yet to take me to the château of Haut-Koenigsbourg, but it is impossible to study a guide of the area and not be drawn to its majesty, sitting as it does high above the country, overlooking the Rhine and beyond that into Germany. Naturally, the language here is a mixture of French and German, but as the French refuse to admit to being a bit German, they try to impress upon you that the other language is, of course, Alsatian. A few staunch people still refuse to communicate in French, despite the passing of time.

Nightlife is distinctly Germanic, with beer being drunk in *bierstubs* and wine in *winstubs*. Having learned a few words of German before I ever studied French, I find it funny to see a famous dish like sauerkraut—thin strips of white cabbage fermented in a sour acid—spelled *choucroute* in French. At least they call the Tour de France *Le Tour de France*.

I Recommend

Hôtel La Diligence (www.hotel-diligence.com) in Obernai (*département* 67). The architecture in this peaceful village will take your breath away, as will the half-timbered building of this hotel-restaurant. The cuisine is typically Alsatian, meaning you can expect to eat very, very well, with dishes featuring pork, sausages, or freshwater fish like trout and pike. The stairs and floors creak a little in this place, so you'll need to send yourself to sleep with excesses of local beers or the *vins d'Alsace*, or even locally made *schnapps*.

The Hôtel La Diligence in Obernai exudes Alsatian charm.

Domaine Langmatt (www.domainelangmatt.com) in Murbach (*département* 68). Located in forested tranquility between Mulhouse and Colmar, this large inn has an indoor heated swimming pool, suggesting a year-round clientele that enjoys summer walks in the Vosges or skiing on the Markstein mountain. The rooms are spacious but simple, as the priority here is exercise, followed by relaxation in the sauna or pool, and then many hours eating and drinking in the lavish restaurant.

Hostellerie Le Maréchal (www.hotel-le-marechal.com) in Colmar (*département* 68). This sixteenth-century dwelling has to be seen to be believed, and better still, it has to be experienced from the inside out. Built literally into the banks of the river Lauch, at the heart of Colmar's half-timbered old town, Le Maréchal offers hospitality of the highest order. Choose between a night in the Wagner or Bach suites and a simpler form of sleeping in one of thirty other rooms. But make sure you go for the host's eight-course Gala menu in the hotel's restaurant, À l'Échevin, with wines chosen for each course by the resident *sommelier*! You'll need a good bike ride the next morning to burn it off.

Regional Specialties: Alsace

Filet de boeuf au foie d'oie en croûte de choucroute: Filet of beef with goose liver in a crust of sauerkraut.

Blanc de turbot duxeline, sauce au vermouth: Filet of turbot cooked in a vermouth sauce.

FRANCHE-COMTÉ

We're heading south now, driving or cycling out of the Vosges—hallowed terrain of the Tour—with first Germany on our left and then Switzerland, to the east of Besançon in Franche-Comté. The Tour comes through here every few years, stopping or starting at Lons-le-Saunier, Belfort, Montbéliard, Pontarlier, or Dôle. Speedsters like Olaf Ludwig and Jerome Blijlevens have won the sprint into Besançon, the capital of the region, which often acts as a staging area for the first alpine stages. Nearby, Lance Armstrong abandoned the race on a nasty wet day in 1996, not knowing his ailment was in fact the onset of testicular cancer. In fact, the Texan returned to Besançon with greater panache eight years later to win his fifth stage of the 2004 Tour, as well as, virtually, the Tour itself.

Visitors to Franche-Comté, possessing a more modest ambition, can choose between hiking or cycling in the highlands of the Jura and driving or cycling up

FACE TIME   *English fans salute Lance Armstrong in Franche-Comté in 2004.*

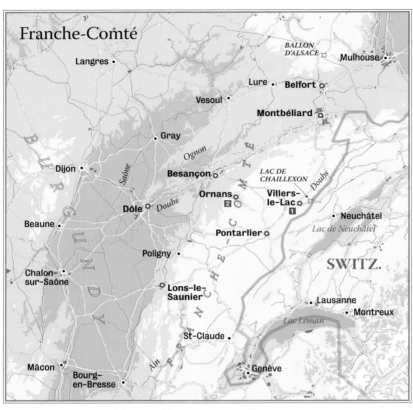

Franche-Comté

Langres

BALLON D'ALSACE

Mulhouse

Lure
Belfort

Vesoul

Montbéliard

Gray

Ognon

Dijon

Saône

Besançon

LAC DE CHAILLEXON

Doubs

Ornans
2

Villers-le-Lac
1

Dôle
Doubs

Neuchâtel

Lac de Neuchâtel

Beaune

Pontarlier

SWITZ.

Poligny

Chalon-sur-Saône

Lons-le-Saunier

Lausanne

Montreux

St-Claude

Lac Léman

Ain

Mâcon

Bourg-en-Bresse

Genève

RECOMMENDATIONS ■ LODGING ■ LODGING and FOOD ● FOOD

1 Hôtel Restaurant le France

2 Hôtel de France

LEGEND 〰〰 ROAD   ---- RAIL   ○ CITY MENTIONED IN TEXT   ⊡ POINT OF INTEREST |‾ 25km ‾|

the Ballon d'Alsace, the first mountain the Tour ever climbed, in 1905. There's a memorial to René Pottier here, the French cyclist who crossed the summit first that year, but who then had to abandon the Tour the next day due to fatigue. The memorial is a tribute to his ascent of the mountain one year later, when he preceded his nearest challenger by a massive forty-eight minutes on his way to winning the Tour outright.

Probably none of these famous cyclists has ever visited the unofficial source of the river Doubs, a thunderous cascade of water on the Swiss border that is guaranteed to deafen you. It's also a thing of beauty, so take a look at the Lac des Brenets (or Lac de Chaillexon, as it is called in France), from which the Doubs flows on its way to join the river Saône at Chalon-sur-Saône.

I Recommend

Hôtel Restaurant le France (www.hotel-restaurant-lefrance.com) in Villers-le-Lac (*département* 25). Walkers and cyclists will love this busy little town on the banks of the Lac des Brenets, and close to the alternative source of the Doubs. They'll enjoy even more the service in this hotel, which is included in the prestigious Châteaux & Hôtels de France chain. Ignore the somewhat scruffy exterior; diners in the cozy restaurant will be spoiled by the choices offered in an area of great fishing, boar hunting, and pheasant shooting, the produce of which is to be found on the restaurant's ever-changing menu. The sommelier is a local, and is likely to offer you a glass of the local *vin de paille* (a kind of "straw wine" made from dried grapes)—especially excellent in that region—before one of the restaurant's more renowned *crus* (vintages). I loved this place!

Hôtel de France (www.hoteldefrance-ornans.com) in Ornans (*département* 25). A self-described simple hotel with twenty-five modern rooms, this is a Logis-de-France address that allows the traveler to experience the beauty of this divine village, whose buildings literally have their foundations in the river Loue! Riverside restaurants compete with the hotel's own excellence, so a two-day stay is a must. Carp and trout from the river and nearby lakes are the local specialty, but the high forests of the Jura provide the ingredients for other dishes such as quail, guinea-fowl, and lamb. The influence of Gustave Courbet, the realist painter born in Ornans, is everywhere, most especially in the museum that was once his home.

Regional Specialties: Franche-Comté

Poulet au Côtes-du-Jura: Free-range chicken marinated in white Jura wine, coated with a buttery mushroom sauce and served with pasta.

Fondue comtoise: A local fondue using Comté cheese, with dry white Jura wine, kirsch, garlic, pepper, and nutmeg to flavor the brew. Crusty bread pieces are used to soak up the tasty melt.

BOURGOGNE, CENTRE

The regions west of the Swiss border form a central band that clearly separates the north of France from the south. In Bourgogne and Centre (as well as Poitou-Charentes; see the next section), you could not find two more different areas to visit. Bourgogne seems to have it all: wheat fields, vineyards, beef, and chicken farming too. *Boeuf charolais* (the meat) takes its name from the region west of Mâcon, *boeuf bourguignon* (the recipe) from the area closer to Beaune, and *poulets de Bresse,* the region's famously tasty chicken, just a little farther south.

The wines are to die for as well—Côte de Beaune, Côte de Nuits, and Pays d'Auxois are revered areas that produce such appellations as Givry, Meursault, Mercurey, Nuits-Saint-Georges, Savigny-les-Beaune, and Semur-en-Auxois. These are either of the red, pinot noir variety—light, fruity, and very expensive—or the white chardonnay—crisp, dry, and also very expensive. This is quite a hilly region of the country, with *vignes* (vineyards) that enjoy long hours of hot sunshine in the summer. So it's far less of a cycling region than the one to its west.

Centre shares the Loire Valley with neighboring Pays de la Loire, but it can boast of the greater collection of Renaissance châteaux, with such masterpieces as Chambord, Chenonceau, Valençay, and Maillant. The region also has a few vineyards of its own—producing *vins de Touraine*—and includes great cities such as Chartres, Orléans, Tours, and Bourges. At its center lies the forested mass of Sologne, an area of about 1,800 square meters that contains wildlife—prey for hunters—and quiet country roads for some very enjoyable cycling. Don't worry, the hunters won't aim at cyclists, at least not before October 1, the official opening of the French hunting season.

< OPPOSITE *The source of the Doubs, near Villers-le-Lac.*

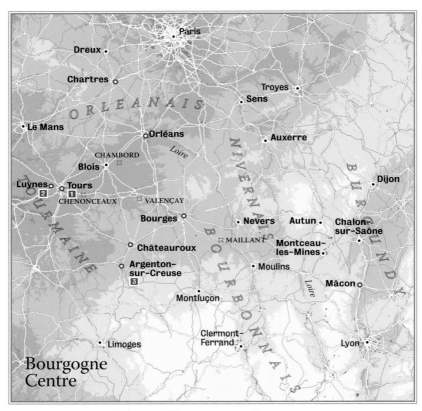

Bourgogne Centre

RECOMMENDATIONS ▪ LODGING ▪ LODGING and FOOD ● FOOD

1 Hôtel de l'Univers
2 Domaine de Beauvois
3 Le Cheval Noir

CENTRE   *The Château de Chenonceau on the river Cher near Chenonceaux is the second most visited château in France, after Versailles.*

I Recommend

Hôtel de l'Univers (www.hotel-univers.fr) in the center of Tours (*département* 37). A jewel of a place to stay, this hotel has been in existence since the nineteenth century, and it is as palatial as anything at the same price that you'd find in the heart of Paris. A gallery of former guests includes frescoes of Ernest Hemingway, Rudyard Kipling, Winston Churchill, Katharine Hepburn, and dozens of others, including many kings and queens of European countries. Eating is best done in the *vieux ville* (old city), ten minutes away from the hotel, where a warren of alleyways and squares conceals a massive choice of cuisines.

Domaine de Beauvois (www.slh.com/beauvois) near Luynes in the Loire Valley. One of several château-hotels in the area, this hotel takes pride of place due to its position above the Loire, and for its year-round exposure to late evening sunshine. Dinner can be enjoyed on the stunning terrace prior to settling down for the night in one of the exquisitely furnished rooms. The wine cellar, built into the limestone rock on which the hotel sits, is a feature in itself.

Le Cheval Noir (www.le-chevalnoir.fr) in Argenton-sur-Creuse (*département* 36). I discovered this beauty during the 2008 Tour, following a mix-up in my original hotel booking that had me scurrying to find any hotel that night. It would be a fabulous place at the best of times, but then it was as if I'd entered a modest version of paradise, with dinner being served to my fellow guests on a charming patio, behind the hotel's gated entranceway. I had already been shown to my country-style room by a willing receptionist, and the same man appeared at my table within minutes, eager to serve predinner drinks and make sure any stress from the day's work was already a thing of the past. A true star in the world of Logis-de-France!

Regional Specialties: Bourgogne

Boeuf bourguignon: Chunks of beef braised in strong red wine and a broth of garlic, carrots, and onions, served with a mushroom garnish and either pasta strips or steamed potatoes.

Escargots de Bourgogne: Poached snails baked in shells with garlic butter, shallots, white wine, and breadcrumbs.

POITOU-CHARENTES

It is when we look at Poitou-Charentes that we begin to see an altogether different sort of France. Gone is the cooler weather, the fertile greenery of the north, the more aloof people who live up there. In Poitou-Charentes, we start to see what I feel is the real France, a land of contrasts, colors, and cultures within a region gifted by its exposure to the warm Atlantic Ocean and enriched further by a heavily agricultural interior. It is here that we start to see the way south toward the Pyrenees, or east into the Massif Central, which is why the French often associate this region with Aquitaine, the region just below, and Limousin, the farming capital of France, just to the right.

In Poitou-Charentes, you can experience such cultural highlights as le chemin de Saint-Jacques-de-Compostelle—the road to Santiago de Compostela—with its line of fine Roman churches and abbeys that motivated pilgrims to continue walking, many centuries ago. The pilgrims may have come down from the north through towns like Parthenay, where the cobbled streets and medieval houses have a hint of the same English flavor as those in Normandy.

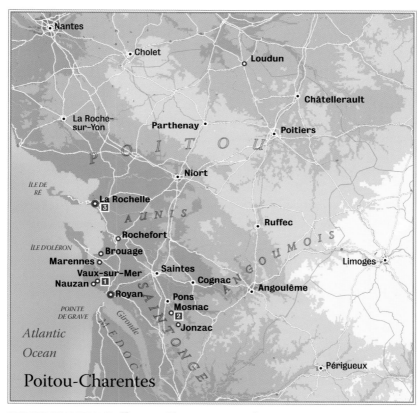

Poitou-Charentes

RECOMMENDATIONS ■ LODGING ■ LODGING and FOOD ● FOOD

1 Résidence de Rohan
2 Le Moulin de Val de Seugne
3 Hôtel François 1er

LEGEND ROAD   RAIL   ○ CITY MENTIONED IN TEXT   ⊡ POINT OF INTEREST   25km

They probably didn't venture into the marshy areas of Marais Poitevin, where today tourists explore the maze of waterways by flat-bottomed boats called *barques*.

Today's pilgrims could, if they were so inclined, venture away from their route to sample the alcoholic warmth that is cognac, except that its potency is likely to slow one down by at least an afternoon's nap in the town of the same name. The town's drink is made from locally grown white wines, and the process of fermentation and aging of fine cognac make for an interesting visit to any of its great distilleries.

The coast of Poitou-Charentes is what most people see in this region, and tens of thousands of vacationers ignore the quiet hinterland and head for its beaches. The coastline is nowhere near as long as Aquitaine's, nor are its beaches as discreet and hidden as those in Vendée. But it is perhaps more interesting, for its tiny seaside resorts are scattered between the world-renowned yachting port of La Rochelle and the estuary of the mighty river Gironde, which stretches all the way back to Bordeaux. Seafood is in great abundance here, with the famous green-tinged *huîtres* (oysters) of Marenne competing for attention with the excellent *moules* (mussels) of Brouage.

Two huge islands, Île d'Oléron and Île de Ré, are linked to the mainland by good roads, and—like most of the islands that the western side of France is blessed with—are well worth a visit, with yet more sandy beaches and seafood to enjoy. Both islands have villages with hotels and campsites, meaning you could base yourself there for a few days and visit the glamorous bustle of La Rochelle, rather than the other way around.

The Tour rarely gets to this coast because of the chaos it would mean for tourism, and it has to be said that the roads into La Rochelle get very busy with cars in summer, making it a less desirable destination for cyclists, even though the town is lovely once you are in it. This is a part of France you must visit one day, just as Riccardo Magrini did in 1983, when the Italian won a stage of the Tour that finished on the Île d'Oléron itself.

< OPPOSITE *A pair of barques in Marais Poitevin.*

I Recommend

Résidence de Rohan (www.residence-rohan.com) near Royan (*département* 17). Located behind the beach at Vaux-sur-Mer, this old hunting lodge has great views over a nearby park; guests have direct access to the beach at Nauzan. The hotel is a member of the 246-strong Relais du Silence chain (www. relaisdusilence.com), which puts a high value on privacy and accordingly has no restaurant. From Royan, a thirty-minute ferry ride takes the traveler to Pointe de Grave, at the very tip of the Médoc peninsula, where some of the world's finest wines await your attention. If you haven't been seduced by a full-blown lunch stop at a winery, then a stroll through Royan's town center will

POITOU-CHARENTES   *But does Armstrong love cognac?*

open up endless opportunities for dinner. All feature seafood dishes; some, like Le Dauphin, go a bit further by offering a mixed dish called *parillada de poisson*, a selection of cod, swordfish, sardines, and salmon accompanied by langoustines and mussels.

Le Moulin de Val de Seugne (www.valdeseugne.com) in Mosnac, close to Jonzac (*département* 17). A converted water mill from the sixteenth century, this place takes your breath away with its country-style accommodation and fine restaurant. The rooms are totally romantic, yet modern and spacious, with some actually overlooking the river Seugne. Specials of the kitchen include duck foie gras dipped in cognac, and lamb cooked with local herbs and butter. This is a good place to try a glass of the famous Pineau des Charentes, the locally grown wine that forms the base for cognac.

Hôtel François 1er (www.hotelfrancois1er.fr) in La Rochelle (*département* 17). An elegant two-star hotel in the quieter backstreets of old La Rochelle, this place triumphs because of its vast courtyard, which doubles as a much-needed parking lot for guests. Just a few minutes' walk from the famous port and its plethora of sidewalk cafés and restaurants, the thirty-eight-room hotel is a great place to relax after a day's traveling on the road or sea.

Regional Specialties: Poitou-Charentes
Noix de coquilles Saint-Jacques dorées à la plancha, risotto safrané à la tomate confite et persil plat, jus de veau corsé: Grilled scallops with dried tomato and parsley risotto and spicy veal gravy.

Parmentier de canard et truffes: Cottage pie of potato purée with duck, foie gras, and black truffles.

AQUITAINE
Aquitaine is a region of France as stunning and tantalizing as its very name suggests, and it's not for nothing that this part of the country has been so fought over by Romans, Germans, Moors, and the English, as well as the French themselves: It has to be one of the greatest jewels in France's overly ornate crown. Where to begin exploring a region that has mountains, beaches, rivers, and forests? That seemingly has more châteaux than the Loire—as well as the greatest wines of our world!

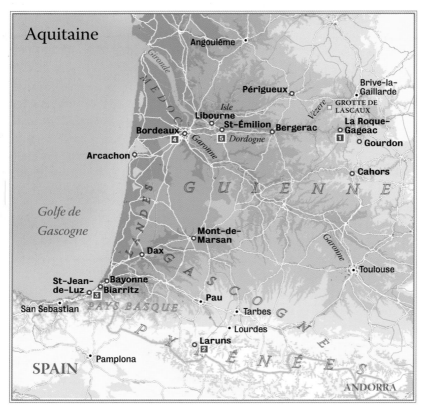

Aquitaine

RECOMMENDATIONS ■ LODGING ■ LODGING and FOOD ● FOOD

1 Hôtel La Belle Étoile

2 Hôtel L'Ayguelade

3 Grand Hôtel

4 Bayonne Etche-Ona

5 Hostellerie de Plaisance

LEGEND ROAD RAIL ○ CITY MENTIONED IN TEXT ❏ POINT OF INTEREST 50km

AQUITAINE *The Basque fishing port of Saint-Jean-de-Luz.*

Let's start with those wines, conveniently squashed into the northwest corner of the area, largely upstream from Bordeaux. Although the French hate the English every bit as much as the English hate the French, the natives must surely be grateful that *les rosbifs* took such a strong liking to the wines of Bordeaux that they opened a worldwide market for French wines that flourishes to this day. The English copied the Romans by using the Gironde to sail boatloads and boatloads of wine around the world via England, a country that still drinks more French wine than any other, with the exception of France itself. I wonder if the English had a hand in defining the borders of Aquitaine as well, for not one vineyard of any note is to be found in Poitou-Charentes; they're all south of the border.

Smaller than Lyon, quieter and more elegant than Marseille, Bordeaux has my vote as France's greatest city, after Paris. You'll find it is a pleasure to base yourself there for a wine tour, but staying in Bordeaux when a stage of the Tour is starting or finishing there makes it an even more enjoyable experience.

BORDEAUX, FRANCE'S WESTERN JEWEL

Because of the way in which Bordeaux is built on the river Garonne, visitors often lose their sense of direction when wandering around this impressive city. It doesn't help that the Tour de France often finishes a stage on the Lac de Bordeaux, further confusing the visitor with more water to consider. If you

stand with your back to the Esplanade des Quinconces— that's where most stages end— and look across the Garonne, you might think that the Atlantic Ocean is just a little farther away. You'd be wrong; it's on the opposite side of the city, and 40 kilometers away! Perhaps there's something about the light in this part of the country that sends out the wrong signal, or maybe it is that mass of water, flowing so powerfully that you're convinced you must be near the sea. And this confusion arises even before most people have had the chance to savor some of the local fine wines.

With Bordeaux's proximity to the vineyards, few people take the time to spend more than a half-day inside the city, preferring to take a one-day guided tour to a series of wine-tasting establishments in Médoc, Blaye, or Saint-Émilion. And who can blame them? Yet Bordeaux has some of the most wonderful architecture in France, so fine that large sections of Paris were modeled on the oldest *quartiers* of the western city. It also has Europe's longest shopping

street in the Rue Sainte-Catharine, a busy and highly successful commercial port on the Garonne, and part of the country's cutting-edge aviation development at nearby Blagnac air base. Bordeaux draws its citizens from far and wide, embracing immigrants from Africa and the Caribbean. Yes, Bordeaux is many things at once: culturally diverse, technically at the top of its game, geographically unique, and particularly blessed by having all that lovely wine on its doorstep!

DINING IN BORDEAUX

Try **La Tupina**, a traditional restaurant offering succulent choices in seafood and meat dishes served in front of a huge fireplace. For a more contemporary setting, look at **Chez Greg**, right on the waterfront; fresh fish dishes are featured, of course, but you can also taste international food like sashimi and chicken kebabs. Haute cuisine is represented by **Le Chapon Fin**, one of the first restaurants to receive a Michelin star in 1933, and reinvigorated in 1987 with equal aplomb in its original belle époque building. Bordeaux has a strong British and Irish heritage—for example, the best cricket team in France is from Bordeaux—so consider an evening at **O'Rowlands**, where Irish stew and Guinness are the house specialties, along with thick and heavy house-made bread.

I'm only able to enjoy Bordeaux many hours after a stage has finished, yet to stroll along the Quai Louis VIII and gaze dreamily into the fast-flowing waters of the Garonne is one of the true pleasures of evening life in this sparkling metropolis—that and the extraordinary choice of fine restaurants to be found in the labyrinth of pedestrianized streets around the Place du Palais, Place de la Bourse, and Place de la Comédie.

The Tour rarely visits the upper wine country of Bordeaux these days, its size and potential to disrupt being a major factor in any planning. It does manage regular passages through towns like Libourne and Saint-Émilion, on its way to or from Angoulême, Limoges, or Brive-la-Gaillarde. But to get it into the peninsula of land called Médoc—the area that contains such legendary appellations as Saint-Estèphe, Pauillac, Margaux, and Haut-Médoc—would cut off the few access roads that exist and threaten to ruin, if only for a day, France's wine supply to the world!

Cyclists of the touring variety will love the area either side of the Gironde— hillier roads on the eastern bank, flat roads on the western bank—and days if not weeks could be spent exploring the warren of quiet country lanes around medieval Saint-Émilion. Many professional teams hold training camps there, preseason or pre-Tour, although I am not sure if they do it so that the cyclists can train in safety or so that the team managers and owners can drink themselves silly every evening. At least you know cyclists are very welcome in these towns; just make sure you drink enough to justify your stay.

Another great area for cycling is Entre-Deux-Mers (Between Two Seas), the area of land that sits between the rivers of the Dordogne and Garonne (the two "seas" that give the area its name). But I wonder if the name isn't a tongue-in-cheek play on words, for this area of the wine country produces predominantly *vins de table* (table wines), has no Grand Crus classés, and therefore finds itself sitting between two oceans of better-quality wine.

Wine is also to be found around Bergerac, but is considered part of the *vins du sud-ouest* (wines of the southwest), the intensely rich grapes of Cahors, Gaillac, and Madiran. If you are in Bergerac, it is probably because you are following the mystical river Dordogne toward its fairytale heartland between

Le Pilar sand dune near Arcachon. OPPOSITE >

Beynac-et-Cazenac and Beaulieu-sur-Dordogne. This is the most beloved area of the Dordogne, with huge *cingles* (meanders) in the river that reveal sights like the châteaux of Beynac, Montfort, and Castelnaud, perched high above the river, or the prehistoric dwellings built into huge overhanging cliffs at La Roque–Gageac.

The Tour delighted the inhabitants of La Roque when it blasted through on its way to Angoulême in 2007, and I believe that is the only time in my career that I've seen the race actually follow the river. The whole area is one of many such places we stumble upon in our travels, but a place I intend to go back to in my next life. I'll be taking my swim gear, for the Dordogne is a tranquil pool this far upriver. Almost all the houses of this area are made from a golden-colored stone, and the combination of reflections from the river and the light of a setting sun turns the buildings a magical shade.

As with the Loire Valley, the name Dordogne actually covers an area much broader than the river itself, taking in towns like Périgueux and Sarlat-la-Canéda, as well as Gourdon in the neighboring region of Midi-Pyrénées. When—not if—you visit this area, you'll want to see the spectacular Grotte de

Lascaux and then travel farther afield to the villages and caves along the river Vézère, as well as the spectacular village of Rocamadour above the twisty and tiny river Ouysse. Beaulieu-sur-Dordogne is further east, closer to the source of the river in the Auvergne, and well worth a look.

The visitor to Aquitaine needs to do a lot of planning before settling on where to go. However, by deciding what you want to do, you can simplify things considerably—you'll find wine tasting in the north, river boating to the east, beach life to the west, mountain life to the south. And of course, the royal bicycle finds a welcome in all of these areas.

The coast of Aquitaine stretches from Médoc to Bayonne, a distance of almost 300 kilometers. There appear to be fewer than ten seaside resorts along that stretch of coastline, which gives you an idea of how long and inviting the beaches are likely to be. Access roads are few and far between, making these beaches even more desirable once you get to them. And if you don't want to sunbathe or swim all day long, prepare a picnic basket and spend a peaceful afternoon drinking, eating, and then sleeping in the adorable shelter of the Landes, a human-made forest that seems to cover almost one-third of Aquitaine, and matches in length all of that wonderful coastline.

Real civilization is hard to find here—just the towns of Arcachon, Dax, and Mont-de-Marsan—making your peace a little more lasting. Arcachon has the country's most revered oyster beds in its bay, and its villa-lined harbor has an enviable number of great seafood restaurants to relax in if forest life is not to your liking. Just south of Arcachon, partly blocking the way out to sea, stands the Dune du Pilat—at over a hundred meters high and almost 3 kilometers long, it's the biggest sand dune in Europe. Dax is a popular spa town with a regency feel to it; Mont-de-Marsan is a popular venue for bullfighting, French style, as well as a vitally important crossroads for the region.

There's one little bit of Aquitaine still to be seen before the visitor can move on to other pastures, the Pays Basque (Basque Country). This area is really a region in its own right, a heavenly tract of land covered with rich, green meadows and bordered by beaches and mountains. Choose between a stay at leisurely Saint-Jean-de-Luz, the bustling port of Bayonne, and so-chic Biarritz if you want some city life for a few days. All three provide a great base for cycling and walking trips. The people here don't just look different than other

AQUITAINE   *The Tour races along the Basque coast near Hendaye in 1996.*

French folk, nor do they just talk differently—they are an altogether different tribe, with their roots spread across the border with Spain. All Basques unite under the controversial flag of Euskadi (as Basque nationalists call the Basque regions of France and Spain), the Ikurriña, whose green, red, and white colors we see waved so proudly on the mountain stages of the Tour.

French Basques are less passionate about the cause of Basque nationalism than the more fanatical Basques over the border in Spain, but in some cafés and eateries in their land, particularly in villages along the valley of La Nive, you won't understand a word that's spoken, and you're likely to feel ever so slightly intimidated by the sight of the Ikurriña. This shouldn't stop you from enjoying a glass of Izarra, or a plate of Bayonne ham with the locals, for in this respect, this part of France is no different from the rest—they love to eat and drink.

If I had to choose one region of France in which to ride my bike, it would be here. On quieter roads than in Rhône-Alpes, but with a choice of rolling coastal routes, high mountain challenges, or traffic-free country lanes, the Basque Country has much to offer the cyclist, including a year-round cycling-friendly weather pattern.

I Recommend

Hôtel La Belle Étoile (no Web site; e-mail hotel.belle-etoile@wanadoo.fr, or phone +33 (0)5 53 29 51 44) in La Roque–Gageac (*département* 24). A stone-walled delight on the very banks of the river Dordogne, this is the nicest hotel in town, and with the best views. The restaurant fits the bill too, with fresh fish from the area, and heavier dishes like *magret de canard* (duck breast), *pâté basque* (a spicy pâté), and *cassoulet* (beef and bean stew). It's a Logis-de-France abode, with prices as modest as other similar establishments that don't happen to have their restaurant terrace overlooking the river.

Hôtel L'Ayguelade (www.hotel-ayguelade.com) in the valley of the river Ossau, close to Laruns (*département* 64). Simple yet tasteful accommodation prepares the traveler for a sumptuous meal in one of the two restaurants here. This is the culinary capital of France, and no effort has been spared to serve the nicest meals at decent prices. *Ris de veau* (veal sweetbread), braised sole, and Aquitaine veal are just a few of the offers at dinnertime. Cyclists can base themselves here before tackling the nearby climbs of the Col d'Aubisque, Col du Soulor, or Col de Marie-Blanc.

Grand Hôtel (www.luz grandhotel.fr), across the bay from the fishing port of Saint-Jean-de-Luz (*département* 64). The name is most appropriate

The Grand Hôtel in Saint-Jean-de-Luz.

for a renovated masterpiece from the belle époque. With fifty-two rooms overlooking the sandy beach on one side or the green hills of the Basque Country on the other, there is no better place to stay, if you can afford the high prices (July rates start at €310). The dinner fare is, of course, of the highest order from Michelin-trained chef

Nicolas Masse, who offers a balance of seafood and local produce in an eight-course tasting menu for €110, or something simpler in the hotel's Rosewood Restaurant overlooking the ocean. A spa attached to the hotel makes this an ideal stopover for the noncycling fan, who might also prefer to browse the town's many boutiques instead of spending all day up a mountain road.

Bayonne Etche-Ona (www.bordeaux-hotel.com) in the center of Bordeaux (*département* 33). This is one of the city's finest hotels, but I've chosen it for its proximity to the historical center of Bordeaux and the Place de la Comédie, where some of the best restaurants are to be found (there is no restaurant in the hotel). A Best Western address, the Etche-Ona has many facilities and the level of quality associated with the chain, yet all its rooms fall under the €100 barrier. Restaurants to visit nearby include Le Bistro des Anges, and Le Pavillon des Boulevards; all offer hearty French fare as favored by every true *Bordelais* (native of Bourdeaux).

Hostellerie de Plaisance (www.hostellerie-plaisance.com) in Saint-Émilion (*département* 33). A member of the distinguished Relais & Châteaux group of hotels, this one defies adequate description, not least because its classy establishment is more than matched by the beauty of medieval Saint-Émilion, the

The Hostellerie de Plaisance.

most famous wine resort in the world. The Hostellerie sits in the heart of town and offers guests rooms that face either the sprawling vineyards or a wonderful hanging garden set within thick stone walls. As befits a hotel of such standing, the restaurant is one of the highest rated in the entire region, with two-star chef Philippe Etchebest at the helm. Over seven hundred different wines await your appraisal in the gated cellar, so you've little need to venture out at all, except to burn off calories by walking the town's cobbled streets and alleyways.

PAU: A TOUR FAVORITE

Definitely the Tour's favorite stopover, Pau is a veritable sporting bastion among France's smaller cities. Through 2008, it had received the Tour on no fewer than sixty-two occasions, making it the third most visited city by the Tour after Paris and Bordeaux. Yet Pau is also very much a rugby town, with a populace utterly in love with the game. It also hosts a series of motor-racing events, with a format akin to Monaco, in that the circuit is laid out on the streets of the city, rather than on an isolated track. It held the world's first Grand Prix in 1901, and still supports Formula Three racing to this day. Pau owes much of its singularity to the British, for large numbers of them settled in Pau at the end of the eighteenth century; their influence can be seen in the belle époque architecture around the Place de Gramont and alongside the Boulevard des Pyrénées.

The Château de Pau, birthplace of King Henry IV on December 13, 1553, was used by Napoleon and has a garden that was a favorite of Marie Antoinette.

At the same time, Pau lies just 60 kilometers from France's southern border, and there is a distinctly Spanish feel to the city. In fact, at one time Pau was part of the region of Navarra. Combine these factors, and you can see why the Tour's cyclists get a very enthusiastic welcome each time they visit, especially the French and Spanish members of the peloton!

In recent years, there's been a determination on the part of the Tour's organizers to simplify the race route, making a three-day stay at Pau quite attractive, as it can offer stage starts and finishes, as well as a watering hole for stages that finish an hour's drive away at Hautacam, Superbagnères, La

Mongie, Pla d'Adet, or the Col d'Aubisque. Not too many years ago, Pau was a slightly isolated city, conveniently close to the Pyrenees but several hours from Bordeaux and its airport. Today, Pau has its own regional airport, with international flights arriving from the UK and the Netherlands daily, making the area a popular headquarters for organized bike tours, and an easy place for the Tour to ferry its VIPs to and from Paris.

With such an international clientele, Pau has an enviable choice of hotels and restaurants to offer, and a summer evening in Pau is not to be missed. Stroll past the magnificent château overlooking the Gave de Pau river, and you'll find yourself in the Place d'État, a crossroads of passageways that meet at the heart of Pau, where the best restaurants can be found. Come Tour time, it is here that locals get the chance to mix with stars of screen and TV, as well as glimpse some of the Tour's cyclists enjoying a late-evening ice cream or beer.

Pau has many fine hotels, but I would particularly recommend Hôtel Villa Navarre (www.villanavarre.fr). A nineteenth-century creation built at the height of the English influence on Pau, this classical enterprise is a five-minute drive from the heart of the city, and sits in its own parkland with views toward the sparkling Pyrenean mountains. Just thirty bedrooms are available in the Villa, yet their size and opulence leave nothing to be desired; it is here that Armstrong and his team and entourage always spent their Tour de France nights when in Pau. Wood paneling in the bar, restaurant, rooms, and reception area gives a lovely country air to the building, and it is quite a surprise to discover this is an address now run by the usually modest Mercure group of hotels.

Regional Specialties: Aquitaine

Parillada de la mer: A seafood mixed grill of sardines, salmon, shrimp, and mullet, seasoned with lemons, peppers, and olive oil. May be prepared over a fire on a grill (open grate) or a *plancha* (griddle). Often served with white rice or a salad of lettuce and tomatoes.

Escalope de foie gras chaud aux raisins: Roasted slice of hot duck foie gras with a raisin and grape sauce.

MIDI-PYRÉNÉES, LIMOUSIN

At some point in our tour of the regions of France, it is necessary to rush through quickly in order to get to more tempting destinations. It is true that Midi-Pyrénées does not make this entirely easy. This is, after all, the largest of France's regions, one that encompasses such contrasting areas as the tranquility of the river Lot and the excitement of Toulouse, as well as the Canal du Midi and almost the entire range of the Pyrenean mountains. Yet outside of these tourist-saturated areas, about which any guidebook can tell you, little else happens in Midi-Pyrénées.

MIDI-PYRÉNÉES   *The Tour passes through sunflower country.*

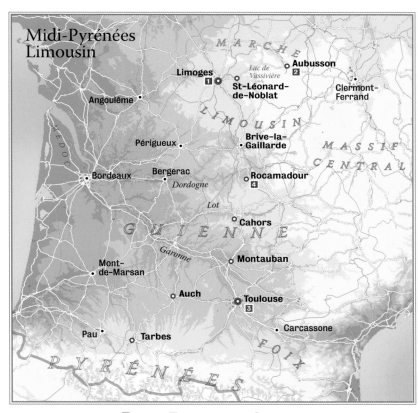

Midi-Pyrénées
Limousin

Angoulême

Limoges 🔳⊙

Lac de
Vassivière

St-Léonard-
de-Noblat

Aubusson 🔳

Clermont-
Ferrand

M A R C H E

L I M O U S I N

M É D O C

Périgueux

Brive-la-
Gaillarde

M A S S I F

Bordeaux

Bergerac

Dordogne

Rocamadour 🔳

C E N T R A L

Lot

Cahors

G U I E N N E

Garonne

Mont-
de-Marsan

Montauban

Auch

Toulouse 🔳

Pau

Tarbes

Carcassone

P Y R É N É E S

F O I X

RECOMMENDATIONS ■ LODGING ■ LODGING and FOOD ● FOOD

🔳 Inter-Hôtel Atrium

🔳 Hôtel Le France

🔳 Hôtel Wilson Square

🔳 Grand Hôtel Beau Site

L

MP

LEGEND   ROAD   RAIL   ⊙ CITY MENTIONED IN TEXT   ⊡ POINT OF INTEREST   50km

It does have miles upon miles of open land that will entertain the cyclist for days on end, and this is the land of sunflowers, those bright yellow wonders that you can see so clearly when driving on one of the region's newer *auto-routes*, but that you can never find once you divert onto slower, more interesting highways. Sunflowers mean beauty to visitors and oil for farmers, for this is a huge agricultural land where little else besides agriculture occurs in an average day. If you've already extended your enjoyment of the Dordogne into Midi-Pyrénées and taken the time to visit Cahors and its mystical Pont Valentre, which straddles the Lot, your exploration of this region is as good as done—except for the Pyrenees, that is (see the next chapter).

The same applies to Limousin; it's a superb area for cycling and farming, but aside from Limoges itself, there's not an awful lot going on. Raymond Poulidor, the eternal second who finished the Tour three times behind Jacques Anquetil, is considered a *vrai Limousin* who was born here and now lives in the village of Saint-Léonard-de-Noblat, where he still rides his bike around the country lanes most days of the week. Limousin is an area still short of the sort of things tourists love, sufficient accommodation being one of them, which is why so many *gîtes* can be found here. At least there is the beauty of the Lac de Vassivière to consider; that's where Greg LeMond and Miguel Induráin have each won time trial stages of the Tour.

I Recommend

Inter-Hôtel Atrium (www.inter-hotel-atrium-limoges.federal-hotel.com), in the center of Limoges (*département* 87). Close to the spectacular main railway station, Bénédictins, this is a fairly modern establishment, easily accessible by car or rail, or on foot. Limoges is something of a gourmet center, and the adjoining Atrium is one of the best-rated eateries in town. But visit **La Cuisine** if you want to try some creative French cooking by chef Guy Queroix, or **L'Escapade du Gourmet** for some formal dishes.

Hôtel Le France (www.aubussonlefrance.com) in Aubusson (*département* 23). A "three-chimney" entry in the Logis-de-France guide, this old-style hotel has elegant rooms at around €80, and a choice of a brasserie or something quite

< OPPOSITE *The Pont Valentre and the Tour peloton in 2007.*

TOULOUSE: TECH CITY

A slow starter in its ascendancy as a major city, Toulouse is now France's fourth biggest city after Paris, Marseille, and Lyon. It owes its emergence to many things, but its establishment as Europe's base for the aerospace industry is the most significant by far. A large proportion of the Airbus fleet is manufactured here, in the same workshops that built the supersonic Concorde airliner in the 1970s, and anyone flying into or out of Blagnac Airport can expect to see some of the world's newest passenger planes being tested years ahead of their official launch. The intense focus on modern technology has attracted a young and dynamic population to Toulouse, which now has one of the biggest university campuses in Europe. Accordingly, the nightlife is particularly notable, and can be enjoyed primarily within the sandwich of urbanization between the river Garonne and the Canal du Midi.

Within this busy enclave are to be found cultural pursuits at the Théâtre National du Capitole, the Ensemble Conventuel des Jacobins (a former monastery enclave that features some outstanding examples of Gothic architecture), and the Halle aux Grains, home of the city's opera house. Lovers of contemporary art can cross the Garonne via the iconic Pont Neuf and enjoy a few hours in the Musée des Abbatoirs, a renovated classic on what Toulouse natives think of as their Left Bank. Tour de France followers will probably not have the time to visit many of these landmarks, nor to enjoy the ninety-minute visit to Aérospatiale's "cathedral" hangar to learn more about the making of the Airbus 380 and Concorde. If you can spare the time, however, you'll not be disappointed!

a bit more extravagant, where the chef specializes in *terroir* (local) dishes like *terrine de canard* (duck pâté) and *Parmentier d'agneau limousin* (ground lamb topped with mashed potatoes).

Hôtel Wilson Square (www.hotel-wilson.com), in the center of Toulouse (*département* 31). Close to the lively Capitole area, this renovated building of thirty rooms offers a nice alternative to the big chain hotels that dominate the city. Toulouse is one of the great dining centers of France, so several evenings there can allow you to experience such temptations as **Les Jardins de l'Opéra, La Brasserie des Beaux-Arts**, or even the slightly tacky **L'Occitania**, a floating barge that departs from the Bayard lock. If you want something lighter than the foie gras, *cassoulet*, beef, and duck dishes Toulouse is so famous for, try **Le Pink Fish**, a quaint little restaurant that specializes in salmon—grilled, boiled, steamed, any which way you want it.

Grand Hôtel Beau Site (www.bestwestern-beausite.com) in Rocamadour (*département* 46). The Best Western folks did their reputation proud by taking over this medieval delight in the center of Rocamadour, a spectacular village built on a towering rock face back in the twelfth century. The new owners have cleverly guarded the stone walls and timbered ceilings of the original property,

LIMOUSIN   *The spectacular medieval village of Rocamadour.*

while adding a contemporary annex across the tiny street, next to the terrace restaurant that serves some of the best meals in the region. From that terrace, you can gaze down into the valley of the Alzou, or crane your neck to take in the steep cliffs far above the village. It helps to have drunk a few glasses of Cahors red to make the neck more supple!

Regional Specialties: Midi-Pyrénées, Limousin

Dinde aux marrons: Roast turkey with chestnuts.

    Foie gras poêlé: Panfried foie gras.

    Croustillant de magret de canard, sauce aux pêches: Crispy filet of duck breast with a peach sauce.

AUVERGNE, LANGUEDOC-ROUSSILLON

Skipping quickly over Limousin and Midi-Pyrénées allows the traveler to spend more time exploring the richer areas to the east and south, Auvergne

Auvergne Languedoc-Roussillon

Moulins

Vichy

Limoges

Puy-de-Dôme

Clermont-Ferrand

Lyon

Puy de Sancy

MASSIF

Périgueux

Brive-la-Gaillarde

St-Flour

Le Puy-en-Velay

Aurillac

CENTRAL

Rhône

Cahors

GORGES DU TARN

Garonne

Tarn

Nîmes

Avignon

Auch

Toulouse

Castres

Montpellier

Arles

La Grande-Motte

Nézignan-l'Évêque

Castelnaudary

Béziers

Cap d'Agde

Carcassonne

Narbonne

Gruissan

Golfe du Lion

ARIÈGE

P Y R É N É E S

Quillan

Port Bacarès

Perpignan

Collioure

Port-Vendres

SPAIN

ANDORRA

Prades

Banyuls-sur-Mer

Cerbère

RECOMMENDATIONS ■ LODGING ■ LODGING and FOOD ● FOOD

1 Hôtel Le Pré Galoffre

2 Hostellerie de Saint Alban

3 Hôtel Les Elmes

4 Hôtel La Frégate

5 Best Western Hôtel Donjon

A

LR

LEGEND ROAD RAIL ○ CITY MENTIONED IN TEXT ◻ POINT OF INTEREST 50km

LANGUEDOC   *The Tour races past the Citadel of Carcassonne in 2003.*

and Languedoc-Roussillon. The two couldn't be more different. Auvergne is a hidden treasure kept secret by the natives for centuries, a land once marked by active volcanoes and dominated by an intense religion. Today it is a tranquil backwater, notable for its lack of population and a beautiful landscape of deep green escarpments split by stone-walled fields, as well as the eye-catching mountain Puy-de-Dôme, which often figures in the Tour.

Its main city is Clermont-Ferrand, at the foot of the Puy-de-Dôme, headquarters of the Michelin tire company, where an excellent Michelin Museum contains mementos of its long history with cycling and the Tour de France. Anyone starved for urban life, however, is better off looking at Vichy—seat of government during World War II—or even more desirable destinations, such as Aurillac, Le Puy-en-Velay, or Saint-Flour, a quaint hilltop town filled with tiny hotels and excellent restaurants. Le Puy-en-Velay is remarkable for its link with ancient religion: It was the starting point of the pilgrim route from France to Santiago de Compostela in Spain, and huge golden statues of the Virgin

Mary adorn volcanic spires. Not a place to forget in a hurry!

Languedoc-Roussillon has a tourist-swamped coastline that runs between the Catalan border town of Cerbère all the way up to Avignon. It is a coastline like no other, made up of little fishing ports such as Port-Vendres and Gruissan; bigger, industrial ports such as Sète; and fortified bastions like Collioure. Sandy beaches are everywhere, when there's nothing in the way, for this coast has purpose-built resorts like La Grande Motte, Cap d'Agde, and Port Bacarès. City lovers can find interests in Perpignan, Narbonne, Béziers,

TOP *The medieval fort of Collioure was enlarged and embellished in the 1670s. The village is now celebrated as a haven for artists.* BOTTOM *The Tour in Cathar country in 2004.*

Montpellier, and even Nîmes, a strength of metropolis that ensures this region is forever crowded.

It is the hinterland, however, that I love most about Languedoc-Roussillon, a treasured land that coaxes one away from the sea to the foot of the Pyrenees, or into Haut-Languedoc, or even further afield toward the Gorges du Tarn. The wines of Languedoc, Corbières, and Minervois lie hidden among rolling, bushy countryside on the way into these uplands, where the ruins of Cathar castles dot almost every ridge or summit.

The Tour often enters the Pyrenees through the Cerdagne, a remote area west of Perpignan that hides some of France's most secluded villages. The road most used takes the great race through the Catalan-influenced Prades and Quillan before turning right into Ariège and hitting the steep climbs for which that region is famous.

If you find yourself watching the Tour in the Pyrenees or near the beaches of Languedoc, make sure you take a day out to visit the Citadel of Carcassonne, the restored fortress city that has dominated life around the river Aude since the early ages. There's probably no other medieval city in Europe that looks as good as this one, but then it has to be said that it almost looks too good—the result of a perfect and very expensive restoration in the nineteenth century. Much of the inner city, called La Cité, is in its original state, with cobbled alleyways and tiny *quartiers* that contain great little restaurants and expensive boutiques.

Carcassonne sits near the Canal du Midi, the popular waterway that carries pleasure boats and working barges between Toulouse and Nîmes, which offers the visitor another form of holiday if watching the Tour is too frenetic. Most cruises or rentals start from Castelnaudary, the market town that argues with Toulouse about the true origin of the *cassoulet*. There's no need for you to get involved in the debate; just sample this sausage-beans-meats dish sometime, ideally in a restaurant overlooking the Grand Bassin (as the port is now called).

I Recommend

Hôtel Le Pré Galoffre (www.lepregaloffre.com) just north of Nîmes (*département* 30). Converted from a farm quite recently, this semicontemporary hotel is a haven of tranquility, just a few kilometers away from the downtown bustle and noise of the city. No restaurant, but a swimming pool and shaded terrace add to the Provençal feel of the place. Go into Nîmes for great food.

Hostellerie de Saint Alban (www.saintalban.com) in Nézignan-l'Évêque (*département* 34). A real gem in the Logis-de-France chain, it features nouvelle cuisine cooking in a *grande maison* furnished in the art deco style. The romantic bedrooms have views over the open countryside or the garden terrace, where guests can be found eating their meals or relaxing by the pool. This nineteenth-century property is a place you'll keep coming back to.

Hôtel Les Elmes (www.hotel-des-elmes.com) in Banyuls-sur-Mer (*département* 66). A gorgeous setting for a gorgeous hotel-restaurant with views of the secluded bay in one of Languedoc's prettiest coastal towns. Another "three-chimney" entry in the Logis-de-France network, the food is as good as the views.

Hôtel La Frégate (www.fregate-collioure.com), in the heart of Collioure (*département* 66). Probably the town's best hotel, and with a sumptuous restaurant to match, La Frégate is a moderately priced choice in which to while away a few days in this delightful seaside resort. Some of the two- and

LANGUEDOC *The rugged coastline at Collioure, a town said by Matisse to have the bluest sky in Europe.*

three-star rooms offer views of the dazzling Mediterranean, while others gaze over the town toward the Pyrenees. This establishment wins because of the quietly efficient nature of its staff, serving seafood dishes and fine Languedoc wines to locals and visitors alike. There is a lively summer dining terrace where you'll be the envy of other town-center visitors who've made the mistake of staying in other hotels or in another town altogether. Don't make the same mistake.

Best Western Hôtel Donjon (www.hotel-donjon.fr) in Carcassonne (*département* 11). One of just three hotels actually inside the ancient *cité*, the Hôtel Donjon is a wonderful blend of medieval architecture and twenty-first-century class. Some of the rooms are on the small side, but all have near-luxury appointments and the softest and coziest beds you'll ever enjoy! The hotel has its own highly rated brasserie next door, but only a fool would go directly there without first exploring the alternatives close at hand—and there are many of them. Car access to the hotel is only possible after 6 P.M., but hotel staff will happily leave the walled city and bring your bags to the hotel if you want to settle in earlier.

Regional Specialties: Auvergne, Languedoc–Roussillon

Cassoulet languedocien: A classic white bean stew made with duck confit and pork sausage.

Feuilleté de rognon de veau et champignons, flambé au cognac: Veal kidneys with mushrooms, flambéed with cognac and served in a flaky pastry.

Dorade grillée, pommes de terre écrasées aux olives: Grilled sea bream with mashed potatoes and olives.

Saucisse sèche d'Auvergne: Dried Auvergne pork sausage, served simply with bread like *charcuterie*, or cooked back to softness with a bacon and herb stew and served on a bed of lentils *(saucisse aux lentilles de Puy)*.

PROVENCE–ALPES–CÔTE D'AZUR

Provence is more than a region; it is a whole country, bounded by the Mediterranean, the Rhône Valley, and the Alps—hence the three-sided official name of the region. It has its own exclusive culture, where native Provençals happily share their cherished land with immigrants and tourists to make this region one of the richest in France, in every sense of the word.

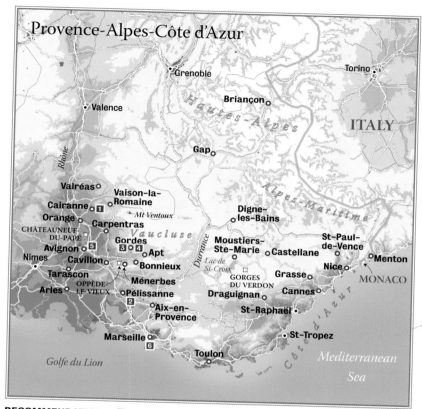

RECOMMENDATIONS ◼ LODGING ◼ LODGING and FOOD ● FOOD

1 Auberge Castel Mireïo

2 Hôtel Restaurant La Touloubre

3 La Bastide de Gordes

4 Auberge de Carcarille

5 Auberge de Cassagne

6 New Hotel Vieux-Port

LEGEND ⠿ ROAD ▬ RAIL ○ CITY MENTIONED IN TEXT ▢ POINT OF INTEREST ⌐ 25km ⌐

PROVENCE   *Sunflowers and lavender—the Tour races through Provence in 2006.*

Provence possesses so many sides, and so many different faces, one would need a full year to experience them all. This is the region of the Pont du Gard, the Palais des Papes in Avignon, the Roman theater in Orange, the Romanesque city of Arles. All of them are accessible from the Rhône Valley, the main gateway to Provence and then all points east and west.

Start your Provençal experience from the airport of Marseille or Nice, and you can enjoy the busy but beautiful coastline all the way to the Italian border at Menton, before turning inland and visiting the hinterland of the Côte d'Azur in historical towns like Saint-Paul-de-Vence, Grasse, Draguignan, and Aix-en-Provence. From Menton you could also investigate the backwaters of the Alpes-Maritimes, where tiny villages apparently lost to the world tempt you to continue north instead, perhaps to the hidden valleys of Tinée and Entraunes, from which all roads lead farther north to the Alps.

Come into Provence from the north, and you'll experience the quieter beauty of this region, in the area that most people recognize as being *vrai* (real) Provence, specifically the piece of land that stretches from Mont Ventoux to the Luberon hills, the Plateau de Vaucluse.

Vaucluse is home to famous hilltop settlements such as Gordes, Bonnieux, Apt, Forcalquier, and Ménerbes, and has strategic market towns such as Carpentras, Cavaillon, and Orange for the inhabitants to do their twice-weekly shopping. Ever since Peter Mayle wrote his best-selling book about life in this area, *A Year in Provence*, places like Ménerbes and Bonnieux have become saturated with busloads of star-searching visitors. Mayle himself soon left, as did some of the film stars and other personalities mentioned in the book. But tourists still arrive en masse, forcing Ménerbes to become a virtual no-go zone for anyone not actually living there—a great shame, seeing how delightful the village is.

PROVENCE *The hilltop village of Gordes and its beautiful white stone buildings.*

Today, tourists will find a greater welcome in towns like Tarascon, Saint-Rémy-de-Provence, and Vaison-la-Romaine, as well as the revered wine village of Châteauneuf-du-Pape—as long as you're buying their expensive, and slightly overrated, wines. If it is wine you are after, or the temptation of eating in a Provençal bistro close to a wine region, then look further afield to Rasteau, Vacqueyras, Gigondas, or Cairanne.

There are also some nice wines to be found on the slopes of Mont Ventoux, called Côtes du Ventoux, as well as in the Massif du Luberon, which is where many of Mayle's famous subjects now live, in secretive villas hidden well away from any roads. Be sure to visit Oppède-le-Vieux, a secluded village beneath the Luberon massif whose two small cafés are favored by reclusive celebrities.

The Vaucluse is a cyclist's paradise, even in the peak periods of summer. Only masochists may wish to climb Mont Ventoux, but there are hundreds of *routes départementales* crisscrossing the plateau that offer flat to undulating terrain for cyclists of a more sane disposition. Cairanne, between Orange and Vaison-la-Romaine, would be a perfect place to base oneself, making a dif-

MONT VENTOUX   *The summit of Mont Ventoux and its observatory.*

ferent circuit every day—perhaps north to Saint-Paul-Trois-Châteaux, east to Valréas, south to Vaison-la-Romaine, then back to Cairanne. A longer route could include visiting Malaucène, a café-strewn village on the flanks of the Ventoux that acts as a perfect rest stop for coffees, pastries, or alcohol, just 15 flat kilometers short of your base.

Sault, to the east of Ventoux, and Apt, to the south, are ideal rallying points for touring, but the terrain starts to get a bit hillier. You could try assailing the Vidauque, a tiny, vertiginous road that climbs away from Cavaillon and takes you to fabulous views over the Luberon massif. Look east from there and you can see the hilltop town of Pertuis, one of a circuit of such towns to be explored on the bike or by car, Manosque, Apt, Bonnieux, and Cadenet being the others. Provence is cycling-friendly throughout, but watch yourself on the Côte d'Azur, where the drivers in summertime are predominantly foreign and liable to tantrums because of the traffic chaos; best to stay in real Provence.

Okay, you don't like beaches, nor big cities, and your only interest in wine is a single glass over evening dinner. Happily for you, Provence has a few other gems up its sleeve, most notably the spectacular Gorges du Verdon. Considered to be the second largest gorge in the world, the canyon occupies a stretch of the river Verdon between Moustiers-Sainte-Marie and Castellane, a partly medieval town, which also acts as a gateway to the Alps as well as a stopping post on the historical Route Napoléon.

The gorge has a depth of 300 meters in some places, and at the bottom runs water that is a beautifully opaque turquoise. Most visitors drive along the northern edge on the D952, stopping at established viewpoints to gaze into the gorge. At the little village of La Palud-sur-Verdon, a narrower D road called La Route des Crêtes takes a loop that gives the traveler even giddier views of the canyon, where large cars and buses have fewer opportunities to stop.

Cyclists might prefer the opposite side of the canyon to enjoy their experience, following the Route de la Corniche Sublime between Aiguines and the Balcons de la Mescla. This is a sinuous, up-and-down road that the cyclist will appreciate more than the motorist, the downside being that after the Balcons, the road goes away from the gorge altogether, forcing you to either retrace your route to Aiguines or pedal for over an hour to reconnect with the main road back to Castellane.

I Recommend

Auberge Castel Mireïo (www.castelmireio.fr) in Cairanne (*département* 84). Typical Provençal cuisine prepared by Bernard Kbaïer and served by his wife Odile on the terrace of a small family château with distant views of Mont Ventoux. Simple accommodation in a separate building. Be warned, the chef and his sous-chef like to drink with their guests after dinner!

Hôtel Restaurant La Touloubre (www.latouloubre.com) in Pélissanne (*département* 13) Country-style cooking with regional specialties, served on a shady garden terrace well away from any roads. Family-influenced accommodation, and therefore a very friendly welcome.

La Bastide de Gordes (www.bastide-de-gordes.com) in Gordes (*département* 84), one of Provence's greatest hotels, with magnificent views over the Luberon massif. Dine in the vine-hung garden or in a discreet corner of the cozy restaurant, which features Provençal and Mediterranean dishes. Relax in the lavish spa, sample one of the hotel's eight hundred different types of wine, or just walk around the town's cobbled alleyways; this is a to-die-for destination!

Auberge de Carcarille (www.auberge-carcarille.com) in Gordes (*département* 84). This stone-walled hotel costs much less than the nearby Bastide de Gordes, but its quality and charm leave nothing to quibble about. A large pool cools guests at the end of a hard day's sightseeing or cycling in the Ventoux, and well-appointed rooms prepare the hungry visitor for the hotel's real attraction: the restaurant. As a "three-chimney" member of the Logis-de-France network, the restaurant has to be able to deliver the very best in home-cooked cuisine that is both innovative and mouthwatering at the same time. It succeeds with flying colors! A three-day stay might be enough to enjoy the basics of the Carcarille's menu, but this is such a perfectly located address that a full week could be spent relaxing here and eating in other nearby kitchens; the proprietor is always happy to make recommendations!

Auberge de Cassagne (www.aubergedecassagne.com) in Le Pontet–Avignon (*département* 84). An exquisite hotel in the Châteaux & Hôtels de France chain—expensive, but an experience you will never forget. True *gastronomie* must have been born here, and it can be enjoyed in the restaurant

< OPPOSITE *The Gorges du Verdon.*

MARSEILLE, THE OLDEST CITY

One of France's great cities, Marseille cries out far louder for a visit than its rivals Toulouse, Bordeaux, and Lyon. This may be a reaction to the disdain once shown the city by the rest of France—Paris in particular—for until recently Marseille had a formidable reputation as a hotbed of racial conflict and strife. Fortunately, today's Marseille enjoys an altogether nicer reputation as a cultural, political, and historical city of great standing. It is also France's premier commercial port, through which flow a rich trade of cargo and passengers from all over the world.

There's a distinctly colonial feel about the city that you don't find nearby in the glitzier Nice, and Marseille's history deserves more than a one-day, one-night look. It won't take much of a stroll around the Vieux-Port (the old, original seaport area) to appreciate the African-Mediterranean influence on Marseille; the city was once the domain of the Greeks, and then the Romans, before becoming France's oldest city in the sixth century. Although the city's immigrant population is made up of Tunisian, Algerian, and Moroccan immigrants, the inhabitants' proudest boast is that the French national anthem, "La Marseillaise," has its roots here.

Marseille never sleeps, which suits Tour de France followers, who can walk off their evening meal by strolling late at night up to Notre-Dame de la Garde and spending an hour gazing out to sea and across the industrial port. But as the night quiets down and the city's *mystère* descends, you can't help thinking of *The French Connection* and Gene Hackman's battle against the mobsters of Marseille.

I love to visit Marseille a few hours after a Tour stage has ended, when the workload has been lifted for a while, to slip into a comfortable seat near the yacht-filled port and sip a few glasses of *kir*, or a beer, or simply some wine, prior to selecting my restaurant for a late meal. Marseille is a people-watching city if ever there was one, with most of the attention centered on the busy junction of the Canabière and Vieux-Port, where so many of the world's cultures mingle

Marseille was a key stop on the Tour's first route in 1903 as the finish to a 374-kilometer stage that started in Lyon. Here, the peloton departs from Marseille in 2007.

in conversation or simply pass each other like ships in the night. The culinary action is centered around this area as well, largely along the Quai du Port and the pedestrianized enclave of Les Arcenaulx. This also happens to be where most of Marseille's better hotels are to be found, meaning one can hoist an extra glass and not have to worry about the drive back.

Locals tend to eat along the Quai du Port in establishments like Le Massena, while tourists and visitors swamp the labyrinth of passageways behind the Quai de la Rive Neuve and choose from a marvelously international table that ranges from genuine bouillabaisse to sushi. Seafood is obviously the recommended cuisine of choice in Marseille, which means one can choose a nice rosé from nearby Bandol to go with the meal before a switch to white, or even a red Bandol, if you're so inclined. Don't be afraid to try a Tunisian dish like Chakchouka (a ratatouille made from tomatoes, peppers, garlic, onions, and a poached egg); it's the perfect accompaniment to an excellent glass of Tunisian red such as Vieux Magon, a full-bodied wine hard to find anywhere else in France.

or beside a most inviting pool in the garden. The rooms are sumptuous, cottage-styled, and overlooking the pool, from which a discreet door leads to the hotel's new spa.

New Hotel Vieux-Port (http://new-hotel.com/VieuxPort/fr) in Marseille (*département* 13). As Marseille grows as an international center, its old hotels have begun to enjoy a new lease on life. Several refurbished beauties are to be found around the port, with the New Hotel Vieux-Port being my preferred accommodation, as it sits close to the yachts and backs onto some of Marseille's enticing backstreets; this location is also responsible for the hotel's reasonable rates. A twenty-second walk will take you to a host of restaurants on the Quai du Port, including Miramar, whose Web site, www.bouillabaisse.com, happily declares that this is Marseille's number one restaurant for seafood.

Regional Specialties: Provence

Filet de rouget au citron vert, salpicon de fenouil et tomate: Filet of red mullet with diced limes, fennel, and tomato.

Filet de boeuf Simmental poêlé à la fleur de sel de Camargue, pressé de pommes amandine, foie gras, et girolles: A filet of Simmental beef boiled in its own juice, flavored with Camargue salt, and served with foie gras, mushrooms, and almond-scented potatoes.

RHÔNE-ALPES

This region of France is probably the most envied of all, even more so than Provence or Aquitaine. Rhône-Alpes does not have a true beach, but it has everything else, literally: rivers, mountains, forests, lakes, wines, and great food, too. Cities like Lyon, Valence, Grenoble, and Saint-Étienne act as the industrial pillars, into which flow goods and natural produce from all four corners of the region, ready for sale around the world.

In those same cities arrive millions of tourists, on their way south to Provence and the Côte d'Azur, westward into the Massif Central, or eastward into the Alps, all of them selecting their particular favorite from a massive playground. Skiing, cycling, swimming, climbing, rafting, caving, kayaking, walking, hang gliding—these are just some of the activities available to those with enough energy.

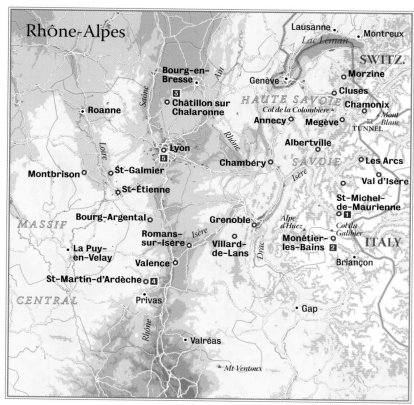

RECOMMENDATIONS ■ LODGING ■ LODGING and FOOD ● FOOD

1. Savoy-Hôtel
2. Auberge du Choucas
3. Hôtel de la Tour
4. L'Escarbille
5. Villa Florentine

LEGEND ROAD RAIL ○ CITY MENTIONED IN TEXT ⊡ POINT OF INTEREST 25km

TOP *The Tour crosses the Lac de Serre-Ponçon, one of Europe's largest artificial lakes, in 2006.* BOTTOM *Fans cheer the centenary Tour through Savoie on a stage to Morzine.*

Wine lovers will adore the Côtes du Rhône wines, particularly the Crozes-Hermitage and Saint-Joseph labels from around Tournon-sur-Rhône and the fruitier Beaujolais-Villages, north of Lyon. There are the subtle wines of Savoie to taste as well, grown on the hillsides around Chambéry. Food connoisseurs will savor so much choice, with local dishes like *raclette* (a Swiss cheese dish) and fondue to be experienced alongside more popular dishes like *Charolais* beef and thick onion soups. Fresh fish are everywhere here, perch, salmon, and trout being the most popular. This is the land of the *gratin dauphinoise*, the potato and cheese casserole baked almost to a crisp, which I will always choose over *frites* (french fries).

The Rhône Valley acts as the main conduit of the region's year-round tourist migration, but its great river is but one of many the region boasts, all of which help to form the rugged landscape and character this area is so famous for. Think how rivers like the Saône, Loire, Isère, and Rhône have divided the land here; it's a compelling geography. Consider too the tributaries of these great arteries—Arc, Romanche, Drôme, Ardèche, Ain, and Drac—along which tiny villages and major towns offer so much to the visitor.

The Isère is the second most important waterway of the region. It virtually splits the Alps in two, gushing away from its source at the top of Vallée de la Tarentaise (the Tarentaise Valley) to separate the Massif de la Vanoise from the northern mountain ranges of Beaufortain. The Vanoise is saturated with ski resorts like Val d'Isère, Tignes, Les Arcs, La Plagne, as well as the Trois Vallées resorts of Courchevel, Meribel, and Val Thorens, all of which host Tour de France stage finishes from time to time.

The Isère continues on its way toward the Rhône, passing through Albertville and then Grenoble, a spectacular city well worth a stopover on the way to resorts in the Chartreuse, Vercors, or Massif des Écrins. Just before the Isère merges with the Rhône, there's a town I adore, Romans-sur-Isère, where sidewalk cafés and restaurants cling to the riverbank, illuminated glowingly whenever there's a setting sun.

The Isère will have skirted the Vercors by the time it reaches the Rhône, but a visit to this peaceful land is a must for anyone who loves unspoiled nature, most especially for us cyclists. The towns of Villard-de-Lans and Pont-en-Royans could not be more different—one distinctly alpine, the other one almost

Provençal, which clings to a cliff face above the river Bourne. It is what runs between them that excites us the most: the Gorges de la Bourne, a 12-kilometer-long passage between 400-meter-tall limestone cliffs. This is not the only gorge in Vercors, but it is the most spectacular, with several tunnels and a natural overhanging roof for most of its length.

Villard-de-Lans is a cross-country skiing center in the winter, and a most perfect place to base oneself in summertime. Once installed, the cyclist or car driver can explore the delights of the Vercors plateau, a vast, green, lush, and forested land

Jean-François Bernard in the yellow jersey in the Vercors in 1987.

surrounded on all sides by sheer walls of rock and traversed by rivers and streams. There is no such thing as a flat road here, but at least there are many to choose from, offering a choice of steep ascents, gentle descents, or undulating meanders through the region.

The Tour has been a regular visitor here for decades, with stages ending at either Villard-de-Lans or Lans-en-Vercors, or passing right through to end in Grenoble or Valence or Saint-Étienne. Try staying at Le Dauphin in Villard, the hotel favored by champions such as Armstrong, Miguel Induráin, and Bernard Hinault, who either based themselves there for pre-Tour training or slept in its rooms after a Tour stage.

Where else to go in this vast and varied region—west into the area around the river Ardèche, east into the southern Alps, or north toward Vienne and then across to Haute-Savoie? The fact is, no one visit will ever be enough to see everything here, I can tell you from my own experiences—and the Tour's been coming this way for years.

< OPPOSITE *A chapel in the Tarentaise valley is decorated by fans in 2007.*

ABOVE *Children dive into the Ardèche river as the Tour passes in 2006.* OPPOSITE *The peloton descends to the Lac de Serre-Ponçon on its way to Digne-les-Bains in 2005.*

Around the Ardèche is a cosseted little area west of the Rhône at Pont-Saint-Esprit, where gorges and forested plateaus enjoy a quieter kind of tourism than other parts of the region. It can get very hot in this part of the country, which is why the Ardèche is popular with locals—its riverbed creates natural pools where people can swim or kayak in safety just a few feet away from the road. In the 2006 Tour, I chanced upon a group of bathing children while chasing the breakaway that changed the course of that year's race. Oscar Pereiro had joined an escape that gained thirty minutes on the Floyd Landis–led peloton. It was a time gap that allowed me to shoot pictures of the escape before clambering over boulders and wading through the stream to set up a rare photograph. I'm sure the kids wanted to get out of the river and cheer the cyclists on, but together with some French colleagues, we managed to persuade them to keep diving in while the peloton raced by, making for some great shots. Yes, I am rather fond of the Ardèche!

A very different France awaits people exploring the area to the north of Chambéry, the capital city of the Savoie, which sits below the southern tip of the Lac du Bourget. There's something quieter and more pristine, something almost Swiss about the whole area, and it's not just because of its Swiss-looking regional flag. This is another part of France that has its own distinctive way of life, with architecture quite different from anywhere else in the country. Great alpine-style wooden houses dominate the hillsides, with ornate flower boxes either hanging from balconies or set on the ground to form a natural fence to protect the property. A dazzling array of native colors can be seen in these boxes—orchids, bellflowers, lilies, and yellow gentians—offering a pleasing contrast to the lush grass, on which neat coils of hay are drying. This is a green and very pleasant land, one that the locals are determined to preserve.

For the adventurer, this region within a region has France's most spectacular mountains as well as some of its deepest streams and lakes. This is the home of Mont Blanc, whose mighty snow-covered peak towers over resorts like

Sallanches, Megève, and Chamonix. Haute-Savoie is also home to the Chaîne des Aravis (Aravis Range), a more rocky outcrop of mountains beneath which the Tour often races, over climbs like the Col de la Colombière, Col des Saisies, and Col des Aravis.

Visitors can base themselves at such famous towns as Morzine, Cluses, Le Grand Bornand, and Saint-Gervais, departing each day on a route that will offer a new view of the Alps. The lakes of Bourget, Annecy, and Nantua offer a milder swim than the mid-altitude lake created by the Barrage de Roselend (Roselend Dam) or any number of other mountain lakes to be found between the high peaks. And the massive Lac Léman (Lake Geneva to English speakers) offers swimming and waterskiing to its visitors, along with the chance to take a boat trip across the lake to the Swiss towns of Montreux and Lausanne. The spa town of Évian-les-Bains on Lac Léman would be a great place to relax or go shopping, though you might find it a little too busy in the middle of July.

Even smaller ski resorts usually reopen in late June, offering a more secluded *séjour* (stay) to visitors than in established alpine towns. Try finding accommodation in such places as Flaine and Les Saisies; you won't be disappointed by the views! My own favorite for a really quiet time is the minuscule Praz de Lys, a tiny settlement of two hotels and one ski lift, just off the road that leads to the Col de la Ramaz. Praz de Lys is where legendary Tour de France climber Lucien van Impe stays when he works the Tour for Belgian TV. He says he slept there by chance during the Tour he won in 1976, and he has been coming back ever since.

As with Provence and Aquitaine, the visitor needs many months to fully discover Rhône-Alpes. Its northwestern edge includes a corner of the Massif Central, where gorges and forests combine their beauty in an area called the Plateau du Forez. The Loire begins its flow not so many kilometers to the west, meaning that contributing rivers and streams permeate the countryside. Little stone bridges carry narrow lanes as well as bigger D roads across the waters, making this a great place for the touring driver.

It is a hilly, testing terrain that cyclists will either hate or love, depending upon how many ascents they've already made that day. A much-needed overnight stop can be found in colorful towns like Saint-Galmier, Bourg-Argental, and Montbrison, but it cannot be stated too often that the horrible city of

ALPE VIEW *A panoramic vista from Alpe d'Huez.*

Saint-Étienne is best avoided altogether, unless it is to dump the rental car and speed away on a TGV to a place more pleasing.

That place should be the opposite end of the region, where the Dauphiné-Alpes awaits your applause. Southeast of the Chartreuse and south of the dividing line that is the Maurienne Valley sits the range of mountains where the Tour has made its greatest impressions. Alpe d'Huez, La Toussuire, Col du Glandon, Col de la Croix de Fer, Col du Télégraphe, Col du Galibier—these fearsome mountains form a ring of vicious yet beautiful ascents absolutely demanding attention from the Tour lover. Once there, the cyclist or driver can go further afield, retracing the flow of the river Arc to the Col de l'Iseran, or heading into Alpes-Provence and experiencing the Col d'Izoard or even the mighty Col Agnel, better known by its Italian name of Colle dell'Agnello.

It's an area so beautiful that I cannot do it justice here. You'll find more detail in the next chapter.

The Tour crosses the Colle dell'Agnello in 2008.

LYON, THREE CITIES IN ONE

Although Lyon enjoys its unchallenged status as France's second city, it has only hosted a Tour stage start or finish on sixteen occasions—a pretty solemn record, which seems at odds with the city's sporting heritage. Lyon is the home of Olympique Lyonnais, currently France's leading soccer team. The city also has a highly rated rugby union team as well as its own ice-hockey squad. Throw in the successful basketball team of nearby Villeurbanne, and you'd assume that Lyon would embrace the Tour more than it does and become the country's premier sporting city, just as it is already the country's leader in gastronomy.

Lyon's apparent indifference to the Tour may be due to its highly complicated, if not chaotic, geography. Two large rivers, the Rhône and Saône, come into the city in tandem but then split to the north and to the northeast, turning the center of town into an island. Lyon's busy road and transport system has to cope with the city's growing population, and travelers on their way north or south do their best to get around Lyon without having to go through the city itself.

Lyon is in fact two cities, one old and one new, with a third one developing independently to the north at Parc de la Tête d'Or. Two major railway stations serve the area, with Lyon-Part-Dieu the most used, as it takes commuters right into the commercial area. Lyon-Perrache is the older station, slightly closer to the old city; it's the terminus for many TGV trains, though if your journey doesn't end there, you may be forced to cross the city and connect at Part-Dieu.

Food is, of course, central to Lyon's identity, and most of Lyon's jewels are on the city's center island, Presqu'île. Partly because of their hectic lifestyles, Lyonais often eat in *bouchons*, which are small, informal, and inexpensive bistros that will see you sit, be served, and leave to go back to work within an hour. The best of these is possibly the Café des Fédérations, right by the Hôtel de Ville (town hall), and one of Lyon's oldest eating establishments of its kind. Unusually for a working-class establishment, the Café is open on Saturday as well. Anyone looking for something a little more showy could try L'Entrecôte, which has sister establishments in Nantes, Bordeaux, Toulouse, and Montpellier but has the flavor of an independent eatery. Lyon's gastronomy at its highest level can be found at a place like Nicolas Le Bec in the deuxième *arrondissement*, or Le Bec's former place of employment, the Cour des Loges, where four different levels of indulgence await the diner. You might want to stay here as well, in rooms adapted from genuine fourteenth-century dwellings, and have an extra bottle of wine to enjoy.

I Recommend

Savoy-Hôtel (www.savoy-hotel.fr) in Saint-Michel-de-Maurienne (*département* 73). The rooms are plain and simple; the restaurant is simple but has superb food. The great attraction of this privately owned hotel is its location at the foot of the Col du Télégraphe, so book early. The owner is a keen cyclist and a photography enthusiast, so he always gets my vote!

Auberge du Choucas (www.aubergeduchoucas.com) in Monêtier-les-Bains (*département* 05). This is a mighty Logis-de-France address that is also listed in the illustrious Johansens guide from Condé Nast. One of the best hotel-restaurants in the Alps—guests will love this old farmhouse just off the road to the Col du Lautaret. No detail has been spared to keep the hotel feeling like a farmhouse, with huge wooden doors and shutters and original furniture, giving the place a unique but casual atmosphere. The food is to die for, served in a very austere restaurant that has original stone ceilings and a massive hearth. Every aspect of a French dinner service is enacted here, so enjoy the education. No need to dress up, either; you're in the country!

Hôtel de la Tour (www.hotel-latour.com) in Châtillon sur Chalaronne (*département* 01). A common name for a French hotel, but this is no ordinary abode. Just south of Mâcon and Bourg-en-Bresse, this is an ideal stopover if you are tasting the wines of Burgundy or Beaujolais. The ornately decorated rooms are romantic, economical, and spacious; many have a four-poster bed. It is on the grounds that you'll learn to relax after a light lunch, napping in a shaded hammock or by the delightful pool. The restaurant will stay in your memory forever, particularly if you want the *traiteur* tasting menu, which requires an advance notice of seventy-two hours.

L'Escarbille (www.hotel-restaurant-lescarbille.com) in Saint-Martin-d'Ardèche (*département* 07). Spend a day in this peaceful Logis-de-France abode to discover the secret paradise that is the Ardèche canyon. A superb place to explore the area through swimming, kayaking, cycling, driving, or walking, the village of Saint-Martin-d'Ardèche features tiny alleyways that lead to the river and its ancient suspension bridge and even more ancient château. Experience the giddy views from above the canyon before settling down for an evening meal washed down with wines from nearby Roussillon, Gard, and Rhône.

Villa Florentine (www.villaflorentine.com) in Lyon. Situated next to the Basilica of Notre-Dame de Fourvière, the hotel has a superb position on the mount of Fourvière, from which guests can enjoy an unparalleled view of the city and its rivers. The rooms are functional in a very classical style, and fitted with the latest high-tech facilities within this sixteenth-century former convent. It might be the restaurant you remember the most, for the Terrasses de Lyon features such uncompromising dishes as a tartare of Brittany scampis, served with a fine accompaniment of caramelized apples for €50—that's just an appetizer!

Regional Specialties: Rhône-Alpes

Brochettes d'agneau: Lamb cubes (kebabs) marinated in olive oil and herbs, skewered with onions and peppers and grilled, served with roast potatoes or *gratin dauphinois* (baked casserole of sliced potatoes, cooked with cream, milk, and either cheese or eggs).

Raie grenobloise: Freshwater skate baked in a fondue of leeks, gruyère cheese, white wine, béchamel, butter, and eggs.

Quenelles de brochet: Small filets of pike covered in a rich, buttery paste called a *panade*, then poached and served piping hot with either a mushroom, cognac, lobster, or crayfish sauce. High in cholesterol, a true specialty of the Lyon restaurants called *bouchons*.

PARIS, ÎLE DE FRANCE

With Paris at its heart, Île de France is the country's most populated region. But there is so much open space once you get away from the city that you could be fooled into thinking Paris was in another part of the country altogether. Almost as soon as you've circumnavigated the dreaded *périphérique—* the ring road that encircles Paris—and branched off toward Lyon, Bordeaux, Rouen, or Metz, lush countryside suddenly replaces the urban expanse, and that is where this relatively new region got its name in 1976. Quite simply, Paris is the island, set among an ocean of forests, agricultural lands, quaint villages, and riverside towns.

If the city is not quite what you want after a few weeks in the vastness of the country, think about staying outside. Towns like Meaux, Mantes-la-Jolie, Pontoise, Rambouillet, Étampes, and Fontainebleau—all within a forty-five-minute train ride from the city center—are charming places to while away the last days of your trip to France, and all of them deserve a visit in their own right if you have the time and are staying in Paris.

Fontainebleau is the most treasured destination of them all, a town set in the middle of the massive forest that bears its name, the forest to which thousands of Parisians decamp on the weekend in order to walk their legs off for a few

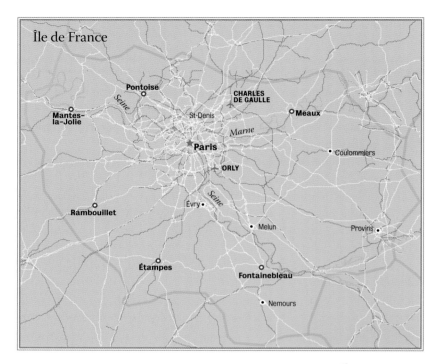

Île de France

Pontoise

CHARLES
DE GAULLE

Mantes-
la-Jolie

St-Denis

Meaux

Seine

Marne

★ **Paris**

Coulommiers

ORLY

Évry

Seine

Rambouillet

Melun

Provins

Étampes

Fontainebleau

Nemours

LEGEND   ROAD   RAIL   ⊙ CITY MENTIONED IN TEXT   ⊡ POINT OF INTEREST   50km

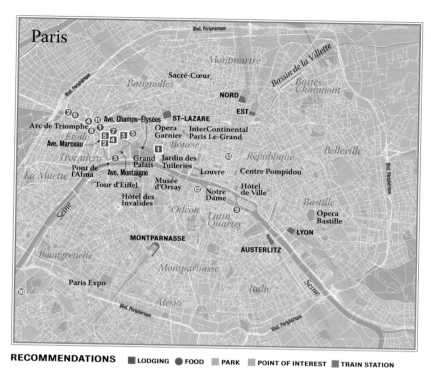

Paris

RECOMMENDATIONS ■ LODGING ● FOOD ■ PARK ■ POINT OF INTEREST ■ TRAIN STATION

1 Hôtel de Crillon

2 Hôtel Élysées Régencia

3 Paris Marriott Hotel Champs-Élysées

4 Hôtel Marceau Champs-Élysées

5 Pershing Hall

1 Chez Clément

2 Bistro Saint-Ferdinand

3 La Maison Blanche

4 La Grande Armée

5 Le Boeuf sur Le Toit

6 Chez Georges

7 Impala Lounge

8 Casa Luca

9 La Tour d'Argent

10 River Café at Issy-les-Moulineaux

11 Restaurant Guy Savoy

12 Le Restaurant de l'Hôtel

13 Pâtisserie Stohrer

LEGEND ROAD RAIL

2km

hours. The spectacular château at the heart of the forest is one of the greatest in all of France, and it is listed as a UNESCO World Heritage site.

If your Tour experience ends in Paris, or Paris is the sole rendezvous you'll make with the Tour, be sure to make it a visit to remember. Fortunately, the Tour ends on the Champs-Élysées, making this famous avenue the base for your Parisian experience. The Champs-Élysées is not the most famous avenue in the world for nothing. It runs through the heart of cultural and historical Paris, sits parallel to the nicest city section of the river Seine, and has along its

TOP *Carlos Sastre wins the 2008 Tour de France in Paris.* BOTTOM *The Tour de France team presentation, held in front of the Hôtel de Ville.*

flanks and side streets some of the nicest boutique hotels in the city—some of the nicest restaurants, too.

As a Londoner, I'm quite envious of Paris, for some clever souls many centuries ago designed the French capital so that virtually all its crown jewels could be viewed and enjoyed from the Seine, and in a single day if need be. Assuming the Tour traveler has taken care to book into one of the hundreds of hotels near the Champs-Élysées, a walk south down the Avenue Marceau or Avenue Montaigne brings one to the Pont de l'Alma, from which your one-day, one-night visit can begin, if that is all the time you have at hand.

Walk over the bridge and visit the Eiffel Tower, or stay on the right bank and walk east to find yourself at the Musée du Louvre (which is best reached by strolling through the Jardin des Tuileries). The Louvre is not for the faint-hearted—it is massive, takes more than a full day to experience, and dumps you among thousands of other tourists, probably like you, wondering why they're wasting an entire day queuing to gaze at paintings that are remarkable for being so ordinary.

PARIS   *The entrance to the Musée du Louvre is through the pyramid.*

Better to walk out of the vast inner courtyard of the Louvre and gaze across the river to the plethora of historical buildings on the other side. You'll have already passed the massive greenhouse that is the Grand Palais, as well as the awe-inspiring Hôtel des Invalides (final resting place of Napoleon), and can now see the grandiose Musée d'Orsay, formerly a railway station, which, until 1939, took passengers from Paris to Orléans and beyond.

It was in the Musée d'Orsay that the U.S. Postal team held their post-Tour parties until Armstrong started winning too often and the parties had to be switched to the bigger but less intimate InterContinental Paris Le-Grand near l'Opéra. The Musée d'Orsay is worth a visit, if only to wonder at the paintings and sculptures in its vast interior (especially if you are a lover of the Impressionist period), or to go into the banqueting rooms and gaze upward at the ceiling murals I last saw through a haze of alcohol in 2001.

Keep moving, keep moving, for the clock is ticking! East of Orsay comes the impressive Institut de France, just as viewable from the right bank if you

do not want to cross the bridge. When, finally, you come to a massive double-towered cathedral surrounded by thousands of gaping tourists, you know you've reached the Cathédrale de Notre-Dame de Paris, a convenient place to break for lunch or supper, unless you are feeling energetic enough to do a tour of the inner cathedral right away. If you are planning on visiting the famous catacombs of Paris, just below, then definitely have lunch first! And don't forget to look left at the magnificent Hôtel de Ville (city hall) before turning your back on both buildings and moving on.

If you stroll across the river, you'll find yourself in the Latin Quarter, a maze of cobbled streets and alleyways littered with enticing eateries. Your sixth sense has to be sharp now, for you have to pick out the Paris *homme d'affaires* (businessman) or elegant *madame* who will be eating at a true bistro, and not at one of the hundreds of tourist places catering to the unwary visitor. Better still, seek out a quieter street beyond the Boulevard Saint-Germain, beyond the reach of the tired visitor, where a decent restaurant is easier to identify. **Les Éditeurs** (4, Carrefour de l'Odéon) and **La Méditerranée** (2, Place de l'Odéon), both near the Place de l'Odéon, or the **Restaurant**

Les Éditeurs restaurant near l'Odéon.

L'Aoc (14, Rue des Fossés St-Bernard) near the Pont de Sully, which crosses the Île Saint Louis on the south side of the Seine, are all worth trying, for this is where the really discerning visitor or Paris businessperson finds worthwhile, unhurried nourishment.

Paris has good restaurants and hotels beyond its vast center, and many visitors feel compelled to visit the area of Montmartre to the north, no doubt drawn there by tales of romantic indiscretions by poets, artists, rock stars, and actors in the establishments scattered throughout its cobbled streets.

< OPPOSITE *The Cathédrale de Notre-Dame at sunset.*

FINAL LAPS   *The Tour's arrival on the world's most famous boulevard,
the Champs-Élysées.*

Montmartre is a city in itself, an area that was once outside the limits of Paris and therefore offered a tax-free and highly intoxicated way of living for the young and talented people who flocked to it. Van Gogh, Picasso, Dalí, Monet, Matisse, Renoir, Toulouse-Lautrec—these are just some of the great artists who set up shop in Montmartre, and who would indulge themselves silly at nightfall or whenever a particular piece of work frustrated their skills.

The Basilique du Sacré-Coeur.

Much of that *esprit* is still in Montmartre today, with art lovers mixing with young Parisians and tourists to fill the hundreds of sidewalk cafés and restaurants. Almost all the action takes place in the shadow of the Basilique du Sacré-Coeur, which can be seen towering above Paris from afar.

THE SEINE *A Bateaux-Mouches cruise boat on the river at twilight.*

Now, if your time in Paris is so short that even a few hours of walking is out of the question, then do what I once did in a hurry: Enjoy an evening's boating-and-dining experience on the Seine, courtesy of Bateaux-Mouches, whose long glass-covered boats ply the river's waters at a leisurely pace. In such a way, one can incorporate the very best of Paris—gazing at some of the most historical sights of the city—as well as eating and drinking your way through a fabulous few hours.

Both Bateaux-Mouches and its rival, Bateaux-Parisiens, offer several levels of indulgence, both during the day and in the evening. My advice is to pay the highest price (about €150 per person) and have a fairly private table for two, with a champagne cocktail to start, a bottle of wine, and a generous three-course meal truly *gastronomique*, while being serenaded by classical music from the boat's quartet.

Seen through the boat's huge glass windows and ceiling, Paris looks dazzling, particularly if you've opted for the twilight cruise that sails from near the Eiffel Tower to a point just past the Île de la Cité and back again, passing beneath about sixteen of Paris's romantic bridges and ending with a showy whirl at the *Statue de la Liberté*, a smaller replica of the Statue of Liberty that France gave to the United States in 1886.

On your way back, you'll sail past the floodlit Hôtel de Ville, possibly Paris's most impressive building, often overlooked by Notre-Dame enthusiasts. If your better half is a noncyclist and needs some tender loving care and attention after days or weeks of your own Tour indulgence, then the Bateaux-Mouches can also serve as a marriage-saving investment. Or, as many people discover, a relationship-making night that will never be forgotten. Just make sure you've left enough on your credit card to pay for a suitably romantic hotel.

The Hôtel de Crillon with a Lone Star flag in 2004.

I Recommend

Hôtel de Crillon (www.crillon.com), on the Place de la Concorde in Paris (*département* 75). I've only managed to eat breakfast here, but because it is Paris's greatest hotel, because it is right where the Tour de France ends, and because I'm a dreamer, I have to mention it before all others, just in case one day I can afford to stay the night! For all its opulence and discreet hospitality, the Crillon willingly embraces the stardom that comes with its visiting guests. Lance Armstrong began staying here at the end of the 2000 Tour, and he persuaded the management to hoist the Texas state flag in place of the French flag when the race arrived on the Champs-Élysées (something that was repeated for the following five years). With Armstrong retired in 2006, the French flag was flying once again in July, only to be replaced by the Spanish flag in 2007 when Alberto Contador won as a member of Armstrong's Discovery Channel team. Contador didn't stay the night, but Armstrong did, and his influence made sure the Spanish winner got a fitting welcome as he pedaled across the Place de la Concorde.

Hôtel Élysées Régencia (www.regencia.com), on Avenue Marceau (*département* 75). A former Best Western address, the Élysées Régencia is now privately owned and doing very nicely for itself. With rooms starting at a reasonable €175, this is a highly desirable four-star hotel on one of the city's quieter avenues, just a few minutes' walk from the Arc de Triomphe. Nearby restaurants feature Lebanese, Chinese, Italian, and "plain" French cuisine, although the exquisite Le Cap Vernet fish restaurant right down the street may top your wish list for a post-Tour lunch or dinner.

Paris Marriott Hotel Champs-Élysées (www.marriott.com), right on the Champs-Élysées (*département* 75). This is the only hotel actually on the famous shopping avenue, and what a gem it is! Outer appearances do not give a clue as to what awaits the visitor or guest inside this nineteenth-century building. With room rates starting at €700 a night in peak summer, only the fortunate few will get to see the decadent upholstery and romantic charm of the hotel's 192 rooms. But the magnificent atrium lobby can be enjoyed by one and all, not least because the hotel's main bar is open to everyone. If you are in Paris only for a one-night, end-of-the-Tour experience, see if you can find a room here. You won't regret it!

Hôtel Marceau Champs-Élysées (www.hotelmarceau.com) on Avenue Marceau (*département* 75). A few doors down from the more expensive Élysées Régencia, this little hotel has rooms starting as low as €135 in the summer, making it affordable for just about anyone. One attraction is its proximity to the Arc de Triomphe and Champs-Élysées, while another is the quiet of its tree-lined avenue the morning after a big night out. As well as putting you in proximity to eateries in and around the avenue Marceau, this hotel situates you a bit closer to the Pont d'Alma with its sprinkling of great *brasseries*, a view of the Eiffel Tower across the river, and the departure point for those famous Bateaux-Mouches and Bateaux-Parisiens.

Pershing Hall (www.mrandmrssmith.com) on Rue Pierre Charron (*département* 75). Any boutique hotel in the Mr & Mrs Smith system is worth a stay of at least two nights, and this hotel is no different. Set inside a converted nineteenth-century mansion, it has too many attractions to list. Suffice it to

DINING IN PARIS

In a city the size and grandeur of Paris, your eating choices are endless, and if my post-Tour experiences are anything to go by, they are usually dictated by the proximity to where you'll end up sleeping. I often settle for the nearest establishment I can find after the last day's work is done, but then plan on finding a truly fine restaurant for lunch or dinner the next day when I have more time—yes, a three-hour extravaganza!

If you avail yourself of any of the hotels I recommend, here are some nearby restaurants to try. To begin with, it is hard not to mention Chez Clément on the Champs-Élysées (123, Avenue Champs-Élysées), for its convenience and location (it's part of a fourteen-restaurant chain, with ten locations in Paris); you can dine on a covered sidewalk terrace or inside a glass-roofed salle for your very French meal and service. Not much farther afield and with perhaps better menu choices are establishments like Bistro Saint-Ferdinand (275, Boulevard Péreire), La Maison Blanche (15, Avenue Montaigne), La Grande Armée (3, Avenue Grande Armée), Le Boeuf sur Le Toit (34, Rue Colisée), Chez Georges (273, Boulevard Péreire), as well as the trendy African-themed Impala Lounge (2, Rue de Berri) or Casa Luca (82, Avenue Marceau), a superb Italian eatery. If you have the time or inclination to explore more distant addresses, try La Tour d'Argent (15–17, Quai de la Tournelle) opposite Notre-Dame, the River Café at Issy-les-Moulineaux (146, Quai Stalingrad), the Restaurant Guy Savoy (18, Rue Troyon) in the seventeenth arrondissement (not far from the Arc de Triomphe), or Le Restaurant de l'Hôtel (13, Rue des Beaux Arts), a magnificent offering on the Left Bank with a view across the river of Notre-Dame. If all else fails, or you are really in a hurry, then go visit Pâtisserie Stohrer (51, Rue Montorgueil); it is France's most famous pastry shop.

say you'll feel utterly seduced by the romantic chic of the hotel's twenty-six rooms, some of which are suites and look out onto a garden courtyard. It is in this courtyard, sitting on cushioned, wrought-iron seats, that you can enjoy a superb dinner prepared by the Japanese chef. The Pershing Hall is the Smiths' offering closest to the Champs-Élysées, making it a superb choice if you are able to book early enough to secure one of the few rooms available.

Regional Specialties: Paris, Île de France

Gratinée à l'oignon: The classic French onion soup, made with beef broth boiled with onions, garlic, and gruyère cheese, with a hint of brandy. Usually comes topped with toasted bread and grated cheese.

Hachis Parmentier: Similar to England's shepherd's pie, the French version features mashed potatoes on a base of minced beef, chicken, veal, or slices of foie gras.

Omelette Viroflay: A traditional egg omelet stuffed with cooked spinach, ham, and cheese.

LEGENDS OF THE MODERN TOUR

JAN ULLRICH

A truly great cyclist named Jan Ullrich raced into my sights during the 1997 Tour de France. I believed I was looking at a man capable of winning the next five Tours de France. Ullrich looked magnificent in my first climbing shot of him, cruising along in front of a group of favorites on the Col de l'Aspin, his predominantly white champion-of-Germany jersey glowing like a beacon against a backdrop of regular team jerseys. Ullrich was clearly working for his team leader, Bjarne Riis, who had won in 1996 and wanted to win again this time. But the camera never lies, so they say, and I could see that Riis's face displayed a little too much anguish for him to be taken so seriously this time. Ullrich looked young, fresh, and eager to turn on the power.

Ullrich's Tour-defining attack came on the Arcalis climb in Andorra, a good 10 kilometers from the finish, which gave me ample time to enjoy his physical excellence as he pulled away from climbing aces Marco Pantani and Richard Virenque. It wasn't just Ullrich's legs

Jan Ullrich in the 1997 Tour, riding a time trial at Euro Disney.

that impressed as they churned a massive gear up the mountain. Nor was it the way his long upper body applied strength and leverage through arms stretched out easily to the tops of his brake hoods. It was a mixture of all this—legs, arms, back, and shoulders acting as one unified force—that was the force of Jan Ullrich at his unbeatable best.

Yet Ullrich never managed again to find and use such colossal strengths as he did in the 1997 Tour. He was formidable throughout the remainder of that race, putting over three minutes into his closest time trial challenger at Saint-Étienne—despite the short distance of just 55 kilometers—and then easily containing attacks by Pantani and Virenque in the Alps, to become the overall Tour winner in Paris by a massive nine minutes.

But the rest of Ullrich's Tour career is a series of what-ifs and maybes. What if it hadn't poured ice-cold rain on the Galibier in 1998? What if Pantani hadn't been so ferocious in 1998? What if Lance Armstrong had never recovered from testicular cancer? Take out Pantani, take out Armstrong, and Ullrich might well have won five more Tours. Yet the suspicion is that there would always have been someone else to upset Ullrich's reign.

So where did it all go wrong? The real problem lay within him, most especially in his inability to train year-round and stay as trim as his rivals. I suspect Ullrich took his awesome strengths for granted, always assuming that his muscular legs and back would be good come July, that he could take months off in the winter and have fun. Yet by 1999, Ullrich's knees were giving way, a reaction to the massive gears he'd depended on when he was younger. He strengthened them sufficiently to scare Armstrong in 2000, 2001, and 2003, but that was as good as it got.

Time trialing became Ullrich's chief commodity when his weight went up and his climbing legs let him down, and it's hardly surprising that the German twice became a world champion in this discipline. It was one of his signature time trials that rocked Armstrong to the core in the 2003 Tour, but Ullrich wasn't able to capitalize on it and attack the American in the Pyrenees. By the last mountain stage of that Tour, Armstrong had recovered his strength, and Ullrich had lost his last great chance to win; it had been five full years since the German's only Tour victory.

Ironically, by challenging and losing to Armstrong so many times, Ullrich became an even more popular cyclist. His annual battle against his rival drew millions of fans to France, and to TV sets around the world, making those years the most popular in the Tour's history. Who can forget their time trial showdowns of 2000 and 2003? Or the sportsmanship they showed to each other in 2001 after deciding the Tour through a mountainous duel lasting over six stages? Ullrich clearly relished the fight; he gave his very best that July to push Armstrong as far as he could. And even when he knew that it would not be enough, that Armstrong was too strong, Ullrich still had the humility to shake his rival's hand in a public display of respect. Little wonder that Ullrich gladly went along to Armstrong's Tour-ending retirement party in Paris in 2005. The applause that greeted the German's arrival on stage at the InterContinental Paris Le-Grand was deafening.

I'll always remember Ullrich as one of my favorite subjects to photograph, for it's not often such a giant of a man is able to race so gracefully yet inflict so much damage. Ullrich was never more graceful than in a time trial, and I thrived on capturing his stealthy, stalking position at its best, side-on, before tucking in behind him and watching those astonishing quads pump untold strength down to the pedals.

There was once a sharp edge to his mountain riding as well, and it became every Tour photographer's hope to capture an Ullrich attack at its best: hands on the drops, shoulders over the bars, a cat-like spring, and that snarling, growling face as the effort began. Sadly, we didn't see nearly enough of such attacks.

In his worst moments, Ullrich was mere cannon fodder, there for Armstrong's pleasure, or as an overweight object for rivals and rival fans to ridicule. Yet on his day, particularly on those great days of the 1997 Tour, I could have fooled myself into believing it was 1969, that Jan was Eddy, that the images I was taking of his attack on the Arcalis were in fact of Merckx soloing to any one of his great mountain victories.

Ullrich retired in 2007 with a huge cloud of suspicion hanging over him. Did he take drugs or didn't he take drugs? Does anyone actually care, I ask? Jan Ullrich brought a unique brand of competitiveness to the Tour, and that's how I prefer to remember him.

MIGUEL INDURÁIN

Miguel Induráin won five consecutive Tours de France from 1991 to 1995, a record at the time. But it seems obvious that Induráin could have won at least six if he'd been allowed to race for himself in 1990. The tall Spaniard had entered Tour life in 1985, and he was coming nicely to prominence when Pedro Delgado suddenly joined him on the Reynolds team in 1988 and won the Tour himself.

Still, Induráin was growing in stature all the time. He won a mountain stage of the '89 Tour while Delgado acted as a decoy to the overall favorites. Delgado made a mess of his Tour defense in '89, and he did it again in 1990; this time it fell to Induráin to sacrifice his own chances and ride for Delgado on a stage where the team leader had missed the vital escape.

It was obvious to everyone that Induráin was stronger than Delgado, as well as the other race favorites, Greg LeMond and Gianni Bugno, but his team management was holding him back. Induráin beat all three men in the Tour's major time trials. The rising star also won a mountaintop stage finish at Luz Ardiden and nearly won at Millau too, adding more credence to the belief that the 1990 Tour could have been Induráin's for the taking. His great time loss came at Alpe d'Huez, to the tune of more than twelve minutes, but that was after Induráin had dragged Delgado back into contention along the windswept valley road before sitting up on the final climb.

When you see how smoothly Induráin cruised through the following five years, when no one got even close to beating him, you can argue that a seventh Tour was a serious possibility, which would have meant that Lance Armstrong would have had to win an eighth Tour to hold the all-time record.

Realistically, though, Induráin was probably past his best in 1996 anyway, at the age of 32 and after twelve seasons as a pro. He'd started the Tour in each of those twelve years, an astonishing record, but one that must also suggest he would have had an accumulation of fatigue in '96.

It's incredibly difficult to look back at Induráin's career and pick certain highlights out of those five Tour victories, for they all looked the same! With a few rare exceptions, Induráin won his Tours by time trialing his way to safe time gaps, before sitting in for a few hard stages in the mountains. There he'd ride protected by his teammates, or by

Miguel Induráin powers to Morzine-Avoriaz in the 1994 Tour de France.

alliances with rivals who saw in Induráin the chance to upgrade their overall positions if the powerful Spaniard would, please, churn those long legs long enough to tow them away from the rest of the pack.

Induráin forged alliances with Gianni Bugno in 1991, with Claudio Chiappucci in 1992, with Tony Rominger in 1993, and with Alex Zülle in 1995. Only in 1994 was Induráin isolated, but he was so strong that it didn't matter. In each of the five Tours he won, Induráin also benefited from the inclusion of a team time trial (TTT) in the route. For some cyclists, the TTT was a virtual guarantee of losing a Tour. For Induráin, although he did the lion's share of the work, it meant a simple time gain over any climbing rivals who awaited him in the mountains. Still, Induráin's power was such that on one occasion, in 1994, his Banesto team got within twenty seconds of winning the TTT, paced by one very strong individual.

You could be forgiven for assuming Induráin was a dull subject for our cameras, yet I found him to be a most awesome Tour champion to photograph. Tall, elegant, gentlemanly, and with a crown of dark, swirly hair atop his handsome face, Induráin was the noble prince who came to France and went away each year with its prized possession. If he did this with dignity and even modesty, he also did it ruthlessly, utilizing his massive body and long, shapely legs to astonishing effect.

For a man who was over six feet tall and weighed 176 pounds, Induráin worked with the grace of a cheetah, and could pedal away from his climbing rivals before they even knew what was happening. In a rare moment in the 1995 Tour, Induráin actually felt threatened by an attack from Zülle, but he bided his time at the foot of La Plagne before suddenly winding up the pace as the road steepened. A string of climbers were blown off his back wheel: Ivan Gotti, Pantani, Pavel Tonkov, Virenque, Rominger, Chiappucci, Fernando Escartin, and Laudelino Cubino. One man, Paolo Lanfranchi, lingered awhile longer, but he too went backward as Induráin raced ahead in pursuit of Zülle.

The champion's efficient climbing style—big meaty hands on the tops of his bars, elbows locked rigidly at 90 degrees, legs pedaling at a very high cadence, face contorted, and teeth flaring—made sure that half of those climbers lost four minutes to him at La Plagne, while the race leader ate over a minute of Zülle's lead to keep the Swiss in check before the Pyrenees. It was probably Induráin's greatest single climbing performance in any Tour, and it enabled him to shed at least some of the stigma that branded him simply as a robotic time trialist.

Nevertheless, the majority of my Induráin archive shows him racing in search of time trial perfection, either on his way into the yellow jersey if it was the first week of the Tour, or actually in yellow if the first mountains had already been climbed; Induráin never left it to the last week to move to the front. Nearest to perfection was the 1992 first-week TT in Luxembourg, where Induráin raced at 49 km/h to take control of the Tour. This was the best time trial Induráin produced in his five winning Tours, and it established a new record at the time.

I remember photographing Induráin on the return leg of the course, before waiting for the next men, LeMond and Bugno, who'd started three and six minutes later. I took shots of them about 30 kilometers from the finish, and even though I had the speed advantage of a high-powered motorcycle to carry me, I never did catch speedy Miguel in time to get more shots of him before the finish.

Induráin's time trialing superiority was certainly copied by Bjarne Riis, who won the 1996 Tour after Induráin blew to pieces in the Alps, and perhaps by Jan Ullrich as well, who succeeded Riis a year later. But the greatest tribute any cyclist paid to Induráin was Lance Armstrong, a man once caught by Induráin for three minutes in the '94 Tour; Armstrong studied and perfected the great man's skills to establish a new speed record in the 1999 Tour, of 49.417 km/h, at Metz.

MOUNTAINS OF THE TOUR

IT'S USUALLY THE TV HELICOPTER THAT TRIGGERS IT—A SURGE OF EXCITE-ment affecting everyone as the noise from the rotor blades drifts up from the valley far below. A cry of delight from some farsighted person acts as the announcement that the peloton has been sighted below that helicopter, provoking a rush of humanity to the vantage point. Sure enough, the peloton *is* climbing the mountain, though its slow, ant-like progress is both hypnotic and frustrating, for it will take many minutes for the race to reach its audience.

The more athletic fans clamber onto rocky viewpoints, abandoning the road-side territory they've been carefully protecting all day. From such a distance, even a pair of good binoculars fails to identify the leaders of the peloton or the team colors in which the cyclists race, adding to the mystery and enjoyment.

The cyclists are getting closer now, just two *lacets* (hairpin curves) below, and the long convoy of silver, blue, and red race cars that precedes them begins to trickle past. Only minutes to go! Suddenly the cyclists are right below the road on which the spectators are standing, their sweat-soaked jerseys and shorts vivid in the clear mountain air. Faces can be seen too, and—*mon Dieu*—they look so striking close up!

This last sighting spurs the spectators to a frenzy of activity, with all semblance of order totally abandoned. People who have been guarding their spot for many a long hour suddenly run to a different spot, triggering a scramble by others

< OPPOSITE *The Tour de France climbs the Col du Lautaret in 2000.*

195

to take their valued places. Other fans try to climb higher, to get away from the maddening crowd, perhaps settling on a patch of lush grass from which they can see the bigger picture of cyclists, spectators, and awe-inspiring scenery.

Finally, the cyclists arrive, their glistening faces illuminated by the startling mountain light, accentuating the strange glamour of their job. To some fans, the Tour is only about the cyclists, their athleticism, courage, poise, and devotion. To others, it is the overall beauty that counts: the beauty of man struggling against the forces of nature, as well as the beauty of nature itself in a truly wondrous corner of the world.

The cyclists are almost past now, cheered on their way by a cacophony of noise and passion and emotion that will be repeated by thousands of other spectators farther up this climb, and on all the climbs that follow. The Tour has entered the mountains at last, and its greatest fans are there to salute the race.

THE GLORY OF THE MOUNTAINS

To many cycling fans, the mountains are what the Tour de France is all about, and even the most serious connoisseur would find it hard to quarrel with that sentiment. Even upon the Tour's first running in 1903, there was an expectation that the race would one day confront France's imposing peaks, that no amount of flat or rolling stages would ever be enough to truly challenge the sport's greatest champions. The same thought applies today, and it is the mountain stages that truly capture the unique drama forever associated with the Tour.

There's a majesty and grace in the Tour that only becomes evident when the race reaches the mountains. Flat stages are good enough for catching a fleeting glimpse of humanity as the race pedals by, and for enjoying the antics of the *caravane publicitaire* a few hours earlier. But the speed of the race on the flats means that there is never a chance to stand back and admire the peloton and its courageous athletes the way one can in the mountains. Gazing down on that snaking peloton far below, one cannot fail to be impressed by the statesmanlike progress as the cyclists make their way up a *col* (pass), preceded by motorcycles, cars, and that helicopter, and trailed a vast convoy of team cars, other motorcycles, and finally, the *voiture-balai*, the broom wagon that sweeps up the riders who abandon the Tour.

ALPE D'HUEZ   *The Alpe is the most populated climb for spectators when the
mountain is a Tour de France stage.*

The mountains bring a different gravitas to the Tour, for it is in the mountains that the race will be won or lost, that reputations will be established for a lifetime or shattered into a thousand pieces. In return, the Tour creates a fearful awe that the mountains might not otherwise elicit. Would the Col du Tourmalet ever have become famous if there had never been a Tour climbing it? Just imagine how much smaller the fame of Mont Ventoux would have been if Tom Simpson hadn't collapsed and died on its slopes in 1967. Even l'Alpe d'Huez was nothing but an underpopulated ski resort during the summers until the Tour began making regular visits to its now-famous twenty-one switchback curves.

In a typical Tour, mountain stages account for about nine days of the three-week total, of which three or four days might be set aside for summit finishes. Although the mountains of the Vosges and Jura offer sufficient challenges for most fit cyclists, it is to the Pyrenees, Massif Central, and Alps that the Tour turns in order to offer a fitting challenge for its thoroughbred athletes.

And it is the first day in the mountains that creates the greatest suspense. After a week of racing where barely a hill worthy of the distinction has been climbed, suddenly the Alps, Pyrenees, or Massif Central is to be assailed with full force. The suspense is shared equally between the spectators following the Tour and the cyclists racing in it, for no one knows what may happen once the climbing begins.

It is the spectators who benefit most; their enjoyment and their adulation of the racing cyclists are quite painless and utterly compelling. For the majority of the racers, however, there's only suffering, uncertainty, and an appointment with fate they could very well do without. Only for a few will the mountains become the greatest stage of their careers.

THE MASSIF CENTRAL

Of the three regions, the Massif Central is sometimes seen as the poor relation, for at best it will only see a visit from the Tour every few years, whereas the Alps and Pyrenees are traversed each year. This is not without its advantages, however, for the Massif Central therefore remains the mystery it has always been to the outside world, a remote land marked by some of the prettiest scenery in France.

Perhaps the Massif Central is visited less often than the other mountain ranges because of its remoteness and apparent lack of climbing options. In fact, there are many hundreds of challenging climbs in the region, but access to and from them is too limiting for the Tour. Such climbs are to be found amid the volcanic areas, scattered above the dense forests, or hidden among rolling green pastures where *burels*—stone huts used by shepherds in times gone by—litter the succulent landscape.

The Massif Central is also home to two exceptional regional parks, the Parc Naturel Régional du Livradois-Forez north of Le Puy-en-Velay, and the more rugged Parc Naturel Régional des Volcans d'Auvergne just to the west, which embraces such Tour playgrounds as the Puy-de-Dôme and Super-Besse (see below).

The bulk of the Massif Central is inside Auvergne, but also stretches out into Rhône-Alpes, Midi-Pyrénées, Limousin, Languedoc, and Centre; for one's sanity, it is best to consider the geographical Massif Central and the historical

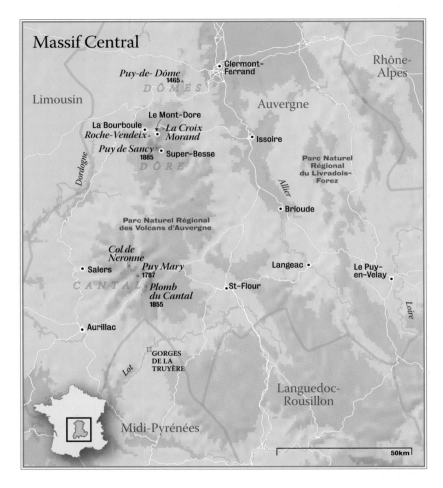

Auvergne as one and the same. From a mountainous point of view, the Massif Central is graced by three different ranges: Monts du Cantal, Monts Dômes, and Monts Dore, and the Tour visits them all once in a while.

Puy-de-Dôme

The best known of the Auvergne mountains, located in the Monts Dômes, is the Puy-de-Dôme, first used by the Tour in 1952, but not included on the

PUY–DE–DÔME *Spectators cheer on the stragglers in the 1998 Tour.*

route since 1988 because of the unsuitability of the road that winds its way to the top. At just four miles long and a bit too narrow for comfort, the road is considered unsafe to accommodate the bulging audience of the modern Tour. At least that's what most people assume; after all, we don't want cycling fans falling off this ancient volcano because there are too many people on the road, now, do we?

Fact is, the nearby city of Clermont-Ferrand holds authority over the mountain and insisted on charging spectators to ascend it back in 1988, a decision that the Tour did not like, for it values its free-to-all attraction. It's high time the city leaders negotiated again, for the Puy-de-Dôme acts as a most perfect summit finish, be it on the way home to Paris or between the stages of the Alps and Pyrenees.

To get an accurate idea of the might of this 1,464-meter-high mountain (that's 4,803 feet), one needs to overfly the Massif Central in an airliner, say from Montpellier to Paris. Seen from the air, the Puy-de-Dôme stands out from the other extinct volcanoes of the Massif as dramatically as Mont Ventoux does from the rest of Provence. For those without wings, it is enough to drive or cycle up the four-mile-long road, and then walk higher still into the crater itself. The views of the Chaîne des Puys, the 40-kilometer-long chain of lava domes erupting from the Massif Central, are awesome!

Farther south, one finds the Monts Dore, a collection of volcanic craters with a more alpine geography than those of the Monts Dôme. Two towns in particular, La Bourboule and Mont-Dore, have enjoyed visits from the Tour. Both are reached by majestic ascents, the first by the Col de la Croix-Morand, the second by the more severe Roche-Vendeix. All the roads in this area are potential leg breakers, but at least the best of them, the D996, makes up for its difficulty by providing a roller-coaster tour of the Puys that is exhilarating and challenging at the same time.

Just off this road between Issoire and La Bourboule is the little ski station of Super-Besse, on the mountain road where I first took a shot of Bernard Hinault in 1978 and was so excited by this act that I didn't notice a fistfight a few minutes later between Jan Raas, the famed sprinter of the TI-Raleigh team, and a spectator who'd apparently insulted the Dutchman.

That was the first time the Tour had gone to Super-Besse, but it went back in 1996 when Rolf Sørensen, who in those days was something of an all-rounder, won the stage from the Portuguese climber Orlando Rodrigues, and again in 2008 when the drugged, and since disgraced, Riccardo Ricco won. Super-Besse must have paid a lot of money to receive these stage finishes; there are not a lot of other reasons to be up there in summer.

Riccardo Ricco wins at Super-Besse in the 2008 Tour; he was later disqualified after failing a drug test.

Puy Mary

The Monts du Cantal are by far the most enchanting area of the Auvergne. They contain a number of spectacular ascents, in particular the Puy Mary, which was climbed by the Tour in 2004 and 2008. If the Puy-de-Dôme has the fame and La Croix Morand the majesty, then without doubt the Puy Mary has the beauty, especially if you have taken your seat on the vast natural auditorium atop the 1,787-meter summit (5,863 feet), and are looking down on the peloton as it struggles its way through the last kilometer of the climb.

This mountain has four different approach roads with four different degrees of difficulty, the worst (or best, depending on your enthusiasm for such things) of which is via the Col de Neronne, heading east on the D680 from Salers. This was the route taken in 2004 by Richard Virenque, who was already alone and in front on the climb, and he virtually strolled to a remarkable stage win in Saint-Flour. Strolling over the Puy Mary was of course impossible, even for this determined Frenchman, yet Virenque made as good a job of his ascent as anyone had through the years, before plunging down into Dienne and then tackling the remaining two climbs to win by over five minutes. I cannot recall seeing or hearing as vociferous a level of support as when Virenque climbed the Puy Mary that year; he turned Bastille Day into a riotous celebration for

Richard Virenque is cheered up the Puy Mary during the 2004 Tour de France.

all of France, not just his cycling fans. It was Virenque's last great ride, for the Frenchman retired after the 2004 Tour, probably with the sounds of those Puy Mary fans still ringing in his ears.

THE ALPS

The Tour has its greatest choice of ascents in the Alps, where over eighty *cols, côtes* (hills), or ski-resort climbs have been used by the race since it first climbed there in 1905. The Alps form a massive landmass impossible to see as one entity unless you are still flying your airliner 30,000 feet above the ground. When a commercial jet heads out of Nice on a northerly route, it requires about thirty minutes to travel between the Alpes-Maritimes—home to such legendary ascents as the Col de la Cayolle, Cime de la Bonette, and Col d'Allos—and the shores of Lake Geneva, in which are reflected the snow masses of Mont Blanc and its associated *grands cols* (great passes) of Joux-Plane, Colombière, Aravis, Saisies, and Roselend. What lies between these two areas of the Alps is an even greater playground for the Tour, with ascents too numerous to mention, including the *cols* of Madeleine, Iseran, Croix de Fer, Glandon, Galibier, and Izoard.

This is already a vast collection of climbs for the Tour to contemplate, but one of the real assets of the Alps is the extensive network of *bas-alpine* ascents that give the tour a double-edged potency. What we know as the Alps—the mighty snowcapped monsters that put the fear of God into anyone climbing them on a bicycle—are surrounded by quieter areas like the Chartreuse, Bauges, Chablais, and Vercors. It is among these officially preserved areas that we might find the Tour climbing the Col du Granier, Crêt de Châtillon, Mont-Salève, Col de la Croix Fry, Col du Corbier, or the Col de l'Écharasson, and then finishing at ski stations like Allevard, Chamrousse, Prapoutel, Villard-de-Lans, and even Orcières-Merlette.

There are many, many, more such climbs, but most of them are too narrow and dangerous to accommodate the mighty Tour, and are instead to be enjoyed in a cozier race like the Dauphiné-Libéré, held three weeks prior to the Tour. If a quiet cycling holiday is what you are after once you've enjoyed the Tour, go and experience these delightful climbs, as well as the scenery all around them; it will be a voyage of discovery and contentment every inch of the way.

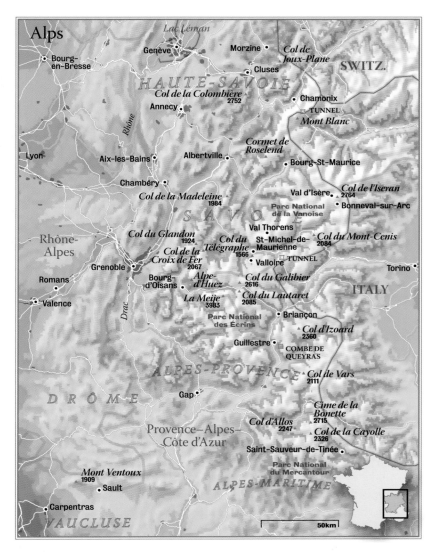

Before I grew up and became a cycling photographer, I once cycled from a thrilling rendezvous with the Tour at l'Alpe d'Huez to Nice by way (mostly) of the Route des Grandes-Alpes. My route took me through Bourg-d'Oisans and

COL D'IZOARD *Stragglers in the 2005 Tour climb through the Casse Déserte atop the Col d'Izoard.*

joined the recognized route on the summit of the Col du Lautaret. For anyone wanting to do a long, place-to-place solo tour, this might be a great idea, but do it without the burden of the camping stove and tent I carried—it's better that way!

If you start from the beginning, in Thonon-les-Bains, and make it to Menton, the official end, you will have covered 660 kilometers and climbed thirteen mighty *cols*, including three of the greatest: Col de l'Iseran, Col du Galibier, and Col d'Izoard. By car, the drive can be accomplished in perhaps three full days, while fit cyclists can expect to reach the beaches in around five or six days—depending on how often they stop to take in the eye-watering scenery.

Going by bike, you can better enjoy such sights as the Massif du Mont Blanc—only viewable on the descent of the Colombière—the stunning Aiguille du Grand Fond overlooking the Cormet de Roselend, the wilderness of the Iseran's long, long ascent, and then the double whammy of the Télégraphe and the Galibier, where you'll be left breathless by the air and the sparkling beauty of the Massif des Écrins.

LEFT *The memorial to Henri Desgrange, just below the summit of the Col du Galibier.*
RIGHT *A plaque dedicated to Fausto Coppi and Louison Bobet on the Col d'Izoard.*

Near the summit of the Galibier stands a memorial to Tour founder Henri Desgrange, one of many such plaques you'll find on your ride south. This plaque is to be found on the southern side of a renovated tunnel, used to allow cars to cross the Galibier if the last five hundred meters are still snowbound or damaged after the winter. However, the extra effort to climb to the real summit is more than worthwhile.

One of the best-known cycling memorials is actually on the descent of the Izoard, on the *faux-plat* (false flat) that takes you through the extraordinary Casse Déserte, all sandstone turrets and loose scree that make it look as if you've landed on the moon. Louison Bobet and Fausto Coppi are as legendary as you can get in Tour history, having won five Tours between them from 1949 to 1955. Their greatest theater seems to have been on the Izoard, so it seems fitting that a joint memorial was created at the top of the 2,361-meter *col* (7,746 feet) by readers of *L'Équipe*.

BONETTE *The Cime de la Bonette, showing the extension above the Col de Restefond.*

Especially amid such an eerie landscape, this is a sacred place for all cyclists, so much so that a mountain gendarme will always guard the memorial when the Tour is passing, as a sign of respect. If you want to spend a quiet few minutes there lost in thought, best to visit the Izoard on another day, such as on your ride to Nice.

By now you will have descended the Galibier at breakneck speed—it's a safe one, but impossible to take slowly—passed through Briançon, and made it up the much easier side of the Izoard. You might choose to sleep in Guillestre, the small town nestling between the Izoard and Col de Vars, but that is after you've enjoyed the splendor of the Combe de Queyras, a mighty rock face that plunges into the rapids of the river Quill. Don't look over the edge of your road too much; you're about five hundred feet above the torrent.

Your next major challenge may not yet be the Col de la Cayolle, for after the Vars has been crossed, the touring enthusiast is faced with a difficult choice between continuing on the Route des Grandes-Alpes and swinging left after the Vars descent and pointing up the road that circles the summit, the Cime de la Bonette, at 2,802 meters (9,192 feet) the highest through road in Europe.

It's a worthwhile diversion to take, if only to see the mountain where Pedro Delgado and Robert Millar were locked in battle in the 1993 Tour and to experience the sparkling alpine lake a few kilometers below its summit. The Tour has climbed the Cime de la Bonette just four times in its history, another reason to experience its wonder.

Strictly speaking, Millar and Delgado were fighting it out on the Col de Restefond, not the Bonette, for they did not swing right to gain the extra hundred meters of altitude that separates the two *cols*—something the 2008 Tour actually did. By crossing the Restefond-Bonette (just why this wonderful climb is not on the official Route des Grandes-Alpes, no one actually knows), the cyclist or driver misses not just the Cayolle—a beautifully wooded climb with thick forests and relative tranquility—but also the Col de la Couillole, although that may be acceptable, given that the time gained could be spent enjoying a

EUROPE'S GREAT HIKES

France caters to all kinds of travelers, especially in its mountain ranges. One of the greatest long-distance walks in Europe, the Grande Randonnée Cinq, or GR5, stretches from Lake Geneva to Nice, passing many of the same *cols* as the cycling route. But without the speed of a bike, it takes the average hiker at least one month to walk the entire way! The GR5 actually starts in the Netherlands and takes the walker through Belgium, Luxembourg, and eastern France before it reaches the Alps. Other alpine routes branch away from the GR5, making one-day or weeklong walks possible as well. Consider the GR54, which starts and finishes in Bourg-d'Oisans and takes the walker on a fantastic circuit of the Écrins national park, featuring peaks like the Galibier and Meije. Other alternatives are the GR58, near the Italian border at Monte Viso, or the GR541, a high-altitude classic that will see you crossing twenty-four passes above 2,000 meters and five passes above 3,000 meters! Check out www.grfive.com for more information, particularly the options on accommodation and the possibility of having your bags carried for you each day.

snack in the Alpes-Provence town of Saint-Sauveur-de-Tinée before continuing south. You also miss out on the mystical ascent of the Col d'Allos, where Thévenet battled Merckx in the 1975 Tour before finally outdistancing the Belgian champion on the climb to Pra-Loup.

My ride back in 1979 took me over the Cayolle but not the Couillole, as I'd decided to ride to Nice instead of Menton. That lovely 70-kilometer descent took me along the Gorges de Daluis, where giant walls of bright red rock guide you gently toward civilization in the south of France.

Alpe d'Huez

Unquestionably, Alpe d'Huez is the grand coliseum of all the Tour's revered mountains, thanks to a modern history that has seen the greatest champions battle—and sometimes win—there. These days, fans automatically refer to the Armstrong-Ullrich duel of 2001, or the nervous ascent of 2003 when Iban Mayo ignited a finale that saw Armstrong struggling to keep pace with Mayo's pursuers. No one who's seen the Tour in recent years can forget the excitement of the stage 16 time trial of 2004, when Armstrong took another step

An aerial view of the final switchbacks of Alpe d'Huez.

LEFT *Marco Pantani powering his way to the fastest ascent of Alpe d'Huez in the 1995 Tour.* RIGHT *Joop Zoetemelk racing Alpe d'Huez in front of a Dutch audience in 1986.*

toward securing a fourth overall victory in front of half a million spectators, most of whom had camped out overnight. People with better memories might recall the Pantani years of 1995 and 1997 as providing the definitive chapters in the Alpe's great legend, not least because Marco Pantani's ride of 1995 is still the fastest *en-ligne* ascent ever made there, in 36:50 at an average speed of 22.48 km/h (13.97 mph).

The fact is, Alpe d'Huez has had a succession of Pantanis and Armstrongs through the years, who have ensured its lasting fame. Fausto Coppi began the story in 1952, and Joop Zoetemelk picked up the legacy by winning in 1976. (Today, with the mountain's legend firmly established, who could imagine the Tour not visiting the Alpe for twenty-four years?) Zoetemelk's win was the start of a golden era for the mountain resort, for the Dutchman's victory launched a migration of Dutch fans to the mountain whenever the Tour put the Alpe on its route.

Conveniently, Dutch cyclists took it upon themselves to save their best Tour performances for the Alpe, inspiring more and more of their supporters to travel

ALPE D'HUEZ   *The Alpe's switchbacks a few hours before the Tour riders arrive.*

to France each summer. Hennie Kuiper, Peter Winnen, Steven Rooks, Gert-Jan Theunisse, and even Zoetemelk again (in 1979, when two stages finished on the Alpe) won there between 1976 and 1989, before the winning streak was ended in 1990 by Gianni Bugno. The popularity of the climb seemed unsurpassable at that time, yet the Armstrong years took spectator levels even higher, to gaudy numbers that may never be beaten.

The success story of Alpe d'Huez owes as much to its strategic location as it does to any stage-winning performances. Less than one hour's drive from Grenoble, the Alpe sits perfectly placed to receive its gladiators after they've crossed over any number of great *cols,* while making it easy for spectators to get there as well. The Tour is too gigantic to end a stage on the summit of the Col du Galibier, the Col de la Croix de Fer, or the Col du Glandon, but it can use those climbs to set up a thrilling finale at the Alpe.

Clever marketing by the Alpe's chamber of commerce has made sure that a rival resort like Les Deux-Alpes has only had one stage finish of the Tour, in 1998; this marketing is funded by the greater wealth l'Alpe d'Huez enjoys from having one of the country's finest ski areas. L'Alpe also has enough hotel space to house the Tour and its 3,000-strong family, as well as the money needed to secure stage-finish rights. Alpe d'Huez has guaranteed itself an eternal fame that ensures the Tour will visit regularly, often in preference to somewhere else.

Just what is it that makes the Alpe so special? Its history, first of all. Second might be the level of excitement its watching public bestows on the Tour as the race begins its ascent out of Bourg-d'Oisans. For me, however, three important things elevate Alpe d'Huez above almost any other mountaintop finish.

First is the series of switchbacks in the last 3 kilometers that acts as a great vantage point for the hundreds of thousands of fans who have made their way so high. From their lofty perch on the banks that flank the road, spectators can see the Tour fought out in front of their eyes, initially from a distance as tiny dots appear between cars, motorcycles, and other spectators, right up to the point when those dots become full-size human beings—legends of the Tour who pass within inches of your face, their own faces showing the signs of wear and tear, determination, and even fear.

Second is that proximity. It's not just that the spectators are so close to incomparable action, but also that on the Alpe, there is nowhere for the racers to hide—and the spectators know it and love it.

Third is that the views from the last few kilometers are simply unforgettable on a good day, with the snowcapped peaks of the Massif des Écrins a permanent fixture on the horizon. If you fall in love with those views as I did, you may want to go back in May, when the panorama of mountain peaks is matched by rich, green meadows, filled with masses of small yellow flowers that further brighten what are generally perfect days.

From a cyclist's point of view, the opening few kilometers act as a launchpad for anyone trying to win the stage or to gain overall time on their rivals. Almost every success on the Alpe has been based on making a ferocious start at the bottom, as Pantani did in 1995, Armstrong in 2001, and Sastre in 2008; only a few of the stage winners have been able to make a successful move later on. The first two *lacets* (hairpin curves) are so steep that they scare most Tour cyclists

Dag-Otto Lauritzen is just visible among   OPPOSITE   >
thousands of fans at Alpe d'Huez in 1990.

Christian Vande Velde launches an attack on Alpe d'Huez in 2008.

into submission—another secret of the mountain—before a relatively calm road allows the gains made below to be consolidated in full.

The road begins to rise significantly again in the last 6 kilometers, with the *lacets* becoming shorter between the corners until that final, spectacular traverse below the waiting masses.

Parts of the climb have become the exclusive domain of partisan supporters. The Dutch have set up a huge presence after those steep opening kilometers, at La Garde, and a massive Dutch flag seems permanently etched into the road there. In their glory days, the Dutch also established their territory on each of the last four *virages*

ACCESS TIP FOR ALPE D'HUEZ

Try accessing the mountain by way of two alternative roads. From Allemont, a tiny road northwest of Bourg-d'Oisans, the D211, takes you to within 5 kilometers of the summit, though part of the road is unsurfaced. From the direction of Les Deux-Alpes and Col du Lautaret, another small road takes you over one *col* at two thousand meters before dropping you into l'Alpe d'Huez itself. Be sure to check with some locals in case these roads are closed on the day of the race. By the way, after the stage ends, both roads make for excellent escapes from the mountain as well.

STAGE WINNERS ATOP ALPE D'HUEZ

Andy Hampsten

1952: Fausto Coppi	1989: Gert-Jan Theunisse
1976: Joop Zoetemelk	1990: Gianni Bugno
1977: Hennie Kuiper	1991: Gianni Bugno
1978: Hennie Kuiper	1992: Andy Hampsten
1979: Joaquim Agostinho	1994: Roberto Conti
1979: Joop Zoetemelk	1995: Marco Pantani
1981: Peter Winnen	1997: Marco Pantani
1982: Beat Breu	1999: Giuseppe Guerini
1983: Peter Winnen	2001: Lance Armstrong
1984: Luis Herrera	2003: Iban Mayo
1986: Bernard Hinault	2004: Lance Armstrong
1987: Federico Echave	2006: Fränk Schleck
1988: Steven Rooks	2008: Carlos Sastre

(curves), only to be replaced by more rowdy Danish supporters in the Bjarne Riis years of 1995 to 1997. Naturally, American fans did their country proud by replacing the Danes from 1999 to 2004; in my opinion, it was nice to see an altogether more discreet level of support offered after too many years of unruly behavior.

Col du Galibier

When you first encounter the wonder that is the Col du Galibier, you sense a certain degree of exposure to the gods, and it's not just because of the thin mountain air or the spectacular views from this roof-of-the-world peak. There's a spirit about the Col du Galibier that seems exclusive to the mountain that carries its name, a spirit so strong I cannot imagine how the Tour cyclists must have felt when they first climbed it in 1911.

The long and very lonely haul away from Valloire is the first challenge, a steep rise giving way to a bumpy road that seems as unending as it is straight.

Unseasonal snow atop the Col du Galibier in 2000.

To your right is the towering peak of the Aiguille de l'Épaisseur, at over three thousand meters, a constant factor in your solitude. You're climbing all the time, not sure of which direction the road will take when it finally reaches Plan-Lachat, a collection of walking huts that act as a refuge for hikers climbing to the Camp des Rochilles, or cyclists climbing the Galibier.

Then you see it, a stone bridge taking the road—your road—over the shallow rapids of the river Valoirette and to an uncertain destination high above. Here starts the real climb: 8 more kilometers of lung-searing agony for the Tour cyclist, or just a mild exposure to heartburn for those with more time on their hands.

If you've the capacity to inspect it, a new horizon has appeared before your eyes, one that has patches of snow on the top edge, rolling meadows with grazing cows at the bottom edge, and the barely definable traces of the road you'll take as the middle perspective (and it is that aspect of your view that occupies your mind the most). It twists, it turns, it sometimes doubles back on itself, but the road always climbs, up and up and up until there's no more road except

COL DU GALIBIER   *Miguel Induráin climbs the south side of the Galibier in 1991.*

the one that will take you over the summit and to another, altogether more
spectacular panorama.

The Tour's competitors can't stop to enjoy the view, of course, for they have
more pressing things to consider, not least the screaming descent that might
lead to Briançon and the Col d'Izoard, or west to either Les Deux-Alpes or
Alpe d'Huez. It's the Tour spectator, photographer, or cyclo-tourist who can

watch the world go by for a while—longer still if you're visiting the climb when the Tour is not there. To your left lies the valley of La Guisane and all points south, and to your right, a look back toward the Grandes Rousses, the range of mountains that supports a mighty skiing industry at l'Alpe d'Huez.

It is the sight directly in front of you that is most hypnotic, a gallery of snowcapped mountains with names like Barre des Écrins, Roche Faurio, and Le Rateau, as well as La Meije, the mountain with the most impressive glacier in the area. It seems appropriate that such a panorama should be on the southern side of the Galibier, as if the knowledge of it being there should be the best inducement to those climbing from the north, the hardest side.

The Galibier was one of the first *cols* I ever climbed as a touring cyclist during the 1979 Tour. Weighed down heavily with camping and camera gear as I was, it was a particularly long ascent I'll never forget, but the exhilaration upon reaching that last 500-meter stretch to the summit was a defining moment in my young life.

I honestly cannot recall even noticing the beauty of the glaciers, but it was somewhere between cycling over the Galibier in 1979, coming back up the very next day to see the Tour follow my route, and then photographing the southern

OVER THE TOP

The first Tour rider over the Galibier in 1911 was Émile Georget, who with Paul Duboc was one of the only riders not to walk over the pass. Georget had earlier crashed heavily on the Ballon d'Alsace and was out of contention for the overall win, but he put in an attack on the Galibier's snow-packed ascent to take the lead ahead of Duboc. The Tour winner that year, Gustave Garrigou, followed closely, alternately walking and riding his fixed gear. According to his first-person account in *L'Auto* at the time, Garrigou was not a big fan of the mountains in that year's edition, observing, "They might suit riders like Georget or Duboc, but for a boy like me who likes his Tours de France nice and easy, getting by without exceptional graft, *eh bien*, it hardly bears thinking about."

Originally, the highest point reached on the Galibier was at 2,556 meters (8,386 feet), but due to the closing of a tunnel in 1976, the road now crests at 2,645 meters (8,678 feet), a bit closer to the mountain's actual peak.

ascent in 1983 as an accredited photographer that I decided the Galibier was best left to the experts. I knew, however, that I could share in some of their glory by capturing the beauty of this mountain on film.

I cannot help but think of the mountain gods whenever the Tour climbs the Galibier these days, for the scale of a meandering peloton set against a backdrop of mountains and glaciers is so overwhelming. My perspective has changed too, and instead of wanting to see a battle royal on the southern side, I'll utter a silent prayer that the peloton will stay together long enough for me to get those vital scenic shots I believe the world wants to see, for the southern side is by far the more spectacular of the two.

A Tour climbing the southern side usually does so in the morning, on its way to many more climbs like the Col de la Madeleine or Col de la Croix de Fer,

< OPPOSITE   *The compact peloton climbs the Galibier in the 2006 Tour, with the Meije Glacier in its sights.*

and perhaps an uphill finish at La Toussuire or Val Thorens; in that case, the peloton is relatively together the whole way up the climb. A Tour that climbs the northern side is almost certainly in self-destruct mode, using the Galibier as a battlefield on which a war, or at least a tough fight, will be engaged in prior to a stage finish in Briançon or a nearby uphill finish. The cyclists will already have climbed a few *cols* that day, and the Col du Galibier is just one *col* too many in the afternoon.

Col de l'Iseran

Stuck far away at the end of the long Tarentaise Valley, the Col de l'Iseran, at 2,770 meters (9,088 feet), is one of the least-used mountains of the Tour de France, yet it is arguably its most beautiful peak. It holds the potential to be as defining a climb for the Tour as the Col du Galibier, but sadly that potential is rarely exploited, for while the Iseran is enhanced by dazzling glaciers on its eastern flank, it also suffers—though not from this photographer's perspective—by only ever having the peloton make its approach from the easier ascent of its western flank.

The Tour rarely visits Val d'Isère, a ski resort that is already far too popular to need the race, but on the few occasions it does, it tends to use the town only as a starting point, which means that the summit of the Iseran is crossed barely one hour after leaving Val d'Isère. As happy as I am to be photographing a fine series of scenic shots as the Tour's compact peloton snakes up the pass, it seems a crying shame that the mountain is not used to its fullest extent. If the race instead climbed the more difficult eastern side from Bonneval-sur-Arc, the Iseran would surely become as well respected in Tour history as the Galibier.

When you study a map of the Alps, several possible routes can be clearly spotted: a stage start in Briançon, followed by a climb over the Col de Montgenèvre, a rapid drop down to Oulx in Italy before a climb over the *autoroute*-wide Col du Mont-Cenis. Depending on the distance required, and the sadism of the Tour's organizers, the race could then start the gradual ascent of the Iseran from Bessans, saving its finale for the Iseran and a stage finish in Val d'Isère; or it could go through the ski town to finish up in Tignes, or farther

The Tour peloton is dwarfed by the peaks above the Col de l'Iseran in 2007. OPPOSITE >

away still, in Les Arcs, La Plagne, or even the Trois Vallées. If Val d'Isère were indeed eager to host the finish, the stage could start farther away in Valloire, Bourg-d'Oisans, or even Grenoble itself.

The Tour first climbed the Iseran in 1938, and then in 1939 the Iseran was the peak in the race's first-ever mountain time trial, a test that started from that eastern side in Bonneval-sur-Arc and finished in Bourg-Saint-Maurice. The Belgian Sylvère Maes won the stage that year and went on to win the Tour by more than thirty minutes. Fernando Manzaneque made a hero of himself way back in 1963, climbing the eastern side of the Col de l'Iseran to win in Val d'Isère with a tasty lead of over five minutes—but that was thirty-five years ago. In 1992 and again in 2007, the western side has been used, in 1992 launching Claudio Chiappucci to victory in Sestrières and then in 2007 elevating Mauricio Soler to a win in Briançon as the most surprising stage winner of that Tour.

The first time I saw the Tour climb the Iseran was in 1992, on the day that the race was to enter Italy on a route that visited five other countries, as a way of celebrating the expansion of the EEC. It's normal for hopeful breakaways to start firing their guns right from the start, if only to make a good start on the climb and not be left too far behind by the summit. But this day was exceptional, and actually put the Val d'Isère side of the mountain into the storybooks for once.

Chiappucci woke up that morning with his head still full of a dream that had convinced him he could race away and win into Sestrières. He did just that, attacking at the foot of the Iseran to begin a 200-kilometer-long lone escape that at one point saw him threatening the overall ambitions of Miguel Induráin. Although most images of that day show Chiappucci winning into Sestrières, or racing among a million Italians on the final climb, my favorite was taken that morning, on the Col de l'Iseran, as Chiappucci pounded away from his rivals. In those days, the Glacier de Rhème-Golette was a substantial size, and I managed to frame Chiappucci exactly where I wanted him, the red-and-white polka-dot jersey he wore as best climber a vibrant contrast to the glacial blue mountain. It was an added bonus when my next shot was just as accurate, of Pascal Lino as he chased Chiappucci, fearful of losing the yellow jersey he'd been proudly wearing for over ten days.

Four years later, 1996 should have been an epic ascent of the Iseran, for summer snows had left the mountain pass looking particularly dramatic. But

LEFT *Claudio Chiappucci attacks on the Col de l'Iseran in the 1992 Tour.* RIGHT *The race leader, Pascal Lino, follows Chiappucci a few seconds later.*

the freak snows had been blown into the Alps by even freakier winds, forcing the organizers to cancel the Iseran and the Galibier, thus ruining the queen stage of that year's Tour.

Eleven years on, the Tour climbed the mountain again, on a day already remarkable for its heat and for the clarity of the mountain air. The peloton more or less played ball with the photographers, inching its way up the long climb with no one willing or able to escape, save for the last few kilometers, by which time almost all the decent scenic shots had been captured.

It was the descent that took my breath away, with a long line of cyclists chasing some unknown kamikaze down the *col*, their aerodynamic poise happily captured against a backdrop of snow and ice of the Glacier de la Grande Aiguille Rousse. If ever the Tour organizers want to bring the race up the other way, preferably with a fat enough peloton with which to work, I'll happily go into retirement afterward—as long as the day is as sunny as it was in 2007.

Cormet de Roselend

When conversations begin about the beauty and majesty of the Tour's mountains, it's hard to find a more suitable candidate for acclaim than the Cormet de Roselend. Except that this beautiful climb also has one of the most dangerous descents in the business. It seems to be a trait of the sport of cycling that something so beautiful can, at a moment's notice, turn into something ugly—and it nearly always does.

Barely a Tour has gone by when the gentleness of the western ascent is not brutally replaced by the savagery of the eastern descent. In 1992, Iñaki Gastón smashed himself into a rock face just beyond where the road makes a vicious left turn; the diminutive Basque had braked too late, unaware of how tight the bend was.

In 1995, it was Johan Bruyneel who misjudged the same corner. The future sport director of Lance Armstrong was going even faster than Gastón, but he miraculously fell through a gap in a concrete wall to land safely on soft ground.

Alex Zülle was the next cyclist to fall under the curse of the Cormet, in 1996. The Swiss cyclist had barely crossed the summit when he went off the

TOP *The curse of the Cormet de Roselend: Iñaki Gastón lies injured after crashing in 1992.*
BOTTOM *Three years later, Johan Bruyneel crashes in almost exactly the same spot.*

wet road into some prickly bushes. The bushes stopped him before he hit the rocks below, and Zülle was able to continue.

Stuart O'Grady was the Roselend's victim in 2007, although his nasty fall came within a kilometer of the end of the descent. A wooden rail stopped O'Grady from falling to a most horrible fate, but a punctured lung, broken ribs, and a broken collarbone are the Australian's sore memories of the mountain.

CORMET DE ROSELEND *The 2005 Tour climbs the Cormet de Roselend with the Barrage de Roselend below.*

When you first start climbing the gentle slopes of the Roselend, it's impossible to even think of the cursed descent. The farther you climb away from the town of Beaufort, the better the view gets. First with the forested valley of Outray, way down on your left, then, after some vertiginous gain to a point where you first start to see the Aiguille du Grand Fond, a towering rock that is as startling as it is scary.

Your awe is calmed by the sight of the beautiful lake created by the Barrage de Roselend (Roselend Dam), a lake filled by the streams and rivers flowing down from higher ground; it's hard not to stop and take in this little picture-postcard gem. Don't stay too long, for what lies ahead of you is even better, on a road that climbs steadily.

To your right is glacier country, highlighted by the 2,888-meter (9,475-foot) Grand Fond, while to your left stands the Crêt des Grittes, a crest made up of a series of sharp rock faces that has patches of winter snow clinging in its crevices in July. You'll pedal over a stone bridge, beneath which rushes a monstrous cascade. A few minutes more and you'll come to the vantage point where that same flow is seen by thousands of Tour fans when the peloton is climbing. This is where you should stop for a while.

Because of the Cormet's lush beauty, it's easy to forget the fact that you are so high up, yet at the Cormet's peak of 1,968 meters (6,456 feet), your panorama changes to a bleaker image, where suddenly there's no greenery, only a gray plateau of scree and rocks. Now starts that fearful descent, so don't dare be distracted by the Aiguille de Prainan, nor the Torrent des Glaciers which flows beside your plunging route. Keep your eyes on the road, as they say.

Col de la Croix de Fer

Any tale about the Col de la Croix de Fer has to have three sides to it, for this great *col* boasts of having three ascents to choose from. It can be climbed from Saint-Jean-de-Maurienne, going in the direction of Grenoble, and can also be approached the opposite way from Rochetaillée, where the average gradient exceeds 11 percent in a few short sections. Or it can be attacked from the north from La Chambre, using the 1,924-meter Col du Glandon (6,312 feet) as a stepping-stone to the Croix de Fer's higher peak, 3 kilometers farther up. All

The eastern side of the Col de la Croix de Fer in 1995.

three sides are endowed with equal degrees of beauty and terror, making the Croix de Fer one of the Tour's favorite destinations, even if the mountain still lacks the awe and fame of its close neighbor, the Galibier.

First climbed by the Tour in 1947, the Croix de Fer ("Cross of Iron"; there's one on the summit) has a location that means it is only used as a gateway to bigger things, or as the penultimate ascent in a day typically ending atop Alpe d'Huez. A Tour climbing the Croix de Fer from the Grenoble side has probably started in Bourg-d'Oisans and is likely to be heading to a stage finish at La Toussuire or to a finale over the Télégraphe/Galibier and into Briançon.

It might also be the first ascent in a long stage going over the Col de la Madeleine and into the Tarentaise Valley, with its vast choice of ski-resort finishes. If the Croix de Fer's 2,067-meter summit (6,781 feet) had enough space for a stage finish, it would more than equal the Galibier's value in Tour folklore, for the mountain has an attraction and difficulty that could give it a much greater role in the Tour.

This was the climb on which Bernard Hinault and Greg LeMond started their famous duet toward the end of the 1986 Tour, and it was here that

Gert-Jan Theunisse about to attack on the Col de la Croix de Fer in 1989.

Gert-Jan Theunisse launched into his fabulous solo escape three years later (both epic breakaways ended in success at Alpe d'Huez). Because of the way the mountain is utilized, it is clear that the 30-kilometer-long eastern side of the Croix de Fer—the side used by messieurs LeMond, Hinault, and Theunisse—provides the toughest challenge, while photographers will tell you the shorter ascent coming from Grenoble is by far the more beautiful.

The version that uses the Col du Glandon has a mixture of challenge and beauty, for there's nothing that's easy about the Glandon's 22 kilometers, especially the last fifteen minutes

Jan Ullrich crests the summit of the Col du Glandon in the 1997 Tour, heading for the Col de la Madeleine and a summit finish in Courchevel.

before the Tour swings left and onto the shoulder toward the Croix de Fer. It is on this section of road that one gets a most perfect view, first of the distant Barrage de Grand'Maison, with its personal backdrop of glaciers, and then the Aiguille de l'Argentière, whose 3,000-meter snowcapped peak stays in your sights until the peloton has passed over the summit and begun the descent to the Maurienne valley. Or to the foot of the Col de Mollard, the vicious ascent recently used by the Tour on its way to La Toussuire, a little-known ski resort now famous because of the manner in which Floyd Landis lost his *maillot jaune* there in 2006.

When one experiences the descent of the eastern side—a nerve-racking plunge on tiny, snaking, dusty roads that take its passengers close to perilous ravines at regular intervals—one quickly realizes the ascending qualities this same route offers when the Tour is traveling the other way.

I first saw this climb in the 1989 Tour, and was lucky enough to be at the point in the ascent, maybe just 8 kilometers up, where Theunisse first broke

COL DU GLANDON   *The Barrage de Grand'Maison is the backdrop as the 1994 Tour climbs the Col du Glandon on its way to Val Thorens.*

away. Here there's a wall of a climb to be conquered before the ascent levels off and tracks the course of the river Arvan, gradually taking its challengers to the crux of the climb in the final 5 kilometers.

In 1989, the Tour was being fought out by Fignon and LeMond, and it was the Frenchman's turn to suffer, as the Croix de Fer played its role to the full. Fignon spent most of those final kilometers yo-yoing off the back of the group that was chasing Theunisse, and the racing was of a kind so potent that any thoughts of doing scenic shots were cast aside for another day or another Tour altogether.

Now that I think of it, I never have seen a *vrai* peloton reaching the summit of the Croix de Fer from this side. Which is a pity, because the crystal-clear pools of mountain water just below the summit would make for some great shots if the peloton were having a really slow day of it. Best to capture this image when the Tour is coming the other way, on descent rather than ascent.

THE CROIX DE FER'S NEW ROUTE

Landslides have affected the difficulty and beauty of the Croix de Fer on the Rochetaillée side. Until 1990, any race climbing or descending this side of the mountain had a straight run at it between the Rivière d'Allemont and the Barrage de Grand'Maison, and one of the climb's great features was a stubborn mound of snow and ice alongside the road that refused to melt, even as late as mid-July. In the spring of 1990, half of the face of the Pic Bunard crashed down the mountain, burying the road forever and forcing engineers to either close the pass for good or build a new way to the Glandon/Croix de Fer summits.

Partly due to the route's importance to future Tours de France, engineers crafted a sinuous alternative on the opposite mountain face, which now takes the Tour on a series of sharp descents and climbs to link up with the older route. This new stretch of road has become known as the Défilé de Maupas, and it creates an even tougher passage for the cyclists. Yet one look at the mountain face above the new road is enough to warn of a similar risk in the coming years. Let's hope any such landslide does not come in mid-July.

ABOVE *A view of Mont Ventoux from its summit, showing the spectacular ranges to the south and west of the mountain.* BELOW *Jacques Goddet lays a wreath at the memorial to Tom Simpson in 1987.*

Mont Ventoux

If the way to judge a mountain's difficulty is by studying the faces of those who have just cycled up it, then Mont Ventoux is the winner going away—at least as far as cyclo-tourists are concerned. I'm not sure the same can be said about today's well-trained Tour cyclists, for the phobia of Tom Simpson's death on the mountain in 1967 has long since faded. For this generation of racers, the Ventoux is simply one of the sport's toughest climbs.

The Ventoux can still make life difficult for the Tour's thoroughbreds, however. If it's stiflingly hot in Bédoin, but cooler once the tree line has been cleared, the climb is brutal but tolerable. But if this part of Provence is having a heat wave, and if there's no wind to clear the air, then the cyclists are in for a real grilling. Such was Simpson's fate all those years ago.

A small group climbs the last kilometer of Mont Ventoux in the 2002 Tour de France.

Other factors contribute to the mountain's fearsome challenge. The Ventoux stage might be a time trial, as in the 1987 Tour. It could be a summit finish after a long day in the saddle, as is most common on the Ventoux. Or it might be the last climb in a long day of mountain ascents, the brutal finale to an *en-ligne* stage ending in Carpentras or Avignon. At least one thing is sure: The Tour will always climb the Ventoux from its harder side, the way it first did in 1951 and the way it has done just twelve times since—and will again in 2009.

Because I first saw the Ventoux climbed in that 1987 time trial, when I could see each suffering individual as he climbed the mountain, capture on film each drop of sweat as it left so many furrowed brows behind, and feel the agony that each of the competitors was experiencing, it is harder for me now to judge the state of mind of the riders bringing up the rear of the peloton. The subjects in my camera these days are the fast men at the front of the race, the winged angels for whom the mountain holds no fear at all—men like Marco Pantani, Lance Armstrong, Richard Virenque, and Iban Mayo.

As for the others, I know they're back there somewhere. They're the less fortunate ones who've struggled from the moment they first glimpsed the bald summit over one hour ago, and are still struggling to finish long after the more gifted men have crossed the line, shared the podium with some pretty hostesses, and are already well into their descent to Malaucène and a cozy shower. It's just that I can't get back there to record their plight the way I once could.

Agony or not, photographing the Tour on the Ventoux is a treasured occupation. It's one that's made all the more exciting because the Tour only visits occasionally, about once every five years since that first ascent, with six crossings and seven summit finishes to date.

It's one of the few mountains that gets me all fired up, right from the moment its name is mentioned at the Tour launch in October; even the Galibier doesn't do that. Mont Ventoux always has a decisive role in the Tour's outcome, and that knowledge is intoxicating. There's never going to be an easy winner on its summit, and Ventoux always acts as *the* great stage on which the race's best cyclists are going to do battle. Great pictures are going to come from any ascent of this monster. What you don't know is who's going to win.

Although I've only seen the Tour climb the Ventoux four times in my career, its more regular inclusion in the weeklong Dauphiné-Libéré stage race that precedes the Tour in June means there's a familiarity about it that makes my work even more pleasurable. Ventoux is one of the few mountains where I can watch the racing as I take pictures.

The opening kilometers are there purely to shed the no-hopers and to focus your mind on the task that lies ahead. It helps that this part of the climb is heavily shaded. The first key place comes about 7 kilometers up, at a sharp right-hand bend. The road is pitched up sharply here, with a gradient of 8.6 percent. It makes this bend a favorite place to stop and see the beginning of the end as the peloton begins to break apart.

The next few kilometers take us to the Chalet Reynard, the steepest and most crucial part of the climb, where the pitch averages just over 7.0 percent

The 6-kilometers-to-go sign near Chalet Reynard, the hardest part of Mont Ventoux.

but includes a ramp or two at 10.3 percent. This also happens to be the most populated area, because of the D164 access road coming from Sault. The ramp that climbs away from the Chalet acts as the final launchpad for many of the Ventoux's stage winners.

Just after the ramp settles down to a more civilized gradient, the road swings right, and at once the shocking face of the Ventoux unfolds before your eyes, a vast mountain of limestone rubble the color of white gold, with the observatory antenna still a distant 6 kilometers away.

It's at this point that I realize all over again how much I love the Ventoux, both as a photographer and a cycling fan. The road just keeps going up, barely turning one way or the other, allowing me to see every pedal stroke the cyclists are taking as they tackle the cruelest section of the mountain. The backdrop is a vista of Provençal *plaine* and distant alpine peaks, which in the late afternoon sunshine is all the more overwhelming.

That same lighting illuminates the sweating faces in a way not seen on other mountains—and, yes, there's definitely a ghostly pallor to even the healthiest cyclists. The limestone acts as a giant reflector, bouncing the sun, the light, and especially the heat back at the Tour's gladiators, as if they didn't already know that there is nowhere to hide on this part of the mountain.

The best ones now ratchet up the pace a little, testing their legs, testing the few rivals left near them. This is where Lance Armstrong delivered the coup de grâce to Joseba Beloki in 2002, firing off a series of attacks that quickly demolished the Basque's failing morale. It was a lesson Armstrong perhaps learned on this part of the climb two years earlier, with just 6 kilometers

TOP *Richard Virenque suffers on his way to winning Mont Ventoux in 2002.*
BOTTOM *Lance Armstrong in full flight a few minutes after Virenque the same year.*

*Marco Pantani beats Lance Armstrong in 2000
after the American paced the Italian up Mont
Ventoux, only to be surprised in the sprint finish.*

to go, when instead of dropping Marco Pantani he let the Italian stay with him, who then went on to win the stage.

Sadly, the last kilometers disappear all too quickly for me. It'll soon be time to calculate the distance I need to make the finish in time—that's if I want to make the finish at all. There's a captivating spirit about the last section of the Ventoux that makes it hard to tear yourself away from the action, a reluctance heavily influenced by the knowledge that the finish shot will literally be just that: the end.

I was a highly disappointed photographer in the 2000 Tour when Pantani surged to the line first but never celebrated his win the way a true Ventoux winner should—arms aloft, head held high, face expressive if not totally split by a wide smile. My preferred plan since then has been to stay with the leaders to the very last kilometer, speed ahead to the final 300 meters, then set up a standing shot with a long telephoto lens just before the final kickback bend to the finish. It's a strategy that never fails, especially if it happens to be a yellow-jerseyed Armstrong pumping out the revs, a rat pack of motorcycle photographers trailing his every move, just as their forebears did with Eddy Merckx in 1970.

As the latest conquerors of the Ventoux pedal past where I stand, it's hard not to feel emotional about the mountain. Men have died cycling up it, while others have found a happier fate doing merely what they do best. As I look down on the land so far below me, I wonder how long it will be before the Tour is back on Mont Ventoux. Not too long, I hope.

VENTOUX: THE TOUR'S TOUGHEST CLIMB

The morning after his seemingly fruitless climb of the Ventoux in 1987, the wise old pro Stephen Roche took the time to explain his post-Ventoux strategy to this naive English photographer. For me to then see that strategy carried out with faultless precision was one of my greater Tour de France experiences. I'd seen Roche lose over two minutes to Jean-François Bernard in the time trial to Mont Ventoux, and I was convinced the Tour had been more or less won by the Frenchman. Not so, according to the Irishman, whom I'd watched win the Giro d'Italia one month earlier. "Graham, you're going to see something today that you'll remember for a long time to come, I promise you," Roche began, at which point he presented a concise, two-minute briefing on how he was going to kick Bernard's backside on that day's pre-alpine stage to Villard-de-Lans. Sure enough, Bernard was given the hiding of his life, losing over four minutes to Roche and his accomplice Pedro Delgado, on a route that straddled four of the worst climbs one could find in the Vercors. To be honest, Roche didn't do it alone; he had engineered his strategy with a dozen other riders, all of them sensing Bernard had extended himself too much on the Ventoux. One day later, Roche found me near the start in Villard-de-Lans and imparted further wisdom by explaining that the Ventoux is so tough, its effect on a Tour rider's legs can linger many days. He believed that the Ventoux is the single hardest climb in France.

STAGE WINNERS ATOP MONT VENTOUX

1958: Charly Gaul

1965: Raymond Poulidor

1970: Eddy Merckx

1972: Bernard Thévenet

1987: Jean-François Bernard

2000: Marco Pantani

2002: Richard Virenque

THE PYRENEES

The Pyrenees present the Tour de France with a very different mountain range in which to play. Even if one includes the entire Spanish side in the calculations, the Pyrenees have a much smaller landmass than the Alps, and there are "only" forty-six *cols*, *côtes* (hills), or *ports* (*port* being a Spanish name for summit) for the Tour to choose from, including twelve ski-resort finishes.

The Pyrenees' peaks fall short of the Alps as well, with the highest Pyrenean climb used by the Tour, the Col du Tourmalet, being five hundred meters lower than its alpine counterparts, the Galibier and Iseran. Thus, Tour followers have no glacial peaks to enjoy while they await the Tour's arrival on a *col*; there might be some patchy old snow on the Pic du Midi, but that's about it.

Yet anyone thinking that the Pyrenees are a weaker attraction for the Tour had better think again, for this range of mountains contains many of the Tour's most feared climbs, with most of them starting from a lower altitude than

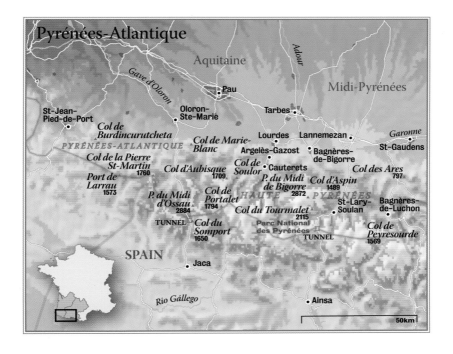

Spectators cheer the 1994 Tour de France peloton as it reaches Luz Ardiden.

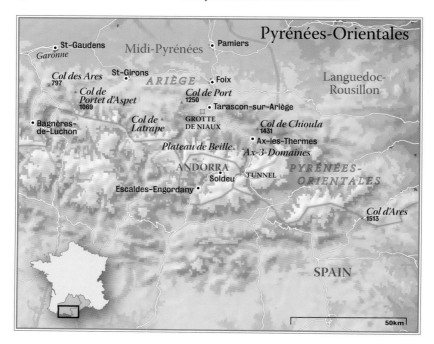

those in the Alps. They are legendary, being typically shorter and sharper than the gradual, 20-kilometer-long ascents in the Alps. True, there are some long, long Pyrenean grinds, like the Col du Soudet and Port d'Envalira, but it is the shorter ones that create the most regular shock waves in the peloton. Uphill finishes at Hautacam, Pla d'Adet, Plateau de Beille, and Luz Ardiden have seen some of the greatest champions win their greatest battles. And the supporting acts of *cols* like the Tourmalet, Peyresourde, Aubisque, Pailhères, and Portillon ensure that the Pyrenees leave their mark on the Tour each time it goes there.

The good news about the Pyrenees is that you don't have to rent an airliner to see its generous collection of peaks. You can see them clearly as you drive south from Toulouse on the A64 *autoroute*, or closer still from a vantage point on the Plateau de Lannemezan. From there you'll see what appears to be the entire *chaîne* (mountain range) stretched across an horizon of green meadows and pastures, its jagged peaks and softer snowcapped mountains even more resplendent if you're viewing the Pyrenees in spring.

PYRENEES   *The 2007 Tour climbs the Col de Pailhères on its way to Plateau de Beille; note the narrowness of the road.*

The Pyrenees can also be enjoyed from the A61 and A64 *autoroutes* that run parallel to the mountains between Narbonne and Bayonne. In fact, even on a clear day, you're only seeing a portion of the Pyrenees; it's the illusion of thinking you are seeing them all that gets one's attention in the first place.

The Pyrenees have a totally different geography from that of the Alps, one that is greener, rockier, more wooded, and most definitely less spoiled by the ravages of tourism. It's an altogether more peaceful place in which to rest or visit, as well as to ride your bike for days on end with little sign of the motor traffic that can afflict one's alpine experience.

If you feel so inspired, there are about ten recognized climbs that can be used to access the Spanish side of the Pyrenees, or perhaps to visit duty-free Andorra, if shopping is on your mind. In colorful market towns like Arreau, Orthez, Laruns, and Cambo-les-Bains are to be enjoyed tiny country hotels and restaurants offering the very best in local cuisines. Strategic towns like Bagnères-de-Bigorre, Saint-Girons, Saint-Gaudens, Foix, and Bagnères-de-Luchon act as perfect bases for journeys into the mountains, by car and by bike. Or on foot, for this is the mountain range that boasts of having the 800-kilometer-long Haute Randonnée Pyrénéenne, a famous hike that runs the entire length of the Pyrenees and takes you into Spain at various points along the route. There is also the more manageable GR10, which allows for walks of single- or multi-day duration.

Just as the Alps have low-altitude ascents in the Chartreuse and Vercors, so do the Pyrenees have some delights to offer in Béarn, Ariège, and the Pays Basque. Climbs like the Col de Latrape, Col d'Agnès, and Col de Marie-Blanc are just waiting to snare the unprepared cyclist on a stage to the Plateau de Bonascre or Ax-3-Domaines, while a plethora of little-known ascents wait to entertain the Tour's cyclists along the Basque border between France and Spain.

It was on climbs like the Col Bagargui and Col de Burdincurutcheta that Tyler Hamilton rode his heart out in the 2003 Tour, soloing to a brilliant stage win at Bayonne after an 87-kilometer epic breakaway. Although Hamilton's career was ruined by his blood-doping offense at the 2004 Tour of Spain, his ride through the Pyrenees in 2003 was the greatest solo performance I'd ever seen in the Tour, and I remember being overwhelmed by the ferocity of the Basque fans as Hamilton crossed the Burdincurutcheta within a few kilometers of the volatile border with

Tyler Hamilton at the heart of his Pyrenean escape in the 2003 Tour de France.

Spain. It's a strange thing, seeing such enthusiastic fans equaled in numbers by the sinister-looking CRS riot squads, but the fans' encouragement for Hamilton was genuine, as it was many minutes later for race leader Armstrong.

I've been lucky enough to see the Pyrenees with no Tour de France in sight, sometimes on pre-Tour training sorties in May, photographing Lance Armstrong or Robert Millar, or when the Tour of Spain reciprocates the visits of the Tour into Spain by ending one of its stages at Luz Ardiden or Cauterets. The Vuelta a España, to give the Spanish race its correct title, comes in September, when one experiences very different Pyrenees from those of May and July. Most of the tourists have left, and the foliage has turned a tempting shade of gold.

Because of these excursions, I've seen the wide-open slopes of the Col du Somport and Col du Portalet where the only observers of my visit were grazing sheep or mountain goats, or where recent snows have added a pleasing element to my already considerable enjoyment. Even on a bad day, there's something mystical about the Pyrenees, like the way the clouds hang between the peaks, darkening the skies and adding a foreboding atmosphere.

With or without its bike races, the Pyrenees are a living paradise of green and pleasant meadows, hills, and stunning mountains, where the sound of coursing streams can be heard in the middle of forested glades, and where fir trees seem to be coming out of every meter of green and brown earth and pointing to the skies. The lighting, so different from the Alps or Massif Central, is misty and moody—just right for the photographer in the way it illuminates the lush vegetation on high ground. The grass-covered peaks beckon you forward, crying out to be scaled by walkers, or simply admired by those watching the Tour pass through, for the Pyrenees lack the intimidating rocky spires of the Alps. I know that whenever I see a stage finish at Luz Ardiden or Plateau de Beille, all I really want to do is take a stroll around these highlands for a few hours, a far more enjoyable activity than spending time in the press center.

A view from the summit of the Col du Tourmalet, deep in the heart of the Parc National des Pyrénées.

Yes, I love the Pyrenees. I love the peace and quiet to be found there, as well as watching the Tour play there. After all, it was the Pyrenees that first gave the mountains to the Tour.

Col du Tourmalet

It's hard to say which side of the Col du Tourmalet is the hardest, or even which side is its prettiest, for both sides have equal merits. A little bit like the Col du Galibier, the Tourmalet sees its best racing on the eastern side, the one coming from Sainte-Marie-de-Campan and passing through the cluttered ski station of La Mongie, leaving the last 5 kilometers to be covered on steep *lacets*, with an all-around panorama that makes one feel very small indeed.

But unless the stage actually ends in La Mongie, as it has done in 1970, 2002, and 2004, the Tourmalet merely acts as a great prelude to a stage finish at Luz Ardiden or Cauterets, meaning its true value is often ignored. Sadly, there's just not enough room on its 2,115-meter summit (6,939 feet) to hold a stage finish,

PYRENEES *The 1993 Tour crosses the summit of the Tourmalet from the east.*

which is why, when La Mongie hosts the finish, race followers are left wondering what might have been had the stage finished on that summit instead.

Coming from the west side, the Tourmalet is usually approached earlier in the day. The peloton is often intact as the climbing starts in Luz-Saint-Sauveur, and will only start to break up in the final few kilometers. The Tour may already have crossed the Col d'Aubisque on its way, and the cyclists may be contemplating the ensuing ascents of the Aspin, Peyresourde, Val Louron, or Piau-Engaly—hence a degree of reluctance on their part to really blast the race open on the Tourmalet.

The west side from Barèges is free of the scruffiness that blights its opposite flank, and the last few kilometers are ridden on a series of switchbacks similar to those on the Galibier, though without the snowy backdrop of the alpine glaciers. Instead, one can appreciate the view of the mighty Pic des Quatre-Termes at 2,724 meters (8,937 feet), whose green and dark gray face stares over the summit like a judgmental mountain god. I wonder what Octave Lapize must have felt when he rode or walked his bicycle over the *col* in 1910, not knowing what fate awaited him on the summit or on the rock-strewn descent that followed.

I first saw the Tourmalet in the 1983 Tour, and I was standing on a grassy mound overlooking the summit when Robert Millar pedaled over it. I had no idea the little Scot was on his way to his first-ever Tour stage win, which he captured at Bagnères-de-Luchon. The Tourmalet was the last climb that day, and I remember standing for ages on that promontory, waiting for a sizable group of cyclists to balance my foreground with the might of the Quatre-Termes. The struggling backmarkers hadn't coagulated into a *gruppetto* as they so often do today, and so I saw a continuous straggle of cyclists pass through my viewfinder and over the summit, one by one.

Each time the Tour climbs the Tourmalet from the west these days, I gaze with envy from my motorcycle at that grassy mound to see if any young photographers are seeking the same shots I sought so many years back, knowing that I cannot take myself out of the race and clamber up there for an hour or two alongside them—wouldn't that be nice!

No matter how hard one tries to adjust history to suit oneself, it is the east side that has afforded the Tour its best racing and this photographer his best images. In 1988, one of my best Tour photos was of Steven Rooks and Gert-Jan Theunisse as they struggled to keep pace with the head of the race. My camera caught Rooks just as he reached for a spectator's bottle of mineral water, his crazed eyes revealing the anguish he felt in a moment of desperate need.

Steven Rooks reaches for a water bottle as he climbs the eastern side of the Tourmalet in 1988.

ATOP THE TOURMALET

It's never had a name, nor does anyone know how long it has been there, but there is a little café atop the summit of the Col du Tourmalet that is well worth a visit. Remarkably open year-round, the café caters to cold and hungry (or thirsty) cyclists in the summer and skiers in the winter, the Tourmalet being a popular resting point between the cycling paths and trails *(pistes)* of Barèges and La Mongie. The interior of this gray stone building has become something of

a shrine to both sports, and old Tour bicycles and wooden skis compete for space and attention in the cozy bosom of the café, which serves meals at peak times and snacks all day long. One wall of the café is a picture gallery, with framed black-and-white and sepia-toned images for fans to ogle. There's one great image of the Tourmalet when the road was first paved, way back when, without a single human being or vehicle to spoil the view. I made a point of visiting the Tourmalet on the rest day of the 2008 Tour—the day after the race had climbed the *col*—to sniff around and see what it felt like to be up there with no Tour. I soon realized the mountain is as popular without the Tour as with it, with the little café doing a very decent business. Someone really ought to give it a name—the Café du Tourmalet, perhaps?

In 1995, a few minutes after Richard Virenque had blitzed his way up the climb in search of a stage win at Cauterets, I homed in on the figure of Marco Pantani, believing the Italian was going to take the victory instead, despite being several minutes down at the time. My race radio had not been working that day, and although I knew there'd been a nasty crash a few mountains and hours earlier, I had no information that one of the injured cyclists, Fabio Casartelli, had died just as the Tourmalet was being climbed. The photo I captured was of a shocked Pantani, who'd just been informed of Casartelli's death, and I felt something of a fool for not knowing the cause of his distress.

Happier days were to come in 2003, for it was on the Tourmalet that Jan Ullrich accelerated away from the peloton, trying to destabilize Lance Armstrong before the final ascent to Luz Ardiden. The American jumped onto his wheel right away, his passive expression a clear sign he was as good as ever. I knew then that Ullrich's challenge in the 2003 Tour would not rise to the level he'd managed in earlier editions.

Port de Larrau

One of the Tour's least-used climbs, the Port de Larrau is, to my mind, the toughest of the race's ascents in the Pyrenees, if not the entire country, with long sections of over 10 percent difficulty, and an average of almost 8 percent over its 15 kilometers to the pass at 1,573 meters (5,161 feet). This vicious ascent was first used in 1996 on a stage that took the Tour de France to Pamplona, Spain, passing right through the nearby town of Villava, site of the family farm of five-time winner Miguel Induráin.

Pamplona had paid a mighty amount of money to get the Tour into Spain, seeing it as a fitting tribute to their cycling hero, who they assumed would be racing in yellow and on his way to a sixth title. However, the Induráin of '96 was not the man of the previous half-decade, and he'd long since lost any hope of winning the Tour before the Larrau was reached on stage 17.

To my mind, there has never been a more impressive climbing spectacle than in that 1996 ascent, although that may be because very few people had any inkling of the Larrau's incredible difficulty. Even before the village of Larrau, the road shot up at ever-increasing degrees, spitting out the weaker cyclists right away. Pretty soon, Induráin was one of those, thanks partly to the wall

The steep slopes of the Port de Larrau split the leading climbers in the 2007 Tour.

of switchbacks at Chapelle-Saint-Joseph, and the attacks made by Bjarne Riis, with Richard Virenque and Laurent Dufaux. The latter two were racing for Festina, a prominent cycling sponsor in Spanish races, for whom a stage win in that country was vital. Induráin, though wholly Spanish himself, was their sacrificial lamb, surplus to requirements, and the perfect script laid out for him by the Tour and the city of Pamplona was totally blown to pieces.

It's not an easy task to focus upon the Larrau's difficulty, for the mountain is as beautiful as it is brutal. As soon as the road climbs away from the torrential river known as the Gave de Larrau, you become aware

not just of the rising gradient, but also of the stunning backdrop of a bright green hillside dotted with gray-brown rocks. The road is in perfect condition, but that doesn't make the pedaling any easier, and soon the peloton will be together no longer, as a series of winding turns takes the Tour onto the forested mountainside, with some brief sections pitched at a staggering 14 percent!

Standing at the roadside taking a picture of the cyclists' torture amid such beauty, you become aware of the sound of a hundred pairs of rasping lungs; even the pure climbers are struggling to maintain some degree of dignity at this point. The backdrop then opens out, meaning there is nothing to interfere with the blissful view across the forested plateaux toward Bayonne and the Bay of Biscay, some 80 kilometers distant.

Still the road rises, and still the race fragments, until only the very best are left at the front. Even for them, the "wall" at the Chapelle seems an impossibility, three or four switchbacks that offer no respite, only more gradient and more agony. Finally, a kilometer or two beyond, the road emerges onto a truly stunning mountainside, with 360-degree views of French mountains and Navarran sierras. The searing gradient has finally leveled off, as if to let the more inquisitive cyclists appreciate the sights. If only they could.

In 1996, this last section of the climb was lined every inch of the way by French, Spanish, and—especially—Basque fans, for whom Induráin had become an absolute *mito*—a myth—living as he did on the delicate frontier at

RIGHT *Abraham Olano and Miguel Induráin suffer on the Port de Larrau in 1996, despite being cheered on by thousands of Basque fans.*

< OPPOSITE *Laurent Dufaux wins in Pamplona in 1996 after joining an attack on the Port de Larrau 100 kilometers earlier.*

Villava—technically part of Navarra, but close enough to the Basque Country for the majority to consider Induráin as one of their own. Only in hindsight can one look back at that day and mark it as the first time we saw such a wave of Basque support for the Tour. Those armies of fans returned each year thereafter, spreading farther away from home to places like La Toussuire, Plateau de Beille, and Mont Ventoux. It's nice to think that the Port de Larrau marked their entry point into the mystique of the Tour, just as Alpe d'Huez had started the Dutch migration in the late 1970s.

Sadly, this great climb has only been scaled once since 1996, in the 2007 Tour, on a huge loop through Navarra that took the Tour back into France over a first-ever crossing of the Col de la Pierre Saint-Martin and then to the summit of the Col d'Aubisque. That was Michael Rasmussen's last appearance as a Tour competitor, on a bad day for the race, a day that saw him winning the stage in the yellow jersey but being sent home later that night by his embarrassed Robobank team—he'd been found to be cheating them. I'm pleased to say I remember that day more for the ascent of the Port de Larrau, for the sounds of so many gasping riders, and for the wondrous views from its summit above the Forêt d'Iraty.

Col du Soulor, Col d'Aubisque

Whether one climbs the Col du Soulor on the way to the Col d'Aubisque, or the Aubisque on the way to the Soulor, it is impossible not to be alarmed by the narrow and winding road that separates the two climbs. In both directions the road is not particularly hard to ride on; it's just that you are cycling on a shelf that was cut into the mountain at the start of the twentieth century and has barely been reinforced since! Appropriately, locals call this stretch of road "La Corniche" (The Shelf); I can assure you there is no better description.

Each time the Tour uses the Soulor-Aubisque passage, I look at the state of the road and marvel that there is anything there at all—that it hasn't fallen into the deep ravine that forms part of the Cirque du Litor. A series of dark, twisty, and unlit tunnels protects the road at its most sinuous point, but the rest of the

A section of La Corniche, between the Col d'Aubisque OPPOSITE >
and the Col du Soulor, in the 1995 Tour de France.

COL D'AUBISQUE   *The western ascent of the Col d'Aubisque is the one used most often by the Tour.*

traverse is undertaken with the knowledge that rocks can fall off the hillside, and that a mighty drop off an unprotected edge is your fate if you are forced to take evasive action or are simply distracted by the awesome view.

It's when the Tour climbs the Soulor side of the Aubisque that this shelf is seen in its most dramatic form, the snaking line of cyclists dwarfed by their surroundings and seemingly at the mercy of the gods as they appear and disappear through those tunnels, their slow progress watched by a waiting public farther toward the Aubisque—for no one in his right mind would dare to watch the Tour on such an exposed part of the climb.

At the end of each winter—which here means late May—the gendarmerie dispatches its mountain engineers to inspect the state of the road before deciding whether to open it as a public thoroughfare for the summer. The Tour passing through in July acts as a good excuse to repair sections of the road that have been damaged by rockfalls or heavy snows, and the tunnels are inspected closely for signs that the roof is not about to fall in unexpectedly on our heroes.

If the Tour is not scheduled to use the Soulor-Aubisque shelf, it's not unknown for the road to stay closed altogether, at least to motorized vehicles, until the following summer. Hence the air of anticipation whenever the race has cleared the summit of the Soulor and begun its hazardous crossing.

The problem with a Tour that is passing in this direction is that the Col d'Aubisque is not much of a climb at all, whether the race has come up the steady ascent from Argelès-Gazost, or used the more spectacular but still steady ascent from the direction of Pau. It is the west side of the Aubisque, coming from Laruns, that the Tour uses the most, but that in turn means the fragmented peloton descends along that fragile shelf, far less of an attraction for photographers and an even scarier task for the Tour's cyclists.

The Aubisque from the west is one of the toughest climbs in the Pyrenees, despite its gentle start in Laruns, from which a series of leisurely switchbacks can fool the innocent cyclist into thinking he is going to have a good day. The road suddenly rears up after Eaux-Bonnes, then enters a long avalanche

The peloton climbs the western side of the Col d'Aubisque in 2007.

shelter that completely covers the road and adds an eerie echo to the cyclists' deep breathing.

Up to this point, the Aubisque is not terribly pretty. It's only when one passes the ski station of Gourette at 1,400 meters (4,593 feet) that a new vista opens up, one that will change imperceptibly but remain quite stunning until the very summit, 6 kilometers farther on. More switchbacks after Gourette give a sudden gain in altitude before a long, winding shelf takes the cyclists out onto the open mountainside.

From here, one can sense, if not actually see, the summit, at 1,709 meters (5,607 feet), but there's some serious climbing to be done before the worst is over. On your left is the impressive Pic de Moulle-de-Jaut, while above you on the right is the massive face of the Pic de Ger, a mountain whose gray rock appears to be shining at you with the reflection from the sun. To those spectators watching from the summit, this is perhaps the most striking view of the

Aubisque, with the ant-sized Tour cyclists completely swallowed by the mountain, yet looking courageous anyway. The final kilometers level off just enough for some cyclists to take in the view, but not those racing in the Tour. For them, there's still that descent along the Soulor-Aubisque shelf to think about, as well as whatever lies beyond.

AND WHAT OF THE OTHERS?

Beauty is in the eye of the beholder, so they say, and this is never more true than when one is choosing one's favorite climbs of the Tour. In this chapter I have picked out my favored few, based on their beauty, history, and difficulty, and also on the satisfaction they give me as a photographer. They are not the Tour's only climbs, of course, but I have little to say about the others. The Col d'Izoard, for example. Despite the astonishing theater it offers to the great race, it has, quite simply, failed to be the significant ascent it should be in modern Tour history, no matter which side it is climbed from, no matter how tough the climbing obviously is. A review of the race's recent results will show that the Izoard has been quite ineffective for the Tour, and until the day that changes, there is little to be said about it.

Similarly, many of the Tour's other fabled climbs fall short, in my opinion: the Col de la Madeleine (pretty, but unremarkable as a challenge), Col de Joux-Plane (a murderously difficult climb, but lacking any sort of beauty), Avoriaz (not used since the 1985 Tour, always overshadowed by the Joux-Plane), Col de Peyresourde (unremarkable for beauty and difficulty), Luz Ardiden (undoubtedly fierce, but hidden from view in the forests and therefore less enjoyable), Col de Marie-Blanc (another difficult ascent, but akin to the Izoard in that nothing ever happens on it), and Hautacam (a vicious ascent that suffers from being unglamorous, with victors like the disgraced Bjarne Riis and Leonardo Piepoli to spoil the tale). My short selection of mountain climbs has been deliberately limited to the ones that have really had an impact on me and my Tours de France. At the same time, I know there are many, many others out there just waiting to erupt onto the stage of the Tour. It's up to the Tour to find them!

< OPPOSITE *Michael Rasmussen is sandwiched between Levi Leipheimer and Alberto Contador before attacking to win the stage on the Col d'Aubisque in 2007.*

LEGENDS OF THE MODERN TOUR

GREG LeMOND

Looking back on Greg LeMond's Tour wins of 1986, 1989, and 1990, it is quite difficult to gauge where the American fits into the bigger picture. Some might say that, succeeded by the five-year reign of Miguel Induráin and three electrifying one-off victories by Bjarne Riis, Jan Ullrich, and Marco Pantani, LeMond's career was then completely usurped by seven-time winner Lance Armstrong, an American who outgunned his compatriot in terms of victories at the Tour. Yes, as of 2008, seven Tours to three is a mighty difference, as is the fact that all seven of Armstrong's wins were back-to-back, indicating the utter dedication of an athlete who staked his whole life on winning the Tour as often as physically possible.

LeMond's three wins, spread over five years, may seem to be a smaller success in comparison. Yet how well would a young and naive Armstrong have coped with having Bernard Hinault as both team leader and rival?

Luck and coincidences play a huge role in creating a multiple Tour champion, and LeMond's luck was against him from the very day he rejoined Hinault, at La Vie Claire, in 1985. Hinault used LeMond's presence on the team to beef up his own motivation, and the wise old *blaireau* (the badger, Hinault's nickname) had no trouble intimidating his colleague into submission. If LeMond had stayed at Renault, with whom he'd begun his pro career in 1981, he'd have been that team's undisputed leader in 1985, and I believe he would have beaten Hinault and taken a Tour victory one year earlier than he actually did. Which would make it four Tours to seven, a nicer score.

It's inevitable that people make comparisons between LeMond and Armstrong; their public disputes beg the question of who was the greater cyclist. But the fact is that they raced in vastly different eras in the sport, meaning that comparisons cannot be made with any accuracy. Additionally, both men were different in character, LeMond the ebullient, slightly crazed guy, Armstrong the calculating, obsessive perfectionist.

Greg LeMond ahead of Laurent Fignon as they climb the Col de la Croix de Fer in 1989.

LeMond raced at a time in the sport that suited his particular style, a time when so much was done on adrenaline alone, when attacks or chases were carried out spontaneously, and when it was the cyclist who called the shots. Greg would have hated today's voice-in-your-ear control by radio from the sport directors—in fact he did hate it, since he continued to race in the Tour until 1994, when radio receivers began to make their presence felt. Armstrong, on the other hand, fitted perfectly into the era of the highly trained, highly motivated, highly scientific athlete; he would have got nowhere in the sloppy, do-what-you-want days of LeMond.

Unfortunately for Greg, science, along with the serious training that comes with that science, was already having a huge influence on the scene in the late 1980s. His youth was disappearing fast as well, and his appetite for the sport was going with that youth. Pretty soon, a talent like Induráin was heading his way, and it was game over. I like to think of LeMond's influence on the Tour as a great thing, something that was good for American cycling, but that also blazed the trail for Armstrong to follow.

It was quite a shock when the *voiture-balai*—the broom wagon that sweeps up riders at the back of the course—rejoined the tail end of the race convoy on a stage of the '94 Tour, its only passenger looking lost and in shock as he sat slumped on one of the dozen plastic seats. Unlike a few of my drama-searching colleagues, I had to look the other way as Greg disappeared up the road, his career—maybe his very life—disappearing with him. One thing struck me right away: Greg should never have let himself start that '94 Tour, his appetite for the race long gone and his health seriously questionable. Remember, this was the Tour during which LeMond's teammate, Chris Boardman, had taken the race lead after a brilliant prologue in Lille, surely a pivotal moment that made LeMond consider whether he had a future in the sport.

I also knew that Greg's team had delivered the final insult, leaving him to abandon the race in the *voiture-balai* rather than hiding him in one of the team cars, as is the norm with a great champion. This is where we could make further comparisons with Armstrong, for Greg was always a handful for his modest French team, playing elaborate jokes on team staff and turning up late for team meetings (or not turning up at all). Yet his importance in Tour history is absolutely massive, and unquestionably respected.

By joining a French team, Renault-Elf, in 1981, Greg broke down some of the barriers that had historically hindered American cyclists racing in France; of course, it helped to have a French-sounding surname. When he won the Tour in 1986, LeMond became a household favorite in France, another important step for English-speaking cyclists.

But it was LeMond's market value after that '86 Tour win that had the biggest impact on the Tour. Suddenly, here was a cyclist reputedly earning $1 million per year, a lot of it coming from endorsements that were also beginning to enrich the Tour itself. American TV paid big bucks for its exclusive access, which in turn brought in other multinational sponsors to LeMond's team as well as to the Tour.

This untold wealth spread across to future winners, particularly Stephen Roche, the 1987 victor, who demanded similar pricing from sponsors. Most noticeably, it was the English-speaking cyclists who benefited the most, with team sponsors paying between 25 and 50 percent more to have their corporate branding on a Tour cyclist's clothing. By the time Lance Armstrong stepped onto the world stage in 1992, his value would have been based on the previous earnings of LeMond at his best, or at least near-best.

Incredibly, LeMond's Tour legacy is still undecided, almost twenty years after he last won the race. If I had any say in the matter, his 1989 Tour win would be his defining legacy, for surely this was the most exciting Tour in modern times, rivaled only by the topsy-turvy adventures of Armstrong in 2003. LeMond against Fignon, Fignon against LeMond, two troubled champions dueling to the death in order to win. See if you can follow the drama: LeMond in yellow after the stage 5 TT, Fignon in yellow five days later; LeMond back in yellow after the stage 15 TT to Orcières-Merlette. LeMond further ahead after the uphill finish into Briançon the next day. Fignon back in yellow one day later at Alpe d'Huez, and fired up by winning at Villard-de-Lans on stage 18. It's not over yet, folks: LeMond wins a four-man sprint to take an alpine stage into Aix-les-Bains, putting torturous pressure on Fignon with two days to go. And finally LeMond wipes out Fignon's fifty-second lead in that unforgettable Paris TT to win the '89 Tour by eight seconds.

Greg LeMond at the moment of realization that he has won the 1989 Tour de France.

Such inspirational racing deserves an impressive ending to a champion's career, yet in LeMond's case this did not happen. Still, had LeMond not managed to get himself shot while hunting in the spring of 1987, that victory in 1989 might have been his fourth Tour win, with a total of five Tours therefore quite attainable. As it is, the world will never know just how good Greg LeMond could have been.

LAURENT JALABERT

It may be over twenty years since a Frenchman last won the Tour, but that fact never stopped Laurent Jalabert from trying to emulate Bernard Hinault and to make something out of the Tour for his country. Jalabert's skills seemed to be one-dimensional when he first rode the Tour in 1991 as a sprinter for the

Toshiba team. Switching to the Spanish ONCE team in 1992, Jalabert then won the green points jersey after winning a stage into Brussels and taking several top-ten places in other sprint finishes. France hadn't had a decent Tour sprinter since Jacques Esclassan's mighty days in the 1970s, and although Hinault had proved he could win a big sprint when he wanted to, it was Jalabert who picked up his nation's hopes with his green jersey success.

No one knows whether Hinault himself ever advised Jalabert to broaden his horizons, but a nasty crash during a sprint finish in the 1994 Tour forced Jalabert to consider his options completely. Sprinting was too dangerous and too limiting for such a talented cyclist, who'd already won mountain stages of the 1994 Tour of Spain.

With his broken jaw mended, his teeth fixed, and some faultless plastic surgery on his damaged face, Jalabert returned

Laurent Jalabert a minute after his high-speed crash at Armentières in 1994, caused when a policeman leaned out to take a photo. Several riders hit him, including Jaja, whose bike was also destroyed.

to the Tour in 1995 as a highly determined all-rounder, having won Paris-Nice and two spring classics earlier that season. The knowledgeable world of French cycling noted that he now attacked in the style of Hinault, prompting them to exclaim that the ex-sprinter was a serious candidate for a place on the final podium of the Tour. Jalabert wanted exactly that, but he was prepared to let his legs do the talking, à la Hinault.

Jalabert never did make the winner's podium, not in '95, not ever. But his efforts to get there turned him into a true French hero each summer, a considerable achievement given that French heartthrob Richard Virenque was at the height of his powers and winning the polka-dot climber's jersey year in, year out. Jalabert, post–1994 Tour crash, bore all the trademarks of a human cannonball, launching himself into risky escapes with 200 kilometers to go or attacking recklessly in the Alps and Pyrenees.

With ONCE, Jalabert had the support of a truly magnificent team, and it was this outfit's strength that helped him temporarily into the *maillot jaune* after a TTT stage of the '95 Tour. One week later, with the race lead now in Induráin's hands, the ONCE team asked for more, and Jalabert obliged as part of an audacious daylong escape, which, to my mind, has yet to be equaled, fourteen years on. Induráin was caught napping when the escape built on the brutally steep climbs outside the stage-start city of Saint-Étienne. Jalabert had three teammates with him and a dozen other riders as well, all of them either part of the ONCE plot or seeking a stage win for themselves. Jalabert coaxed them all the way south toward

Jalabert races to a famous victory at Mende in the 1995 Tour de France.

Mende, helping him build a lead that forced Induráin's team to pay other teams to chase and save the situation. They saved the yellow jersey, but Jalabert stormed away on the finish climb to take a memorable victory. It was July 13, the eve of Bastille Day, and Jalabert was the most popular man in France.

It was impossible to photograph Jalabert in those heady days and not see the similarities between his riding style and that of Hinault. Only the results were different. Like Hinault, Jalabert relied on his stocky legs to propel him forward; he was typically out of the saddle for long moments at a time, or kicking hard to hurt his rivals over the summit of a climb. On flatter stages, those same legs pushed a mighty gear, enabling Jalabert to ride at a much higher cadence and save energy.

Jalabert seemed as mentally tough as Hinault as well. His willingness to attack or sprint, to suffer more than his rivals, was clearly a major plus. His face, dull and impassive at rest, changed completely in competition, with a snarl and a pout so Hinaultesque it defied belief. Yet Jalabert lacked the imperious contempt of the man who was probably his hero, preferring to remain one of the boys in the peloton that he could otherwise have ruled.

But Ja-Ja could also be aloof, even cold, when he wanted to be. Unlike Hinault, who embraced the French media and used them as his personal megaphone, Jalabert mistrusted the press and did his best to avoid contact. By choosing to race with the Spanish ONCE team and then the Danish CSC team, and even choosing to live in Switzerland for a few years, Jalabert risked incurring the serious displeasure of his many fans.

It's a mark of his excellence as a Tour cyclist that those fans still love him today, both as a color commentator for TV and as an ex-*guerrier* (warrior) of the Tour. A *guerrier deluxe*. If, in my dreams, I were a Tour cyclist, I'd rather be Hinault, of course. But I'd then opt for the twin-pleasured post-Tour life of Jalabert: TV commentator as well as respected triathlete and marathon runner.

PHOTOGRAPHING THE TOUR

W HEN I FIRST SAW THE TOUR DE FRANCE IN 1977, I WAS LUCKY IN that I was already a professional photographer. At that time, I was making a living photographing aristocrats and their extended families in London. As you might imagine, I was already thinking about switching to another form of photography and another subject matter altogether, and so I went to France, solely to photograph the Tour and its glamorous athletes. This unbridled ambition proved to be a valuable asset, for it gave me a purpose beyond simply standing at the roadside, my jaw wide open, my eyes popping, my body language very much that of a fan overcome with joy. A fan I was, of course, yet I was there with one distinct aim in mind: to get the best possible pictures of the Tour.

In many ways, such a plan is easier with today's automatic, do-everything-for-you cameras, but today's Tour is also ten times the monster it was back when I began. Ten times bigger means massive crowds, total road closures, increased security, and distractions in the form of a bigger publicity caravan that wants to shower you with a spray of water and free gifts. There's also the issue of photographing cyclists who travel about 15 percent faster than they did thirty years ago.

A PHOTO HISTORY

As it has in all walks of life, photography has played a major role in defining the glorious history that has shaped today's Tour de France. There were no TV

Octave Lapize is forced to walk on the Col du Tourmalet in 1910.

cameras when the first Tour set off from the Café au Réveil Matin in 1903. Instead, a handful of news photographers shot some mundane (for them) images of the sixty or so competitors as they wobbled off down the gravel road to the southeast of Paris. It's a very good bet that not one of those photographers had any inkling of the importance those images would one day attain.

When the Tour first climbed a true mountain pass, the Col du Tourmalet in 1910, it seems that just one lone photographer from *L'Auto* was there, gracing the world with a grainy, soft-focused shot that acted as an early declaration of the brutality and bravery of this new sporting event. In the photo we see a lone cyclist, Octave Lapize, spare tire around his chest, goggles atop his greasy, windswept head, making a slow, painful walk up the dirt track, his progress witnessed by only a small posse of journalists and officials in a following car. I assume the photographer had been on the same vehicle, but had jumped off to run past the weather-beaten cyclist and set up a shot. I'm guessing he did that several times on the following climb, the Col d'Aubisque, climbing back into the car to chase the cyclist down before jumping off again and again.

Bit by bit, photographers gradually became an intrinsic part of the Tour. Their progress was slow, in part due to the logistics of following the early Tours, in part due to the cumbersome nature of cameras made from wood and canvas and glass, and in no small part because *L'Auto* wanted to keep its race to itself (*L'Auto* was the failing newspaper whose editor, Henri Desgrange, created the Tour as a publicity stunt to attract more readers).

A quick scan through some of the Tour's history books reveals epic shots like the one of a group of cyclists in 1947, half in, half out of a village water trough, filling their bottles to the brim while basking in the coolness of the flowing water. A famous shot from the 1949 Tour shows two Italians, Fausto Coppi and Gino Bartali, sharing a *bidon*—a water bottle—as they climb the Col d'Izoard in a double-fronted attack against the diminutive French race leader, Jean Robic. The image is remarkable in that it records the athleticism and beauty of the Tour as it climbs between high banks of melting snow. But for cycling fans everywhere, that memorable image captures the moment when two archrivals, both Italians, buried their differences to defeat the French on home soil. It is a scenario that has been repeated, albeit through a slightly different script, with other rivals since—Bernard Hinault and Greg LeMond in 1986, Miguel Induráin and Claudio Chiappucci in 1992, Lance Armstrong and Jan Ullrich in 2001—but without that iconic 1949 image, the modern versions would have far less meaning.

My first glimpse of the Tour was on British TV in 1967, when news footage showed Tom Simpson dying at the side of the road that climbs Mont Ventoux.

ABOVE *Tour cyclists raid a village water trough in 1947.* BELOW *The motorcycle accident involving Alex Virot and René Wagner in 1957.*

The shaky camera work mesmerized a nation that, even back then, was more interested in soccer, cricket, and rugby. It certainly captured my interest for good; as a 12-year-old I remember waiting for the next day's newspaper to be delivered to our Surrey house, wanting to read more about the bravery and tragedy associated with such a colossal sporting event. The striking black-and-white image on the front page was even more dramatic than the TV coverage had been. A photographer using a fill-in flash had highlighted Simpson's sad features, his face as white as snow, his eyes staring wide open, his very life evaporating as doctors gave him the kiss of life.

A similarly evocative image shows a radio journalist and his *motard*—his driver—close to death after accidentally sending their BMW motorcycle over a cliff in the 1957 Tour; the journalist, Alex Virot, died immediately, while his driver, René Wagner, perished on the way to the hospital.

One of the most poignant images of the Tour is of Roger Rivière, a French cyclist, being rescued after crashing into a ravine in the Cévennes, a mountain range in south-central France, in the 1960 race. A photographer has caught the spirit of the Tour perfectly, for it shows a relay of team managers, mechanics,

The evacuation of Roger Rivière in 1960.

doctors, and a motorcycle policeman lifting Rivière to the roadside atop a stretcher. Rivière suffered a severe spinal injury in the crash, ending his career.

Another image of the Tour, taken in 1970, shows how the media had grown since its infancy in the early decades. Eddy Merckx is climbing Mont Ventoux. The Belgian is in the yellow jersey, struggling to maintain a brutal pace that only he feels must be maintained, for his rivals are far, far behind. It's hot—the sweat on his face and body clearly shows that—and the anxiety in Merckx's face is also clear as he pummels his way to victory, followed by an armada of cars and motorbikes, their passengers leaning out the windows or standing through sunroofs or on the footrests to witness the performance.

This was the first time the Tour had climbed the Ventoux since Simpson's death two years earlier, which partly accounted for the armada trailing Merckx, most of them anticipating a similarly haunting drama. Fortunately, nothing did go wrong, despite the stifling temperatures and the bad spirits now said to be in permanent residence up there. Merckx won the stage, and virtually won the Tour that day; he even managed to nod his head in respect and make a sign of

Jacques Goddet places flowers on Tom Simpson's memorial as Eddy Merckx rides past in 1969.

the cross as he passed the spot where Simpson had collapsed, another moment brilliantly caught on camera.

Looking now at that black-and-white shot, I feel an affinity with the motor-cycle photographers privileged to have been there that day. Then, as now, it was the photographers who had the best view, muscling their way to the front behind Merckx, their state-of-the-art Rolleiflex cameras capturing the moment for eternity.

There's little difference between today's rat pack of Tour photographers and their more gentlemanly forebears who followed in Merckx's pedal strokes on the Ventoux; it's just that there are many, many more of us! And we are a far more international clique than was allowed into the race back then.

One official photographer traveled with the Tour in 1903; perhaps two or three followed the race ten years later, when Belgium's Philippe Thys won the race, and perhaps one more by the time a yellow jersey was created for the race leader in 1919. A maximum of six photographers would have followed Merckx in 1969, some of them actually journalists armed with cameras, for this was a burgeoning period of photojournalism. Today's moto-mounted paparazzi amount to sixteen in all, a big gain over 1969's total, yet a tiny percentage set against the two hundred or so accredited photographers who now sign on at the start of a twenty-first-century Tour and who shoot the race from the sidelines.

Somewhere between 1903 and 1986—the year America's Greg LeMond won—the Tour became a gargantuan attraction on a worldwide level, which in turn created an equally enormous media entourage. More than half of today's Tour photographers are foreigners—*étrangers*—who have been drawn to the race by the exploits of Merckx and LeMond, as well as the handful of other foreign winners who've helped turn this French event into a worldwide phenomenon. Joop Zoetemelk (1980 winner) reinforced a Dutch media already tuned in to the Tour after attempts by Hennie Kuiper to win in the years immediately preceding. Pedro Delgado (winner in 1988 and a close challenger in 1987 and 1989) cemented a Spanish media presence, which grew even bigger when Miguel Induráin began his five-Tour winning streak in 1991. The influx of Danish and Scandinavian photographers almost swamped the Tour when Bjarne Riis won in 1996, but that was nothing in comparison to what happened when Jan Ullrich followed Riis in 1997, for the German media is the biggest, ugliest, most outspoken tribe in Europe.

THE MODERN CIRCUS

Just as *L'Auto* had done back in the formative years, its modern-day incarnation, *L'Équipe*, jealously guards its status, hogging three of the sixteen motorbikes in the race. *L'Équipe* says it needs all three: one for the newspaper, one for its in-house photo agency, Presse Sports, and one for its monthly bike magazine, *Vélo*. In fact, this claim is a desperate, insecure attempt to safeguard jobs in Paris and thwart the ever-present menace from Agence France Presse, the state-owned news agency that is the oldest of its kind in the world, one that would happily kick everyone else off the Tour if it had its way. AFP claims two motorbikes these days, which has a multiplying effect on its rivals, principally Reuters and the Associated Press, who each demand two bikes in the race as well (though they don't always get them).

Already, you can sense the clamor of the photographers wanting to record

TOP *Motorcycle photographers up close and personal in the 1999 Tour de France.*
BOTTOM *Photographers and TV cameramen trailing Miguel Induráin in a Tour time trial in 1994.*

this massive annual circus, be it for themselves or for their agencies. The organizers are surprisingly respectful of the attention given their event, yet remain staunchly loyal to news organizations or photographers who follow the entire cycling season. They allocate one motorcycle each to national agencies like Spain's Agencia EFE and Germany's Deutsche Press Agency (DPA), as well as modern-day news organizations, such as Getty Images (USA/UK) and PhotoNews (Belgium) and the Italian sports newspaper, *La Gazzetta dello Sport.* Aware of its national responsibilities, the Tour keeps a spot open each day as well for the principal newspaper of the region the race is passing through, bringing such illustrious titles as *Le Dauphiné Libéré, Midi Libre, Ouest-France,* and *La Voix du Nord* to the race.

You'll be excused for believing there is little room for the specialist cycling photographers in this mighty jungle. In fact, a few of us remain, something that we hope will never change, despite the race's popularity. Just how we all coexist in a very hostile and competitive environment is best left unexplained for now. Suffice it to say, my days on the Tour were a lot simpler when I was a roadside admirer with one camera and one lens, and one chance at getting a decent shot of the race.

Moments before you catch your first glimpse of your first Tour, and long after you've enjoyed the prerace spectacle that is the *caravane publicitaire,* you'll spot today's Tour photographers as they speed past where you're standing. Some of you will be annoyed, for if any of those photographers is actually working at the time, his motorcycle might well be the only thing you see instead of the cyclists, the photographer twisting around over his left shoulder to shoot whichever Tour favorite is in front, pedaling just a few feet behind the photographer. But none of you can fail to be impressed by the sight of a dozen specially equipped motorbikes, their engines purring despite the low revs and the thin mountain air, their *motards* (drivers) gazing steadfastly at the route ahead in anticipation of crazy spectators who might run into the road. All the while, the drivers must also listen for their masters' nervous demands to get closer to the cyclists or to get away altogether.

There'll be another half-dozen snappers right after the race has gone by— the ones waiting for crash shots, or those who have been pushed out of the ruck by the primeval nature of their competitors. Whether you are a competent

SPLIT SECOND　*Michael Schumacher crashes at Super-Besse in 2008, a lucky shot taken from behind the crowd barriers by a German photographer, Hans-Alfred Roth.*

photographer with a brace of SLRs or a fledgling enthusiast with a compact digital camera, your success rate depends on how you get a clear shot of the race without one of those *motos* in your shot.

FRAMING THE TOUR

Photographically, the Tour de France has many distinctive features—color, scenery, athleticism, and drama among them. I consider these four to be the cornerstones of the sport. Even if you are an amateur photographer, you can strive to capture them all in your shots.

Color is everywhere, from the cyclists' jerseys and shorts to the matching shades on their helmets and glasses. Color is in the deep tan on their arms and legs and faces, as well as the team cars that follow in their wake. Most colorful of all is the peloton of two hundred cyclists as it meanders up an alpine pass or between fields of bright yellow sunflowers in Périgord.

Scenery is everywhere, under a blue French summer sky dotted with puffy cumulus clouds. Scenery and color are a ten-man escape racing over a small stone bridge in deepest Auxois, their flight from the peloton cheered on by villagers waving "*Vive Le Tour*" banners. Scenery can be something even more French than that, perhaps the Tour passing through the Normandy fishing port of Honfleur on Bastille Day, the blue, white, and red flags hanging proudly from half-timbered houses. Scenery and color and athleticism are the Tour as it climbs a Pyrenean *col* like the Soudet, a 30-kilometer-long brute that broke the spirit of Induráin in 1996, yet which is ranked as one of the Tour's prettiest ascents. The thousands of fans who find viewing platforms high above the zigzag road on the Pic Soulet will testify to that.

Drama is everywhere, acts of daring, tragedy, or comedy just waiting to erupt on the roads of the Tour. Drama can be a cyclist as he plunges down a mountain pass with a speed and irresponsibility just demanding to be punished. Drama is a packed sprint gone wrong, a pedal that's touched a wheel, a bicycle that's been knocked into the path of another, a pile of sweaty, pulsating bodies hurtling to the tarmac. Drama can be a bloodied cyclist arriving at the stage finish twenty-five minutes after the winner has won, chased and then engulfed by a gaggle of journalists, TV reporters, and—of course—photographers desperate to record the reasons this particular cyclist came to be so delayed. In this modern, often tarnished Tour de

The Rabobank bus is surrounded by the press in the 2007 Tour.

France, drama is a Rabobank team bus surrounded by an even bigger mob of media people, their cameras, mikes, and lenses a mass of confusion and energy in the hunt for news about the latest drug bust.

Drama takes other forms, like the arrival at the Tour of French president Nicolas Sarkozy, just weeks after winning over the voters of France, his security team staring aghast at the wall of Tour watchers that might contain a madman.

NOT SO FAST   *A small boy infiltrates the Tour on a stage start from Arras in 1991.*

Drama can be funny too, like a 10-year-old boy sneaking into the 1990 Tour peloton on his tiny bicycle—drama for his parents, at least!

So, just where do you begin your work as a Tour photographer? The most serious among you must plan each day where to be and when to be there, as well as what to do when in place at your chosen location. It helps to follow all three weeks of the Tour, for that way you get a second bite at the apple if something goes wrong on the first attempt. Trying to cram everything into a ten-day visit leaves less room for errors, and there will be plenty of those!

The Tour has a conveniently logical stage on which its cyclists perform, with time trials at the beginning, middle, and end, as well as flat stages that take the race into and out of the mountains. This gives four distinct opportunities for photographers, if you also consider the stages that are neither flat nor mountainous—what the French call *moyenne-montagne*. These stages often turn out to be the most productive for roadside photographers, not least because fewer spectators are there to get in your way and because the cyclists themselves are more relaxed than on other stages. A relaxed Tour cyclist, particularly a star, can often be seen nearer to the front here than on other stages, a genuine plus for the roadside photographer.

CHASING THE TOUR

It's most likely that you will follow the Tour without accreditation, which means that you must do an awful lot of planning to get around the challenges facing a photographer.

First of all, you should always arrive at your chosen location as early as possible—even the day before, if necessary. The best map reading and most skillful driving won't be of help if you've tried to get onto the race route less than five hours before the Tour is due to pass by. The moving vacuum that is the Tour stretches ahead for over 20 kilometers at times, and gendarmes tend to close the roads completely around breakfast time, even if they are 200 kilometers from the start line. The best plan is always to do a reconnaissance the evening before, stopping on the route if you see a desirable location, or coming back to that point the next day on alternate roads.

The Tour rarely uses the main N routes through France, staying mainly on D roads to allow other traffic more freedom. But there are thousands upon thousands of other D roads that will connect you to the race route, or near enough to it that you can walk or cycle to the exact point you want.

If you've dedicated your trip to getting some great images, you are likely to be frustrated when things go wrong—and they will go wrong, believe me! Closed roads, slow drivers, traffic jams, awkward gendarmes or police, radar traps, bad map reading, and just straightforward bad days will take their toll if unchecked.

One way to avoid problems if you are driving is to stick rigidly to the speed limits. To reiterate the caution I gave in Chapter 2 ("Getting Around"), let me emphasize again that France has really cracked down on speeding tourists, fining them on the spot or hauling them to the nearest ATM machine to pay their fines in cash. If you drive too fast through villages or towns (which almost always have a 50 km/h limit), you can also expect to have your car confiscated and your license withdrawn until you've returned to make a court appearance—it really has become that tough in France.

THE PROLOGUE

The fact that the Tour insists on a 100 percent lockdown for its prologue course should not deter the camera enthusiast from getting some great individual action shots early in the race. Your main priority for this short-distance time trial should be to walk around the course twenty-four hours before the event starts; that's what the pros do, so that's what everyone should do. You need to find the best place to work from and, as importantly, where the light will be coming from at exactly the same time next day, when the race is on for real.

If you are lucky, your reconnaissance will coincide with that of the Tour cyclists who, being professionals themselves, will need to spend an hour or two the day before studying the corners and characteristics of the prologue course. They'll repeat their research on the morning of the prologue, and indeed they will keep circling the course right up to the moment when the first cyclist begins his race.

You have to be in position many hours before the prologue begins, so your look-around the day before is vitally important; it will dictate the lens you

Lance Armstrong and Udo Bolts survey the prologue course in Luxembourg in 2002.

choose, and whether you go for a panning shot from the side or a head-on, balls-to-the-wall cornering shot. You may even get really lucky by finding a long, curving bend that allows you to alternate between panning and head-on shots.

When you are making your reconnaissance, try to put yourself inside the cyclists' heads, anticipating where they'll set up for the corner, where they'll start to turn in, and where they'll exit once they've passed the apex of the corner. In this way, you can decide whether to stand at their exit point with a longer lens—where they'll be aiming right at you—or whether to be at a 90-degree angle to the apex of the corner, in which case you may want to use a shorter lens for that panning shot.

Thor Hushovd in the 2006 Tour prologue in Strasbourg. A side-on shot like this is attainable from behind crowd barriers if you have mild-mannered neighbors and a clear view of the cyclist.

It's most likely that you'll be shooting from standing height—barriers tend to be covered in their entirety by sponsors' boards or banners, and even if free of banners there might be official photographers sitting against the inside of your barrier, blocking your view even if you could shoot between the barrier's slats—so my recommendation is to go for the side-on shot, in which elevation is less important than simply getting a clear shot. A head-on shot with a long lens requires certain skills from the photographer—composition, anticipation, and oodles of self-confidence—but it also requires huge amounts of luck—there must be no preceding gendarme motorcycle to spoil the approach, and you must have faultless neighbors, who do not wave banners, who do not clap at full arms' length, and who never, ever, wave those green cardboard hands tossed out by the publicity caravan. You'll find that many shots are spoiled by overenthusiasm from your fellow fans, and this day is too special to be spoiled.

The organizers will have put the crowd barriers in place before you do your pre–race day walk, which will help you to calculate the distance to the cyclists

A classic cornering prologue shot of Chris Boardman in 1994. A medium-length telephoto lens will capture images like this if you have chosen your place carefully.

and therefore determine your choice of lenses. Typically, a prologue course uses the full width of the existing road, so you do not absolutely need to wait for the barriers to be erected to do some preliminary work; take a look around thirty-six or even forty-eight hours before the race, if you have time, then make any necessary adjustments later. And if you see any of the camera pros looking closely at a particular corner, take a close look yourself; they may have seen something you've overlooked.

Bear in mind that once you are in place on race day, your chances of moving to another location are virtually nil. For every one photographer doing the same thing you are, there will be at least fifty thousand fans also seeking to safeguard their hallowed ground. So find your place and plan to stay there for the duration.

If you've found a really good spot, you'll find the official photographers showing up on the other side of the barrier to take advantage of the location, too. You will find them parking themselves right in front of you before the prologue begins, but all of them will sit down in the road once the first cyclist starts his race. So don't panic and start shouting at them; they'll be out of your way when the cyclists race past.

Children are of more concern; they have a habit of crawling in front of you, or sitting between and on your feet when you're trying to balance yourself for a shot. It's still illegal to thump young children in France, especially if they are not your own. Just tell yourself the prologue only lasts about three hours . . . plus waiting time.

THE SPRINTING STAGES

Sprint finishes are the stages that torment the roadside photographer the most, for there really is no good place to stand when a pack of cyclists is hurtling for the finish line at eighty kilometers per hour across your line of vision. Most of the Tour's flat finishes have barriers along them from about five kilometers out, meaning that even if you have managed to get a place right at the barrier, you're going to be too close and totally at the wrong angle to get any sort of decent shot.

I think there are two ways to approach this situation. One is to find an elevated position in the last kilometer where you can shoot the sprint with a degree of freedom, either by zooming in tight on the leading half-dozen sprinters or zooming out wide for a generic image of the whole pack. Perhaps from a hotel balcony overlooking the finish?

The other solution is to walk away from the finish to the point where either the barriers end or the road bends or curves and where you see a gap to stand in among the expectant public. Most flat stages finish close to city centers, where there are bound to be corners, but the last few kilometers should be straight; that's what the sport's rules say, anyway. In practice, this doesn't always happen, so it is here that the well-placed, well-prepped photographer has the best chance of shooting images of a massive crash.

Your chances of seeing a mass fall are extremely small, for crashes rarely take place where you expect them to. If it makes you feel any better, the same frustration applies to accredited race photographers, no matter how experienced they are. One of the most spectacular stage-finish crashes in living memory was at Armentières in the 1994 Tour. This was a near-straight finish, but there was a gentle, yet distinct, right-hand drift in the last 200 meters. It was here that the Tour's fastest men raced for the line, cutting off the angle to gain an extra meter's advantage. Problem was, it was on the racing line that a local policeman decided he should stand, back in the days when the finish straight had a policeman stationed every 20 meters to keep an eye on the public and to show a ceremonial presence to the watching world. What transpired was as near to outright carnage as the Tour has ever seen: Wilfried Nelissen led the way, head down, full of aggression against Laurent Jalabert and Djamolidine Abdoujaparov. Nelissen only saw the policeman at the last split second, and

Be prepared to shoot images of a sprint some distance from the finish. This crash came 200 meters from the line in Koblenz in 2005, but it could easily have come at 800 meters or 2 kilometers.

the policeman, who had stepped forward to take a photo himself, never saw Nelissen—and one big bad fall was captured brilliantly by Eric Gaillard of Reuters, using an autofocus camera for the first time in his life!

No one else got as good a shot as Eric, because most of us were still shooting manually, and therefore had our focus on the finish line instead of the moving death wish that was Nelissen. Gaillard sensed Nelissen was the quicker sprinter, and locked his autofocus on the demented figure as he sprinted toward the line. Gaillard didn't just get Nelissen's crash to the ground—he also got the actual moment of impact with the policeman, the moment another policeman jumped for his life over the barrier and into the crowd, and the spectacular collision and somersault of Jalabert, who hit Nelissen and the policeman before

smashing his face into the ground. The rest of us got a mediocre shot of a bewildered Abdoujaparov as he crossed the line without challenge.

Abdoujaparov himself had had a spectacular Tour crash two years earlier after hitting a plastic Coca-Cola sign in the last 200 meters in Paris. *L'Équipe* had four photographers on the finish line that day, but it was a fifth photographer from the newspaper who took an astonishing series of shots. Christian Rochard had been sent away from the finish line by *L'Équipe*'s chief cycling photographer, who had a long-running feud with Rochard, the paper's chief tennis photographer. Rochard walked back 200 meters, fitted a long lens on his camera, and pointed it at Abdu' as he led the sprint out—with great results, for Rochard won a major photography prize with his crash shots.

It is rare for someone behind the barriers to get the shots that the pros do not, but, as Rochard proved to his jealous colleague that day, it does happen. A few years back in the Tour of Italy, or Giro d'Italia, there was a pileup at a stage

A sprint finish has two sides: the lead-out, as in Châteauroux in 2008 (above), and the actual finish, as in 2007 in Tours (below). Stand at a point where you can get a clear view of the action without needing to lean over the barriers and risk injury to the cyclists. Look for a slight bend in the road or the final corner to take your shots.

PHOTO TIP: Standing behind the barriers may seem too tame, but as long as you have found a point with an unobstructed view of the road, you are better off there—at least on your first attempt. If you do not want to use a long lens on this first outing, try your luck with a medium-length zoom lens (70–200 mm), and try a panning shot as the cyclists come racing past. If you use a flash while doing this, and a shutter speed of at least 1/250, you might capture a uniquely "racy" image, slightly blurred but eye-catching all the same. If your camera works with flash at 1/500 or more, then use that as an option. Just be wary of your fellow fans waving their arms and clapping their hands; they're a constant threat to getting a clear shot!

finish, the epicenter of which was too far away for the Giro's finish-line photographers to see clearly. But a keen photographer had got himself a good position in the public grandstand, 200 meters from the line. Armed with two cameras, the Australian tourist caught the exact moment when Mario Cipollini lost his grip on the wet surface. This enterprising shutterbug then switched to a camera with a wide-angle lens to catch the aftermath as Cipo hit the crowd barriers, bounced back into the path of a dozen other cyclists, and caused a nasty pileup. The Aussie photographer then managed to sneak into the media room after the stage and sell his images to *La Gazzetta dello Sport* for about $400—not a bad day's work! If by any rare stroke of luck—your luck, not the cyclists'—you capture a crash in the Tour and feel no one else has the shot, you can usually make contact with one of the Tour's officials by getting close to the security cordon near a green sign saying "*Salle de Presse/Permanence*." Show him the digital image in the back of your camera and he'll figure out what you are trying to achieve.

THE TIME TRIAL

Apart from the starts and finishes, and around any dangerous corners along the route, a time trial takes place on roads totally free of crowd barriers. Time trials also tend to be the least populated stages, meaning there is a lot of open space in which to find your preferred shooting location.

A classic side-on shot like this one of Sylvain Chavanel is easily achieved if you have found a quiet section of the road. A telephoto lens, 200 mm or 300 mm, works best to frame the cyclists traveling at about 30 miles per hour.

The choices are basically the same as for the prologue—head-on, side-on, cornering shots—but your scope is much wider, regardless of which angle you go for. The most important thing is to match your camera skills and your equipment to the type of shot you envisage taking. It's no good trying to take a side-on shot of a speeding cyclist if your lens was intended for close-up shots of flowers or for weddings.

Because the road on which the TT will take place is likely to be closed early on, the serious photographer has to consider skipping the previous day's stage to do a full reconnaissance of the course. But you might also be able to do adequate research after the previous stage has ended, if the TT is in close proximity to the previous day's finish. You'll find many professional photographers doing the same thing—those who have escaped the post-stage purgatory of the press room—as well as Tour enthusiasts looking to park their campers or tents in the best place possible for the time trial. Since a time trial stage puts you more in control of your work than a flat or mountainous stage, you have to make days like this count, for there'll be many stages when you go away completely empty-handed.

If you have not had the luxury of doing a full reconnaissance twenty-four hours before, you need to be flexible in your approach to location. Ideally, you want the best of both worlds, finding a place that will allow you to do cornering and side-on shots within a few hundred yards of each other, in case your preferred choice does not work out.

Even then, whether you've chosen a place the day before or a few hours before the TT begins, there is still the possibility that the weather, and the lighting that comes with the weather, will completely alter your plans. So try to have a second option available nearby.

There's been a trend in recent years for cycling photographers to go for the long-lens, side-on shot from the middle of a wheat field or, better still, from the center of a sunflower field. Variations of this shot are vineyards, sand dunes, lavender fields, even cemeteries, depending on how desperate the photographer

The author half hidden during a time trial stage of the 2008 Tour. A low angle adds something extra to your image, especially if you have found a neutral background.

has become in his search for something different. The idea is to place the time-trialing cyclist against an isolated or neutral backdrop, so that the physics of the cyclist are of secondary importance to the overall image.

Agency photographers like the long-lens shot because it increases their chances of getting it published on a general interest page of a newspaper or magazine. Specialist cycling photographers tend to go for a close-up action shot, knowing that their pictures are more likely to be published on the sports pages of a newspaper or in cycling magazines and on Web sites, as well as sold to long-term clients such as sponsors or manufacturers of bike equipment.

Laurent Fignon in a time trial to Avoriaz in 1983. For images like this, you need a clear space that's hard to find in the modern Tour. I used a medium lens, about 50 mm. Flash removed the dark shadows on Fignon's face.

Unless you are as well staffed as AFP or *L'Équipe*, however, with one photographer for action, one for ambience, and another for post-finish exhaustion shots, you have to make a choice, one in which luck plays a huge role. It's not for nothing that official photographers scouting the course on their motorbikes will often stop when they see a roadside photographer squatting in a useful-looking place; this is the one stage where roadside camera pointers have opportunities equal to their in-race colleagues. One of the most flattering things that can happen to a roadside photographer is when you suddenly have a posse of official photographers for company at your chosen location. If this ever happens to you, you know you've made the right choice; just don't let the pros push you off your spot!

First thing is to make sure you're going to get a clear view of the cyclist as he races past at more than fifty 50 km/h. Normally, this seems to prohibit shooting on a corner or on a spectator-crowded climb; there'll always be someone in your way just as you put your finger on the shutter release. But consider a shot taken with a short lens on a steep climb, where the photographer is lying on the ground or sitting in a ditch on the inside of a curve or bend, where few spectators bother to stand. You see the cyclist at the last moment, true, but he will be going fairly slowly by then. He'll be grimacing too, a wonderful sign of emotion that you'd normally only ever get in the mountains. Of course, you've got your flashgun all set up to illuminate that grimace, along with the sweat that comes as a result of that grimace. Don't mind that your fellow spectator is laughing at your prone position; he hasn't traveled anywhere near as far as you have and almost certainly knows nothing about the finer skills of sports photography.

The same stance can be employed even better on a quiet ascent free of spectators, and you may even have the space to use a longer lens and isolate the cyclist completely—perhaps against an empty sky. I photograph about twenty-five time trials each season, and the shot taken from below road level with a long lens is still one of my favorites.

One time trial image I'm particularly proud of is Lance Armstrong in the 2004 Tour at Besançon. It was taken with a 400 mm lens about 3 kilometers from the finish—away from the soul-destroying crowd barriers that ruin many a photographer's shots—and it seems that Lance is staring right at me in the last minutes of his winning ride.

I took the shot while lying on the ground among spectators' legs, having arrived a few minutes before Lance and before they'd had the chance to complain. It was pure instinct that made me stop at that place, for at first glance the long, flat, wide road was totally unsuitable for any kind of shot, let alone one set up without the benefit of having photographed the preceding cyclist. The secret lay in identifying the gentle curve of the road, the fact that Lance would be taking the shortest line possible—where I was lying—and the certainty that he'd have his head up to look through the turn. That the photo was shot at the

> **PHOTO TIP:** Towns and villages do not make good vantage points for TT photography; there are too many uncontrollable factors like disruptive fans, awkward policemen, and the risk that a late-afternoon shadow from a tall building will ruin your shot just when the Tour's best riders are due to arrive. Seek out the quietest stretch of road you can find so that you have more than one option of lens or position if the light changes. In a typical Tour stage, 190 cyclists starting at two-minute intervals might take over six hours to come past, so make sure you have water and food to last that long in the open and a decent hat and a waterproof jacket at hand in case of exposure to the elements. Try to buy a copy of *L'Équipe* before you begin your work; the starting order of the cyclists is printed in it, a vital guide to your photography so you won't miss anyone famous.

end of the stage he had won, close to the end of the Tour he went on to win, and that he was on his way to becoming the first man ever to win six Tours means the expression on his face was as near-perfect as I could have hoped for.

In fact, Lance is not staring right at me—he's staring at the road surface on which my head was resting, perhaps a half-inch to my left. Go try a shot like this, especially if you know you've already got some great shots in the bag. It doesn't do any harm to take risks sometimes; you never know when it might pay off.

FLAT STAGES

Capturing a great shot during a flat stage is a photographic challenge, and how good a chance you have to meet it depends on how much time you spend with the Tour. A typical Tour de France has about ten flattish stages in it, meaning a photographer following the Tour for three weeks has about ten varieties of shots to achieve. The fewer days you are in France, the fewer chances you have to get it right.

< OPPOSITE *A simple head-on, long telephoto shot of Lance Armstrong in the 2004 Tour at Besançon. How did I get him to look at me? See text.*

A fortuitous shot from the 2004 Tour. Images like this cannot be planned; they just happen—about once every ten years! When you are looking for a place to stop on an ordinary stage in the middle of nowhere, you might find an opportunity like this.

Flat stages seem to have little of interest for the Tour photographer; images spring to mind of go-slow cyclists, complete stops at water fountains, games or even fights along the road, bunch sprints, mass crashes when half the peloton is daydreaming. Yet these are the days when France opens its hidden beauty to the outside world. A lily-covered canal in Poitou, the medieval parapets of Vannes in Brittany, the rolling fields in Champagne, the lazy river Dordogne at Domme, the humid traverse across Languedoc-Roussillon: days that are one day out from the Pyrenees, two days in from the Alps. On each of these days, the Tour photographer has the chance to show a peloton in proximity to something extraordinary. The racers may be to the side of it, beneath the shadow of it, or above the waterline of it. But to miss these flat stages is to miss the very essence of the Tour in summertime France, to miss the subtle adulation a nation bestows on its greatest treasure, *Le Tour*.

Because of the logistics of tracking the Tour on such flat and, usually, long stages, the photographer has to make crucial choices. Some might choose to

CAMERAS AND COMPUTERS

Cameras and lenses improve all the time, although as I write these words in the fall of 2008, I find it hard to believe that much more progress can be made; our gear is spectacularly good already!

My current stock of equipment for a Tour de France consists of two Nikon D3 camera bodies, each loaded with two Lexar 4GB memory cards. A Nikon SB-900 flash is fitted to one of the bodies.

I carry five lenses with me all day:

- 16 mm fish-eye for ultra-wide panoramic shots
- 14–24 mm zoom for landscapes and close-up human-interest shots prestage
- 24–70 mm zoom for side-on shots from the motorcycle and some landscape shots
- 70–200 mm zoom for head-on/side-on shots from the motorcycle, and for tightly cropped landscape shots
- 300 mm f4 fixed-length for capturing landscape images, action shots from the roadside, and finish-line and podium shots

I also have a 200–400 mm zoom lens for time trials as well as for finish shots when it's going to be a big sprint. As an extra, I carry either a 1.4x or 1.7x extender that allows me to increase the focal length of the longer lenses. The extender is useful for finish-line shots when a lone cyclist is about to win.

All this gear is either on my shoulders, in a set of waist-belt pouches, or in one of the motorcycle panniers.

I also use a Nikon D1X body for specific shots with fill flash, usually on mountain stages, as I find the results with flash much better than those with the D3. I use a Quantum Turbo SC charger to accelerate the recycling time of the flashgun.

If rain seems likely, I'll squeeze an AquaTech cover into the panniers as well; the cover slips over the camera like a glove and keeps the rain out for a few hours, yet still allows me full usage of the camera functions. A good old-fashioned piece of chamois leather is always in my pocket to wipe away dirt or water.

continued >

CAMERAS AND COMPUTERS *continued*

The author enjoys a day with his raingear.

When I finally get to the media room postrace, my assistant has already set up my laptop and connected it to the Internet by cable or wi-fi. I use a MacBook Pro laptop computer, the latest 15-inch glass-screen model, with Adobe Bridge to select the images and Adobe Photoshop as my editing software.

My clients are a mixture of Web sites, magazines, newspapers, and sponsors, all of whom require different services each day. I'll spend one to two hours selecting, editing, and transmitting Web-sized images directly to clients that require such a service, before selecting, editing, and then uploading all my high-resolution images to a password-protected database, from which magazine and newspaper editors can help themselves.

Total time in the media room depends on the kind of stage that's just finished, but three to four hours per stage is a good guide, though I may quit after three hours to find the hotel and get dinner, before using the hotel wi-fi to finish off the remainder.

miss the start and head for a known landmark 40 kilometers down the route, having checked maps in order to avoid the worst of the parallel traffic and gain at least some access to the race route. They might then look at the chances of making the finish well in advance of the race, or trek across country to capture an image of the race as it crosses the Loire, the Tarn, the Oise, or the Garonne, while forfeiting the finish altogether. They might drive the race route the evening before, becoming completely disillusioned at the unremarkable Picardie

Consider the feed zone as a subject for your camera. It is often the soigneurs *(or* soigneusse *in this case) who offer the best emotions as they prepare the hand-ups for the riders.*

landscape only to spot, at the last minute, an unforeseen water mill astride the river at Aire-sur-la-Lys.

To experience the majesty that is the Tour among this hidden array of beauty, and then to successfully capture it on camera, is one of life's great pleasures; you've rescued what might have been a wasted day and captured something that is unique and exclusive to you! So when you plan your precious holiday time in France, when you focus in on the obvious double whammy of the Alps and Pyrenees—together with the finish in Paris—spend a few hours considering the unknown, though far from guaranteed, surprises that await in deep France, France *profonde*. You won't be disappointed.

Days spent in the countryside of France are days when you must have total mastery of your choice of equipment. When you are surrounded and quite likely overwhelmed by the beauty of rural France, this is not a time to reach for that ultrawide lens in order to make a decent picture out of something very ordinary. Instead, it is a time when the photographer must use the most

TOP *If you discover a wonderful panorama miles from the peaks, don't be afraid to stop and risk your luck. Such places are usually free of cars and crowds.* BOTTOM *The same applies for a shot of the peloton, taken on a bend in the road and from ground level to get the best composition.*

> **PHOTO TIP:** Picture editors won't be impressed by a single-shot masterpiece, no matter how fabulous it may appear to be. The flat stages of a Tour make a great contribution to a three-week portfolio of images, because you do need to show the more subtle side of the Tour and its surroundings. Even if you feel some landscape shots lack sufficient interest, include at least a few in your final selection after the Tour. After all, the quiet, unassuming countryside is what many people associate with France.

fundamental skills—composition, lighting, and positioning—to bring out the best of what is already a beautiful scenario.

Your choice of lens should be ultralong for the tightly cropped shot that balances the cyclists against the silhouette of a hilltop castle or château, as well as for those classic shots of sunflowers or lavender. Or a moderate wide-angle that allows you to make full use of a colorful foreground and dazzling blue sky. In both instances, the secret is to make the peloton and scenery equal partners in your envisioned shot: Too much peloton detracts from the beauty, while too much beauty overwhelms even the Tour's *grande* peloton.

That said, landscape photography does need a focal point to attract the eye, and the scenery within your composition must draw in the viewer. Thus your shot must be scenic as opposed to purely sporting. On the flatter stages of the Tour, a lot more thought goes into creating the perfect shot than it does in the mountains, where everything is scenic anyway! Even on days when the countryside seems monotonous, or when you've had the bad luck to see France under leaden, gray clouds, there's always a shot to be had—perhaps a timeless shot of some weathered country folks watching the race?

THE SUNFLOWER STAGES

Without doubt, it is the sunflower shots that all photographers want most. If the Tour has 200 accredited photographers on its roster, you can be sure all but a small handful of them will be out hunting in earnest if word gets out that the race is in sunflower country. Here, unaccredited snappers have a huge

I discovered these sunflowers a few minutes before the 2005 Tour went flying through and was lucky to have Armstrong leading the way. Even the overcast skies failed to spoil this image, so don't be put off if the sun is not shining!

advantage over their credentialed colleagues, in that they can drive down the course the evening before to survey potential sunflower fields. Some photo agencies dispatch a spotter to do this for the professionals left working in the press room, but in most cases it is purely luck if the accredited photographer chances upon these brightly colored delights in the middle of a stage.

Based on my thirty years' experience, anyone finding acres upon acres of sunflowers the evening before should stop there and then; it might be the only sighting you'll get! There's simply no logic to where these sunflowers are to be found, except that they tend to be in moist, hot areas of southwest France, and usually on rolling or partly hilly terrain. To be more precise is difficult, for we are dealing with a phenomenon of nature. But if you draw an imaginary rectangle that stretches east from the Atlantic at Dax to central Provence at Avignon, with a northern edge at Angoulême and a southern base at Saint-Gaudens, you're in the right area!

Sunflowers offer photographers a variety of opportunities, be they with a moderate zoom lens and a high vantage point (above) or with a fish-eye lens at ground level (below).

The French name for sun-flower is *tournesol*, meaning "turn to the sun"—which, like many things in French life, is in fact an exaggeration of the truth. What they are trying to say is that the flowers twist their heads toward the sun. What they should add is that mature sunflowers only do this

in the morning, turning toward the rising sun before keeping their heads in shade for the afternoon. This is bad news for Tour de France photographers, seeing as how most stages of the Tour start late morning, leaving only a few hours of reliable sunflower time.

What's worse is that sunflowers wither and die after the first heat wave of the summer, reducing their photogenicity still further. Basically, a Tour that passes through southwestern France before the Alps has a better chance of getting itself photographed amid such yellow splendor than a Tour that arrives in the southwest after the Alps, when the moisture has dried out of the flowers.

I had some early success with sunflowers in the 1988 Tour, but I then had to wait until 1994 for the next decent image. Yet in 2004 and 2005, my sunflower archive was bursting after two particularly fortuitous Tours. I'd managed to get long-lens shots, wide-angle shots, even shots with a fish-eye lens, which all seemed to work. And then I got a shot of the peloton racing between fields of yellow, with the man in yellow, Lance Armstrong himself, leading the way.

Tour photographers are completely obsessed with sunflowers. As with searching for a sacred bird of prey, it is the hunt that absorbs us the most, for there are too many occasions when the bird has fled the nest by the time we arrive; the flowers are either dead or hiding from the sun!

If you've found your way into a really decent sunflower field, you can amuse yourself by watching the official photographers as they too see the potential. They arrive in cars or on motorbikes, trying hard to hide their vehicles so other Tour snappers won't see what they've seen. A lone photographer becomes two, then three, followed by another four at the same time. Before you know it, the field of yellow has dark spots all over it—the heads of the Tour's photographers submerged in the foliage, each determined to get the best angle.

PHOTO TIP: A word of caution to anyone hunting sunflower shots: Bees love the pollen in this flower. It's a risk that comes with the job for us pros, but it could spoil your trip if you get stung badly. The other thing to note is that sunflowers can grow to over eight feet tall, and you may need a ladder to get a clear shot. Although you can always do what some Japanese photographers do: Drive your rental car into the field, clamber barefoot onto the roof, and use it as a huge tripod!

The Tour climbs the Col du Lautaret in 2002 against a backdrop of snow, rock, and puffy clouds in a blue sky. I captured this image after a short hike up a sheer, scree-covered slope—well worth the effort!

The funniest scene of all is when photographers arrive too late to get a decent shot, because the Tour is on their heels. This is the moment when prima donna agency photographers are best left alone, for they can be a mightily sensitive lot at the best of times!

THE MOUNTAIN STAGES

At last, you've arrived in the mountains, probably the main event of the Tour for you, as well as for those competing in it. So where to begin your photography? If you're in France long enough to do both the Alps and Pyrenees, you have a lot more scope than anyone having to choose between the two. A typical Tour has five or six full-on mountain stages, of which at least a few will feature mountaintop finishes.

First of all, isolate those summit finishes in your planning; those are where you can go for some killer action shots featuring the battle for overall victory,

Andy Hampsten and Stephen Roche duel in the 1987 Tour, one of dozens of such climbing battles that litter the Tour's history books and make life distinctly pleasant for photographers.

your ultimate aim being to get at least one great image of the race leader in his *maillot jaune*. You'll best achieve this by finding a suitable location in the last few kilometers of such a climb, using your experiences from the prologue to select a place behind the barriers where you can get a clear shot (always choose the outside of a bend).

The Tour finds its greatest fans in the mountains, but they are also more numerous, more crazy, more volatile, and therefore more unpredictable than anywhere else. So be extra careful whom you stand next to; that quiet, gentle lady from Munich, the one wearing the "I once loved Jan" T-shirt—she'll probably turn into your worst nightmare when the riders arrive.

If you are brave enough to stand away from the barriers among a half-million Tour fans and expect to use a long lens to get your shots, I can tell you now that you'll fail. Unless, that is, you've chosen a day when the rain has kept half the fans away, or a year when half the cyclists have already been drummed out of the race after a drug raid, taking half of the audience with them. In the absence of that kind of luck, my best advice is to use a camera that has a medium-zoom lens, maybe a 35–70 mm. Make sure you have a flash as well to illuminate the shadows formed by the late-afternoon sun.

If you've a second camera body, by all means fit a longer lens—70–200 mm—and use that to pick out some of the chasing cyclists, the ones who don't have motorcycles in front and behind, and who definitely don't have a pack of Dutch fans running alongside them all the way to the finish!

By using the wider-angle lens, you can pop out of the crowd at the last moment and grab a shot or two of the leaders as they race by, before pulling your head back in to avoid the motorized entourage that always threatens to scalp you if you are not quick enough. It takes practice to get it right, but you'll get at least one more bite at the cherry before the Tour leaves the mountains behind.

Once the race favorites have passed your spot, think about switching locations, perhaps climbing a rock or getting onto another vantage point. From there, your longer lens can be used to close in on the next group of cyclists, taking care to show the depth of the crowds as well—a vital record of the Tour's popularity. Finally, go back to ground level for individual shots of the stragglers; these are the real heroes of the Tour, the ones who suffer day in, day out, and who appreciate the support your fellow fans will give them. Make sure you get some of it on camera.

On stages that do not end atop a mountain, your choices expand considerably. Most people are tempted to stand on the final ascent, wanting the best of the action and atmosphere for their portfolios. But as there will be several stages like this, ones where the finish lies in the valley, long after the final climb is over, you need only take this type of shot once. Change your plan next time to take a scenic shot on a preceding mountain, when the peloton is still more or less together, enabling you to fill the foreground with cyclists while your main focus is on the alpine backdrop. Shots like this live on forever, long after that year's Tour winner has retired and banked his fortune and fame, and long after you yourself have stopped and banked your fortune, if not your fame.

It is important to figure out which mountain to stop on, before the racing starts to break up the peloton and ruin your shot. It's impossible for me to calculate the number of times I've had such images spoiled by misjudging the racing, or through sheer bad luck, when someone decided to attack a few kilometers

earlier. As a general rule, if the previous stage has been a leg-breaking
blockbuster, the chances are
today's will at least start more quietly; in that case, go for an early
mountain stop. If the previous day
has seen gentler racing, then go for
the penultimate climb of the day;
by the time the race reaches you,
the peloton will have regrouped
after a ferocious day in the saddle.

I often follow an escape over
the summit of a mountain, using
the opportunity to scout a suitable *virage* (switchback turn) on
the descent where I can shoot
descending shots of the overall
favorites—and most especially the
race leader—as they race in pursuit. I always wonder why it is just
I and a few wise colleagues who
are in activity on the descents.
Surely every race-following photographer has a great opportunity to get some crystal-clear
action shots, free of the worry
that a spectator or photographer's
motorcycle will get in the way. Yet
I rarely see anyone but us on these
descents and curves.

If you only try it once, you have
to take the chance to photograph
the Tour on the descent of a moun-

TOP *Thomas Voeckler, captured with a long
lens (200 mm) as he descends the Pyrenees in
2004.* BOTTOM *Official photographers lie low
on an inside corner to shoot Michael Rasmussen
in 2007.*

PHOTO TIP: If you're shooting on a descent, remember that riders start to eat as soon as they've crossed the summit. I still forget this and get angry when I focus on a top cyclist racing elegantly into view only to see his mouth is full of an apple slice or face-distorting fruit bar.

If you see some loose gravel or melting tar on a downhill bend, don't assume the cyclists will fall off for the benefit of your photography. The Tour rider on a descent is far too alert to not see or anticipate such hazards, and your shot may well be spoiled by his taking a different line through the turn.

If you are photographing the overall favorites on a descent, make the yellow jersey your first target, as he will always be one of the first cyclists to pass you. Use any preceding cyclists only as a practice run for your first shot; if you start firing off images of every one of them, your concentration will be flawed when it matters the most. Once the yellow jersey has passed, you can throw caution to the wind and see how many other stars you can capture.

tain. Consider that on an 80 km/h descent, each of the Tour's cyclists will pass you one by one, whereas on the preceding ascent, 165 of them might pedal by as one entity. Consider too, the double-edged gain of photographing the race favorites one by one, before climbing to a vantage point and getting a wide-angle shot as a large group of cyclists swoops down the descent against a stunning backdrop (remember, scenic shots are not restricted to the ascents).

If you position yourself on the inside of a bend, you can also shoot with two cameras—a long-lens shot as the cyclist approaches the bend, then a wide-angle shot on the bend itself. And if you do this on a second mountain stage, you can position yourself on the outside of a bend to get a different perspective. Just take the precaution not to stop on the first corner you get to; cyclists need a few kilometers to spread out on a descent. Also be aware that on cooler days, even in July, cyclists often put on warm tops for the descent, obscuring their jerseys and race numbers. So if the weather forecast hints at cooler air in the mountains, you may want to save your descending shots for another time.

Only official photographers get on the road at the Arc de Triomphe, but spectators on the outside of the turn can get superb images if they have a long lens (70–200 mm or more).

PARIS

Home at last—well, almost! You're in Paris, you've photographed the Tour all over France—in the mountains, on the plains of Provence, and among the ravines of the Cévennes. What more is there to do?

First thing is to decide where you're going to shoot the final stage. The Champs-Élysées is the only logical place, seeing as the Tour usually ends with about ten laps of the long circuit. But you still have to choose between the top end at the Arc de Triomphe and the lower end at the Place de la Concorde—or anywhere in between, for that matter.

If you've signed up with one of the official Tour operators, you have a reasonable chance of a good seat at the Place de la Concorde, where a huge grandstand gives you a view up the Champs-Élysées toward the Arc de Triomphe. From there, you can take shots of the Tour as it enters the circuit, and again when it exits the Champs-Élysées at high speed. That's a particularly good place

TOP *The victorious CSC team in 2008. The Arc de Triomphe is a great place to enjoy the closing hours of racing, with or without a camera.* BOTTOM *The peloton races onto the Champs-Élysées. This is a shot that can be taken from a grandstand reserved for premium-paying clients in the Place de la Concorde.*

Carlos Sastre savors his moment of victory in 2008. This shot was taken from the ground amid official photographers and mingling tourists.

to be if you have a very long, super-telephoto lens (400 mm or more) that allows you to close in on the eventual Tour winner and his teammates as they lead the way across the cobblestones. You may not be allowed down onto the roadway itself, but your view from an elevated position is still worth a lot.

Most photographers prefer the top end of the avenue, where the race does a massive U-turn in front of the Arc de Triomphe. If you have managed to get there early enough—and some avid spectators camp out all night near the finish line to get a clear view—you have probably found the best place to take pictures.

At this point, whether on the right-hand side as the cyclists climb the gentle ascent to the top of the

PHOTO TIP: Security is tight in Paris, and even the Tour's accredited entourage find themselves under scrutiny from the city's police force. But there is a place where the public can get close, right after the race is over, at the point on the Place de La Concorde where the team cars have to divert to where their buses are parked on the Avenue Gabriel. The road is kept open for the cars, but the security forces cannot cope with the aftermath of the Tour, when fans, families, and well-wishers swamp this area. Sneak in there with your camera, and you might get some intimate shots of the stars, right after they've finished.

avenue or on the left-hand side as they turn to go back down, you can get a clear view of the race action, as well as the last-lap scramble by sprinters' teams, and the final farewell as each team carries out a complete lap of honor. Each team assumes an official pose at the top end of the circuit, making this area a place of great atmosphere when the Tour is finally over.

The Champs-Élysées is a very wide avenue, and a long lens is required to get satisfactory action shots, but the cyclists do ride close to the barriers as they climb and descend, so even a compact digital camera will afford you some clear images. When choosing your spot behind the barriers, repeat your prologue thinking by working out where the cyclists will turn into the corner, and where they'll exit on the way out (the way in affords a slightly better angle, I think). VIP and sponsors' grandstands make it hard for the weary Tour follower to get anywhere near the finish area one-third of the way up the avenue, but if you have decided to see the final stage on that part of the circuit, you might be able to get close enough to find a good view of the final awards ceremony.

AFTER THE TOUR

Your Tour is over. You can go back to your Paris hotel and relax—perhaps take a nap, take a shower, and prepare for another mid-evening dinner. In Paris, all the world's great cuisines are at your beck and call, and you may feel tempted to go for an Indian, Chinese, Thai, or Vietnamese alternative to the traditional French meals you've been enjoying for the past few weeks. But have you downloaded, edited, and transmitted today's images yet? If you were really serious about your photography, you'd do this before entertaining any notion of relaxing for the night.

So spare a thought for the professional Tour photographer who is probably on the twenty-third consecutive day of such postrace drudgery. Each year, the Tour arrives in Paris, and all you want to do is go and have a few beers with your mates, and a wind-down meal with your really best mates, before closing the curtains for a deep, deep sleep, not caring if you ever see another Tour de France in your life. In reality, those drinks won't touch your lips before 11 P.M., and you'll be lucky to see the inside of a decent restaurant—any restaurant—on the good side of midnight. It's been like this for the entire Tour, save for those two precious rest days and the days in preparation before the Tour start.

It is at times like this that I try to remember my predecessors, the pioneering legends on the Col d'Aubisque in 1910, the news-hungry snappers who caught Simpson's tragic death in 1967, the privileged few on Mont Ventoux who witnessed Merckx's single best effort in the 1969 Tour. I think of photographers I looked up to when I began, men like the dapper Henri Besson of *Miroir du Cyclisme*, Aldo Tonnoir of *Sport 80*, Cor Vos of *Wieler Revue*, and many, many more such characters. Would they have complained back then? Probably not!

Cycling, and the Tour de France in particular, is one of the most beautiful sports in the world, and we're all lucky to be a part of that sport. By becoming a photographer of the Tour, professional or otherwise, we all become part of the process of establishing and recording its history. This is what brings each of us back, year after year, as if missing a Tour will omit a piece of history from our lives.

The chances are that you and I, photographers both of us, missed an awful lot of great shots this July. Chances are those misses will haunt us for days, weeks, even months to come, right up to the time next July rolls around. So treat your mistakes as a learning curve, the way I treat mine—and tell yourself you're going to get it right next time.

LEGENDS OF THE MODERN TOUR

LANCE ARMSTRONG

Whether you base your opinion on his eye-opening victory of 1999, the superhuman brilliance of his 2003 victory, or the entire series of the seven Tours he won, it is almost impossible to do justice to the importance of Lance Armstrong's Tour de France reign. Seven Tours, a total of twenty-five stage wins, eighty-three days in the *maillot jaune*, as well as his countless efforts to win more—Armstrong's dominance places him at the very top of the league of Tour winners, beyond even Eddy Merckx, the greatest cyclist of all time.

Armstrong's sporting record alone should be enough to establish his standing within the bigger history of the Tour's almost hundred editions. Yet the broader attraction of his involvement with the Tour, to my mind, makes the Armstrong legend greater still, ensuring that he can rightly stand alongside the great men who were such pivotal figures of the Tour's first century. Henri Desgrange, cofounder of the Tour, was such a fellow, as were Jacques Goddet and Felix Lévitan, the dual successors to Desgrange who together guided the Tour through its next fifty years. Jean-Marie Leblanc, general director from 1989 to 2005, owns a special place in the Tour's rich history because of his deep passion for the Tour, as well as his handling of the race through the troubled 1990s. I rate Armstrong up there with these iconic men, beyond even the athletic influences of Maurice Garin, Jacques Anquetil, Louison Bobet, Merckx, and Bernard Hinault.

When Armstrong won that 1999 Tour, the race was still in shock after the Festina drug scandal of 1998, which had sent the race's sponsors looking for the nearest exit. It

FIRST WIN   *Lance Armstrong celebrates his victory in Verdun in 1993, the American's very first Tour success.*

hadn't helped that the '98 Tour winner, Marco Pantani, had been caught cheating in the 1999 Giro d'Italia, barely one month before the start of the Tour. Armstrong was seen by most observers as the savior of the Tour.

But it was the big business that followed Armstrong's first win that had the greatest influence on the Tour. American TV came back in 2000 with more money and much greater ambitions, which benefited the Tour de France at least as much as the man who had to tough it out on his bicycle to secure his wealth. That TV interest in America spurred an even greater worldwide audience, bringing many more millions of dollars into the Tour's coffers.

Before long, there wasn't one English-speaking country in the world that didn't broadcast the Tour live, and as Armstrong's tenancy grew and grew, countries in the Far East and Middle East joined the West by buying into the Tour's potency. Armstrong, not the Tour, was their prime motivation, his battle against cancer and subsequent triumph in the Tour a marketable attraction. But the Tour saw a massive gain as well.

Race and team sponsors suddenly had their corporate image brought to a truly worldwide audience, while new sponsors came rushing to France to grab whatever opportuni-

CELEBRITY MAGNET *Arnold Schwarzenegger with Armstrong in 2003.*

ties were left. With those sponsors, many of whom were attached to Armstrong or his team, came an entourage such as the Tour had never before seen. Private jets flew into France's regional airports each day, to be met by a fleet of Tour-registered helicopters, which would then fly the VIP guests over the racing peloton to enjoy a summit stage finish. Those same guests would then be whisked away to a suitably distinguished château or resort hotel in the mountains; the extra-special ones would end up dining alongside Armstrong at the team's more modest abode. Film stars became regular visitors to the race, with big names like Will Smith, Robin Williams, and Arnold Schwarzenegger wanting to rub shoulders with Armstrong.

The Tour had never seen anything like this in its life, and it was barely able to cope with the pressures and the security headaches that came with it. By the time romance had brought rock singer Sheryl Crow into the world of the Tour de France, creating an even greater media frenzy than the film stars, the race organizers had probably had enough—even though some bean counter back in Paris was deliriously tallying each dollar that had poured into the Tour's bank accounts.

What was remarkable was that Armstrong played his role to the fullest extent, winning year after year, as per the script laid out before him. Happily, it was a script that made him as much a star as any one of those Hollywood visitors.

Many of those TV networks and race sponsors have stayed involved with the Tour after Armstrong's retirement, aware that the Tour has become a magnet for viewers who'd originally switched on their televisions purely to watch the Texan race. It seems incredible that the same Tour organizers could heap so much scorn on Armstrong's achievements in France. The billions of dollars, euros, yen, and pounds earned from TV and sponsors gave the race an extraordinary wealth.

It is a wealth that has allowed the Tour to survive in these difficult years as a viable commodity, when most other sporting organizations would have declared ruination. Armstrong's potential return to the Tour in 2009 could replenish the organizers' lost income, yet even now they seem unable to muster much warmth for the former champion.

I suspect the organizers' cynicism is an orchestrated attempt to lessen the embarrassment of not having enjoyed a single French victory all these years. They insinuate that drugs were what made Armstrong so good and that not taking drugs, as they would have us believe is the norm on French teams, is the reason for a total lack of local success. If only those sad people making the accusations knew the mindset of Lance Armstrong, they'd never fall for such propaganda.

Illness in the form of cancer got in Armstrong's way a few years after he won a stage into Verdun, yet the man returned in 1999 to begin his metamorphosis into the most accomplished Tour champion of all time. I am proud to recall the good, glorious, and golden days of cycling that accompanied Armstrong's string of victories. His dedication to training, along with his super self-confidence, is what won him those seven Tours de France.

Many people ask me to pinpoint one particular highlight of Armstrong's reign. The fact is, there are too many to make that easy. I could say it was the man's audacity when he offered a cheeky wave and a smile to me while setting a record-breaking speed in a time trial stage of the '99 Tour. Or the gutsy, face-contorting effort he had to make when he blew up on the Col de Joux-Plane in 2000. It might be the playacting scene on stage 10 of the 2001 Tour, the day Lance fooled most people, including me, into thinking he was dead meat, only to then attack Jan Ullrich at Alpe d'Huez and take one of his most spectacular stage wins. The next year, 2002, can only be remembered for the total dominance of his easiest Tour victory, whereas 2003 was, without doubt, his toughest.

Perhaps 2003 is the best memory: Armstrong winning after a tumultuous three weeks when he'd been far from his best, yet was still tough enough to hold off Ullrich. This was the Tour when lady luck smiled on Lance on more than one occasion, when a diversion across a farmer's field on an alpine descent competed for jaw-dropping drama with a spectacular crash at the foot of Luz Ardiden. The rain-soaked time trial that finished that Tour has no equal in terms of nerve-racking energy. I never want to experience such tension again, and I was merely an unbiased photographer doing his job. Yes, 2003 was a Tour to remember for a long lifetime and more.

If there is one unfulfilled moment of the Armstrong years, it is that we never enjoyed a long solo effort in the mountains, the kind of effort his forebears had had to make in order to win, the kind of effort Armstrong was capable of if he'd raced in a more primitive era.

The 2004 Tour was the closest we came to seeing the Merckx that we all knew was inside Armstrong, yet instead of any long escapes, we saw a demonstration of power and ruthlessness that established Armstrong's win as the most compelling of his seven Tour victories. The American put himself in control right from the start, actually easing off to avoid winning the prologue, because he'd already put seventeen seconds into Ullrich. Armstrong and his U.S. Postal team were in a rampant mood, attacking across

Lance Armstrong in 1999, following his first Tour de France victory.   OPPOSITE   >

the cobblestones of Paris-Roubaix fame on stage 3, before annihilating their supposed rivals in the team time trial at Cambrai. Having let France's Thomas Voeckler enjoy a full week in the race lead, Armstrong tore into the Pyrenees midway through the Tour, then sprinted like a starving alley cat to win the stage and take the race lead at Villard-de-Lans. Armstrong's body language at that stage 15 finish spoke of a desire to put on a truly dramatic performance for his public, with the result that he went on to win three consecutive stages in the Alps, plus the final TT at Besançon—this after having already won on stage 13 at the Plateau de Beille. Even Merckx hadn't been able to win in such a dominating way.

It has already been several years since Armstrong retired from the sport. Yet a series of drug scandals and disqualifications at the Tours that have followed mean that his solid reign is even more prominent in our minds. I for one don't mind this vacuum at all, as it allows me to dwell a little longer on the glories of his unblemished career and take the time to appreciate what it meant to have such a special guy to work with.

Lance cast a spell over all those around him, and he was able to elicit a loyalty from his believers that was so intense it was almost scary. That same energy could be employed against any rival he chose, and I am not at all surprised that Armstrong was never bettered in those seven Tours. He had all the ground covered and plans to allow for every eventuality should it be necessary.

It would be no exaggeration to say Armstrong literally took over the Tours of 1999 to 2005, monopolizing the event to the extent that he eventually made enemies of the organizers. He was a champion cyclist, for sure, and a champion of the hundreds of thousands of people who flocked to the roadsides of the Tour each July to watch their man perform.

Until today, the Tour has been a much smaller, quieter, and perhaps duller affair without Armstrong. It is a Tour that has owed much of its continuity to the man who came back from the dead to secure his own personal place in history. With Lance now racing the 2009 Tour in his incredible comeback year—even if he doesn't race it to win—I'll be one of the most avid observers. It'll be as if he never went away in the first place. And he just might win it, too!

MENU DECODER

abbachio: young lamb.

abricot: apricot.

acajou: cashew nut.

affiné: matured, aged (of cheese).

agneau: lamb.

> **carré d'agneau:** rack of lamb.
>
> **côtelettes d'agneau:** lamb cutlets or chops.
>
> **agneau de pré-salé:** lamb raised on the salt marshes of Normandy and the Atlantic coast, the flesh of which has a delicately salted flavor.
>
> **épaule d'agneau farcie:** stuffed lamb shoulder.
>
> **gigot d'agneau:** leg of lamb.
>
> **navarin d'agneau:** lamb stew with vegetables.
>
> **agneau de Pauillac:** specialty of the region, with a slightly salty taste.

agnelle: baby ewe lamb.

aiglefin: small haddock; also called *églefin*.

aigre: bitter, sour.

aigre-doux: sweet and sour.

aiguillette: a long, thin slice (usually chicken, duck, or goose breast; may also be meat or fish).

ail: garlic.

aile: wing (of poultry).

aillé: with garlic.

aïoli: garlic mayonnaise; a specialty of Provence, served with fish or vegetables.

algue: seaweed.

aligot: a dish from the Auvergne; mashed potatoes, often seasoned with garlic, blended with melted *tomme*, a kind of cheese.

alose: shad.

alsacienne, à l': in the style of Alsace; usually with sauerkraut, sausage, or foie gras, simmered in wine.

amande: almond.

amuse-bouche: appetizer before serious meal.

ananas: pineapple.

anchoïade: an appetizer dip of puréed anchovies with garlic and olive oil; from Provence, usually served with raw vegetables or toast rounds.

anchois: anchovy, the best coming from Collioure in Languedoc.

ancienne, à l': in the old style; usually a dish with meat and vegetables in cream sauce, or cooked in red wine.

andouillette: sausages made from tripe; a Provençal dish, best served grilled.

anglaise, à l': in the English style; usually means plain or boring.

anguille: eel.

> **anguille au vert:** eel poached in a green herb sauce with shallots, onions, spinach, mint, thyme, tarragon, parsley, chervil, butter, and crème fraîche.

AOC (Appelation d'origine contrôlée): a national standards system specifying the characteristics a wine, butter, cheese, or fruit must have and the area where it must be grown if it is to carry the name of a specific location on its label.

armoricaine, à l': in the style of Armorica (Brittany); in a sauce of white wine, cognac, tomatoes, and butter.

artichaut: artichoke.

asperge: asparagus.

assaisonné de: seasoned with.

assiette: plate.

> **assiette de légumes:** vegetable plate.
>
> **assiette de charcuterie:** a plate of cold meats, usually ham and other pork products.
>
> **assiette du pêcheur:** platter of the fisherman; fish platter.

aubergine: eggplant.

auvergnate, à l': in the style of Auvergne, with cabbage, sausage, or bacon.

avocat: avocado.

Portions of this decoder are adapted from the Patricia Wells French/English Food Glossary, available at www.patriciawells.com.

baba au rhum: sponge cake soaked in rum syrup.

baguette: long, hard-crusted loaf of white bread.

ballottine: boned, rolled, and stuffed meat, fowl, or fish.

banane: banana.

bar: sea bass; also called *loup* in the south.

barbotte: catfish.

barbouillade: eggplant stew.

barbue: a flat fish from the turbot family.

basilic: basil.

basquaise, à la: in Basque style; usually prepared with tomatoes and red peppers.

bâtard: football-shaped loaf of bread.

bavette: a skirt of steak (flank steak), often braised because of its toughness.

béarnaise: a popular steak sauce made of egg yolks, tarragon, shallots, and vinegar.

béchamel: white sauce of milk, flour, and butter.

beignet: deep-fried dough sprinkled with sugar and wrapped around a variety of desserts, fruits, or meat.

 beignet de fraises: strawberry fritter.

beurre: butter.

 beurre demi-sel: lightly salted butter.

 beurre des Charentes: fine butter from the Poitou-Charentes region.

biche: female deer.

bien cuit(e): well done.

bière: beer.

 bière blonde: light or pale beer.

 bière en bouteille: bottled beer.

 bière brune: dark beer or stout.

 lager: lager.

 pression: draft beer.

bifteck: steak.

biologique: organic.

bisque: thick, creamy soup of puréed crab, crayfish, lobster, or shrimp.

bistrotier: bistro owner.

blanc de volaille: chicken breast.

bleu: cooked rare (blue), usually of steak; also the name for a variety of cheeses.

boeuf: beef.

 boeuf à la mode: cubes of beef marinated and braised in red wine, served with carrots, onions, and mushrooms.

 boeuf bourguignon: beef stew with red wine, onions, mushrooms, and bacon.

 boeuf Charolais: high-quality beef from Burgundy.

boisson: drink.

 boisson (non) compris: drink (not) included.

bonbon: candy.

bordelaise: in the style of Bordeaux; may refer to a red wine sauce of shallots, mushrooms, thyme, and bone marrow.

boudin blanc: white sausage of veal, chicken, or pork.

boudin noir: pork blood sausage.

bouillabaisse: Mediterranean fish stew. Typically includes at least three local fish—*rascasse* (scorpion fish), *Saint-Pierre* (John Dory), and *galinette* (gurnard), and sometimes *lotte* (monkfish), *dorade* (bream), or *turbot*—cooked in a broth of water, olive oil, onions, fennel, garlic, tomatoes, parsley, and saffron. Langoustines (see below) are added in expensive restaurants, but they are not part of the original recipe.

bouillon: stock or broth.

boulangère, à la: in the style of the baker, which originally meant any dish baked in the oven; today it generally refers to potatoes and onions cooked with meat in a stock.

boule: large, round loaf of bread.

boule de Lille: Mimolette cheese; a hard, round cheese produced near the city of Lille.

boulli: boiled.

bourgeoise, à la: in bourgeois style; with carrots, onions, braised lettuce, and diced bacon.

bourguignonne, à la: in the style of Burgundy; often with red wine, bacon, onions, and mushrooms.

brandade de morue: puréed salt cod with milk.

bretonne, à la: in the style of Brittany; a dish served with white beans or bean purée; may also refer to a white wine sauce with carrots, leeks, and celery.

bretzel: a large pretzel with a soft, doughy center; a specialty of Alsace.

brioche: unpretentious, buttery, egg-enriched yeast bread served at breakfast.

brochette: cubes of meat or fish and vegetables on a skewer.

brocoli: broccoli.

brouillé: scrambled, usually describing eggs.

brut: very dry or sugarless, particularly used in reference to champagne.

buffet froid: variety of dishes served cold, sometimes from a buffet.

cabillaud, dos de: the back of a codfish; also called *dos de morue* in southern regions.

cabri: young goat, kid.

cacahuète: peanut.

Caen, à la mode de: in the style of Caen, a town in Normandy; a dish cooked in Calvados and white wine and/or cider.

café: coffee.

café au lait: espresso with warmed or steamed milk.

café décaféiné: decaffeinated espresso.

café express: espresso.

café noir: black espresso; same as *express*.

café serré: extra-strong espresso, made with half the normal amount of water.

caille: quail.

cajou: cashew nut.

calmar: small squid, usually served in batter.

Calvados: a famous (and very potent!) apple brandy from Normandy.

camomille: chamomile herbal tea.

campagnard: literally, country-style, rustic; used to describe an informal buffet of cold meats, terrines, and the like.

campagne, à la: in country style.

canard: duck.

cannelle: cinnamon.

câpre: caper.

carafe d'eau: pitcher of tap water; served free with all meals in France.

caramélisé: caramelized; cooked over high heat to brown the sugar.

carbonnade: braised beef stew with beer and onions.

carotte: carrot.

carpe: carp; a freshwater fish.

carré: rib or loin.

carré d'agneau: rack of lamb.

carré de porc: pork ribs.

carré de veau: loin of veal.

carte: menu; *à la carte:* dishes to be selected individually, not as part of a set menu.

casseron: cuttlefish; tiny sea creature from the family of octopus and squid.

cassis, crème de: black currant liqueur; used with champagne to make *kir royal.*

cassolette de: a small casserole of something.

cassoulet: popular meat stew of white beans, cooked with combinations of duck, goose, lamb, mutton, pork, and sausages.

céleri: celery.

cèpe, cèpe de Bordeaux: applied to several species of edible wild mushroom, especially porcini.

céréale: cereal.

cerf: male deer.

cerise: cherry.

cervelle: brains of calf or lamb.

champignon: mushroom.

chanterelle: yellow-orange, fruity wild mushroom.

chapon de mer: Mediterranean fish, in the *rascasse* (scorpion fish) family.

charbon de bois, au: charcoal-grilled.

charbonnade: charcoal-grilled beef or horse meat.

charcuterie: pork products cured with a preservation process that allows such meats as bacon, ham, sausage, and patés to age with greater flavor than if they were refrigerated. Generally offered as an appetizer, or as a light lunchtime meal.

chasseur: literally, "hunter"; used to describe a white wine sauce with mushrooms, shallots, tomatoes, and herbs.

châtaigne: chestnut.

chateaubriand: thick fillet or rump steak; often served with sautéed potatoes and a rich sauce of white wine, beef stock, butter, shallots, and herbs.

chaud(e): hot, warm.

chaud-froid: roasted fish, meat, or poultry coated with a cream sauce while cooling.

chausson: a turnover, such as a *chausson aux pommes* (apple turnover); may also have a savory filling.

cheval: horse meat, a delicacy for French meat lovers when served *tartare* (raw).

chèvre: goat.

chèvre, fromage de: goat's-milk cheese, often served hot in *salade de chèvre chaud.*

chicon: endive.

chiffonnade: ribbons or strips of leafy green vegetables.

chipiron: a small squid from the southwest coast, often cooked in its own ink.

chipolata: small, fresh pork breakfast sausage.

chocolat: chocolate.

chocolatine: croissant with chocolate filling.

chou: cabbage.

chou de Bruxelles: Brussels sprout.

choucroute: sauerkraut; famous dish from Alsace.

chou-fleur: cauliflower.

cidre: hard cider.

citron vert: lime.

claire: oyster placed in salt-marsh oyster beds, called *claires*, to fatten up before it is sold; *fine de claire* indicates a longer, two-month spell at sea.

cochon: pig.

cochon de lait: suckling pig.

coeur: heart.

colin: hake, an ocean fish related to cod; known as *merluchon* in Brittany, as *merlan* along the Mediterranean.

complet: full restaurant; no room for more customers.

compris: service included; *non-compris:* service not included.

concombre: cucumber.

confiserie: candy, sweets, confectionery; a candy shop.

confit: pieces of duck, goose, or pork cooked and preserved in their own fat; also fruit or vegetables preserved in sugar, alcohol, or vinegar.

confit de canard: preserved duck.

confiture: jam.

consommation: literally, "consumption"; drinks, meals, and snacks available in a café or bar.

consommé: clear soup or broth made from beef or poultry.

contre-filet: beef sirloin roast.

coq: rooster.

coq au vin: rooster cooked in a wine sauce, with mushrooms and garlic.

coque: cockle; a tiny clam-like shellfish.

coque, à la: served in a shell.

coquillage: shellfish.

coquille: shell.

coquille Saint-Jacques: breaded and sautéed sea scallops with lemon juice, pepper, butter, and garlic, baked and served in their own shells.

coriandre: coriander.

cornichon: a gherkin, or small pickle.

côte d'agneau: lamb chop.

côte de boeuf: rib-eye steak.

côte de veau: veal chop.

côtelette: thin chop or cutlet of meat.

cotriade: a fish stew from Brittany, usually made of conger, mackerel, mullet, whiting, leeks, butter, and potatoes, often served over toasted French bread.

coulis: vegetable or fruit purée.

courge: yellow squash.

courgette: zucchini.

couscous: popular North African dish of steamed wheat, with broth, vegetables, and lamb or chicken.

couvert: a place setting, including dishes, silver, glassware, and linen.

crabe: crab.

crème: cream.

crème anglaise: light egg-custard cream.

crème brulée: rich custard dessert with a topping of caramelized sugar.

crème caramel: vanilla custard with caramel sauce.

crème de cassis: black currant liqueur.

crème catalane: creamy anise-flavored custard from southern Languedoc.

crème chantilly: sweetened whipped cream.

crème fraiche: thick, sour, heavy cream.

crêpe: thin pancake; served covered with a variety of sauces, hot chocolate and orange liqueur being the most popular.

creuse: crinkle-shelled oyster, sometimes called rock oyster; long and thin but tasty.

crevette: shrimp.

crevette grise: tiny shrimp that turns gray when cooked.

crevette rose: shrimp that turns pink when cooked.

crique: potato pancake from the Auvergne.

croissant: flaky, crescent-shaped breakfast roll made with puff pastry and butter.

croque-madame: toasted ham and cheese sandwich with a fried egg on top.

croque-monsieur: toasted ham and cheese sandwich with no egg.

croquette: sausage-shaped fried roll of ground beef, fish, or vegetables cooked in egg and potato and covered with breadcrumbs.

croûte: crust.

en croûte: food cooked in the crust, that is, enclosed in a pastry shell.

cru: raw.

crudité: raw vegetable, as in *plat de crudités.*

crustacé: crustacean, usually lobster or crab.

cuisine bourgeoise: home cooking, or dishes in that style.

cuisine campagnarde: country cooking, or dishes in that style.

cuit(e): cooked.

bien cuit: well done.

très cuite: charred (for meat).

cure-dents: toothpick.

darne: a rectangular portion of fish filet, or fish steak; best-known kind is *darne au saumon* (salmon steak).

daube: a beef, lamb, or mutton stew with red wine, onions, and tomatoes; specialty of many regions, particularly Provence and the Atlantic coast.

daurade: sea bream.

décaféiné: decaffeinated coffee.

dégustation: tasting, sampling, as in *menu-dégustation* (tasting menu) in restaurants.

déjeuner: lunch.

petit déjeuner: breakfast.

demi: half.

demi-bouteille de bière: half-bottle of beer.

demi-bouteille du vin: half-bottle of wine.

demi-glace: very rich, concentrated stock of beef, lamb, or duck, usually used to thicken a lighter sauce.

demi-sec: semi-dry; used to describe wines or champagnes, but also some food dishes.

demi-sel: lightly salted butter.

demoiselles de Cherbourg: small lobsters from Cherbourg, cooked in a court bouillon and served in their cooking juices.

dieppoise: in the style of Dieppe; usually, with white wine, mussels, shrimp, mushrooms, and cream or cider.

digestif: after-dinner drink, such as Armagnac, Calvados, cognac, or marc.

dijonnaise: in the style of Dijon; usually, with mustard.

dinde: turkey.

diner: dinner; to dine.

dos: back; also, the meatiest portion of the fish.

douceur: candy.

doux (douce): sweet.

dur: hard, as in *oeuf dur*, hard-boiled egg.

duxelles: minced mushrooms and shallots sautéed in butter, then mixed with cream.

eau: water.

eau gazeuse: carbonated water.

eau minérale: mineral water.

échalote: shallot or sweet-tasting onion; sometime seen as *échalotte* on menus.

écrevisse: crayfish.

églefin: small fresh haddock, a type of cod; same as *aiglefin*.

elzekaria: Basque bean and cabbage soup.

émincé: thin slices, usually of meat (*émincé de boeuf*).

enchaud: pork tenderloin with garlic; specialty of Dordogne.

entier, entière: whole, entire.

entrecôte: rib steak.

entrecôte maître d'hôtel: rib steak with sauce of red wine and shallots.

entrée: first course.

épaule: shoulder of lamb, mutton, pork, or veal.

épice: spice.

épinard: spinach.

escalope: thin slice of meat or fish.

escargot: snail.

escargot de Bourgogne: snail baked with butter, garlic, shallot, and parsley.

espadon: swordfish.

espagnole, à la: in Spanish style; a dish usually made with tomatoes, peppers, onions, garlic, and rice.

estouffade à la provençale: beef stew in the style of Provence, with onions, garlic, carrots, and orange zest.

estragon: tarragon.

étoffé: stuffed.

façon de, à la: according to the custom of, in the style of.

faisan(e): pheasant.

farci(e): stuffed.

faux-filet: sirloin steak.

favorite d'artichaut: classic vegetable dish of artichoke stuffed with asparagus, covered with a cheese sauce, and browned.

fenouil: fennel.

fermé: closed.

fermier: farmer; as an adjective, describes farm-made products, such as cheese, free-range chickens, milk.

feu de bois, au: cooked over a wood fire.

ficelle: thin loaf of bread.

ficelle picarde: thin crêpe wrapped around a slice of ham and topped with a cheesy cream sauce; specialty of Picardy.

figue: fig.

fines herbes: mixture of herbs, usually chervil, parsley, chives, and tarragon.

flageolet: small white or pale green kidney-shaped dried bean.

flamande, à la: in Flemish style; usually with stuffed cabbage leaves, carrots, turnips, potatoes, and bacon.

flammekueche: specialty of Alsace; a savory tart with a thin crust, covered with bacon, cream, and onions; also called *tarte flambée.*

flet: flounder.

flétan: halibut, caught in the English Channel and North Sea.

fleur de sel: fine, delicate sea salt, from Brittany or the Camargue.

florentine, à la: in Florentine style; made with spinach and cream.

flûte: loaf of bread, similar to a baguette but shorter and wider.

foie: liver.

foie blond de volaille: chicken liver.

foie gras de canard: liver of fattened duck.

foie gras d'oie: liver of fattened goose.

foie de veau: calf's liver.

fond d'artichaut: the artichoke's heart and base.

fondue: melted cheese (usually gruyère, comte, or beaufort), cooked in an earthen pot. There is also a meat dish called *fondue bourguignonne*; cubes of meat are boiled in a buttery oil and flavored with dipping sauces.

forestière, à la: in the style of the forester; with a garnish of wild mushrooms, bacon, and potatoes.

fougasse: a crusty bread associated with Provence but available everywhere; generally includes olives, cheese, anchovies, and onions, like the Italian focaccia.

four, au: baked in an oven; usually describes pizza, but may be sausages or beef.

frais (fraîche): fresh.

fraise: strawberry.

framboise: raspberry.

fricassée: fricassee, typically using white meats, with the ingredients braised in wine sauce or butter with cream added; a modern variation uses fish in the place of meat, and is served on a bed of rice.

frit(e): fried.

frites: french fries.

friture: deep-fat frying.

froid(e): cold.

fromage: cheese.

fromage blanc: a smooth low-fat cheese similar to cottage cheese.

fruit confit: whole fruit preserved in sugar.

fruits de mer: seafood platter, usually a mix of shellfish and sardines.

fumé(e): smoked.

galantine: pressed meat, served cold.

galette: a round flat pastry, typically from Brittany, on which are spread savory sauces or sausages or chicken; like a crêpe, but drier.

gamba: large prawn.

garniture: garnish.

gâteau: cake.

gâteau basque: a pastry crust filled with black cherry preserves or pastry cream.

gâteau suisse: cheesecake.

gaufre: waffle.

gésier: gizzard; gizzard of chicken or other poultry is considered a delicacy.

gigot: leg of lamb or mutton.

gigot brayaude: leg of lamb studded with garlic, cooked in white wine, and served with red beans, braised cabbage, or chestnuts.

gigot de pré-salé: a leg of lamb from a sheep grazed along the coast of Normandy, the flesh of which has a delicately salted flavor.

gingembre: ginger.

glace: ice cream.

glacé: iced, crystallized, or glazed.

glaçon: ice cube.

gourmand(e): a person with a weakness for good food, all kinds; applies to most French people and discerning visitors!

gousse d'ail: clove of garlic.

goût: taste.

graisse: fat, the noun.

grand crème: milky coffee; enjoyed by many French instead of café au lait.

grand cru: top-ranking wine.

gratin: crust formed on top of a dish when baked or broiled; also the name of the dish itself.

gratin dauphinois: baked casserole of sliced potatoes with butter, milk, cream, and cheese.

gratin savoyard: baked casserole of sliced potatoes, with butter, Swiss cheese, and beef stock or bouillon.

gratinée lyonnaise: a version of onion soup made with chicken stock, caramelized onions, and a baked cheese crust.

gratinée à l'oignon: onion soup.

gratuit: free.

grecque, à la: in Greek style; cooked in seasoned mixture of oil, lemon juice, and water.

grenade: pomegranate.

grenouille, cuisses de: frogs' legs.

grillade: grilled meat.

grillé(e): grilled.

gros sel: coarse salt.

haché(e): chopped or minced.

hareng: herring; a salty fish found in the Atlantic and the English Channel.

haricot blancs à la Bretonne: white beans in a sauce of onions, tomatoes, garlic, and herbs.

haricot vert: green bean, usually fresh; probably the most commonly used vegetable in French cuisine.

haute cuisine: classic high cuisine, richly served.

herbes de Provence: a mixture of ground dried herbs, usually including lavender, rosemary, basil, marjoram, thyme, and bay leaf.

hochepot: a thick stew, usually of oxtail; specialty of Flanders.

hollandaise: sauce of butter, egg yolks, and lemon juice; used in eggs Benedict in the United States, but primarily served over asparagus in France.

homard: lobster.

homard à l'armoricaine (or à l'américaine): lobster served with a sauce of white wine, cognac, tomatoes, and butter. The *américaine* version uses a quicker preparation, first used by a French chef once based in New York. Few people can tell the difference these days.

homard cardinal: baked lobster with a cardinal sauce of béchamel and truffles.

hors-d'oeuvre: appetizer; hopefully the precursor to a great meal!

huile: oil.

huile de noisette: hazelnut oil.

huile de noix: walnut oil.

huile d'olive: olive oil.

huître: oyster.

île flottante: floating island; a beloved dessert that uses the whites of eggs, with sugar and vanilla extract, to create a meringue that floats on a sea of custard sauce that is often called *crème anglaise.*

indienne, à la: in the style of India; a dish with curry.

infusion: herbal tea.

jambon: ham.

jambon blanc: lightly salted, unsmoked ham, served cooked but cold.

jambon cru: salted or smoked ham that has been cured but not cooked.

jambon fumé: smoked ham.

jardinière: jardiniere; a garnish of fresh cooked vegetables.

jeune: young.

joue: cheek.

julienne: long, thin strips of vegetables, ham, or chicken.

jus: juice, gravy. Meat *au jus* is cooked in its own juices.

kascher: kosher.

kir: an aperitif made with *crème de cassis* (black currant liqueur) and most commonly dry white wine, but sometimes red wine.

kir royal: a kir made with champagne.

kirsch: wild black cherry eau-de-vie or brandy.

lait: milk.

lait demi-écrémé: semi-skimmed milk.

lait entier: whole milk.

laitue: lettuce.

lançon: tiny fish, served fried, often in salads.

langoustine: a slim, clawed crustacean of the lobster family; fast becoming a hard-to-find delicacy because of overfishing. Its tail is served as deep-fried scampi in some countries, but live, whole langoustines can be found at the best French seafood restaurants.

languedocienne: garnish of eggplant, tomatoes, and wild *cèpe* mushrooms.

lapin: rabbit.

lard: bacon.

lardons: tiny cubes of bacon, found primarily in salads.

lavaret: lake fish of the Savoie; similar to salmon.

léger (légère): light.

légume: vegetable.

lentille: lentil.

> **lentille de Puy:** green lentil from the village of Puy in Auvergne, grown in volcanic soil without fertilizer.

lieu noir: black cod; a pleasant, inexpensive fish found in the English Channel and the Atlantic.

lièvre à la royale: hare cooked with red wine and shallots, then rolled and stuffed with foie gras and truffles; specialty of the Poitou-Charentes region.

lotte: monkfish; a large firm-fleshed ocean fish.

loup de mer: sea bass.

louvine: striped bass.

lyonnaise, à la: in the style of Lyon; dish usually includes onions cooked golden and seasoned with wine.

macaron: macaroon; small cookie of almonds, egg whites, and sugar.

magret de canard (d'oie): breast of fattened duck (of goose).

maigre: thin, nonfatty.

maïs: corn.

maison, de la: literally, of the house; used to describe a specialty of the restaurant, as in *vin de la maison* (house wine), *apéritif* (pre-dinner drink), or *dessert.*

maître d'hôtel: headwaiter; may also mean the proprietor.

maltaise: orange-flavored hollandaise sauce.

mandarine: tangerine.

mange-tout: literally, "eat it all"; a snow pea.

mangue: mango.

maquereau: mackerel.

marbré: striped sea bream.

marennes, huîtres de: flat-shelled green-lipped oysters, found primarily on the west coast of France, near La Rochelle.

mariné: marinated.

marmite: a dish cooked in a small casserole.

marron: chestnut.

matignon: a garnish of mixed stewed vegetables.

médaillon: medallion; a round piece or slice of meat.

mélange: mixture or blend.

menthe: mint.

menu fixe: a set menu in a restaurant.

merguez: small spicy beef or lamb sausage.

meunière: sautéed in butter and, usually, lemon.

mi-cuit: half cooked.

miel: honey.

millefeuille: puff pastry with many thin layers.

minute, à la: quickly grilled or fried in butter with lemon juice and parsley; may also mean "prepared at the last minute."

mirabelle: a colorless fruit brandy made from yellow plums.

mirepoix: cubes of carrots and onions or mixed vegetables.

morceau: piece, small portion.

morille: wild morel mushroom; often served as an accompaniment to steak dishes.

mornay: white béchamel sauce enriched with cheese and egg yolks.

morue: fresh cod; also called *cabillaud.*

mouclade: mussel stew from Poitou-Charentes on the Atlantic coast, based on *moules marinière* but thickened with cream and flavored with curry.

moule: mussel.

> **moules marinière:** mussels cooked in white wine with onions, shallots, and butter.

mousseline: a hollandaise sauce lightened with whipped cream or beaten egg whites; also used to describe a dish with a light, airy texture.

moutarde: mustard.

> **moutarde à l'ancienne:** old-style mustard, with unground grains included.

mouton: mutton.

nature, à la: prepared in a simple, unadorned way.

navarin: lamb or mutton stew with vegetables.

navarraise, à la: in the style of Navarre; with sweet peppers, onions, and garlic.

noilly, sauce: a vermouth-based sauce.

noisette: hazelnut; also a dessert flavored with hazelnuts.

noix: nut; also, anything nut-sized, as in *une noix de beurre* (a lump of butter).

non compris: service not included.

normande, à la: in the style of Normandy; a dish of seafood or meat served with cream.

nougat glacé: classic bistro dessert of frozen whipped cream and candied fruit.

nouilles: noodles.

nouveau, nouvelle: having the characteristics of nouvelle cusine.

oeuf: egg.

> **oeuf brouillé:** scrambled.
>
> **oeuf dur:** hard-boiled egg.

oeuf de la ferme: free-range egg.

oeuf poché: poached egg.

oeufs à la neige: literally, "eggs in the snow"; a soft vanilla custard dessert served with puffs of meringue.

oie: goose.

oignon: onion.

ombre chevalier: lake fish, similar to trout.

onglet: hanger steak, or butcher's steak; a tasty but tough piece of meat found close to the animal's diaphragm and best cooked anything but well-done.

oreille de porc: grilled pig's ear.

origan: oregano.

ouvert: open.

pain: bread.

> **pain au chocolat:** croissant with chocolate filling.

> **pain complet:** whole-grain bread.

> **pain grillé:** toast.

> **pain aux raisins:** bread, most often rye or wheat, filled with raisins (raisin brioche).

palette: pork shoulder.

palombe: wood pigeon.

palourde: clam.

pamplemousse: grapefruit.

panaché: beer and lemonade; quite refreshing in summer.

panais: parsnip.

papillon: small oyster from the Atlantic coast with a creamy flavor.

papillote: cooked in parchment paper or foil.

paquet, en: wrapped in pastry, like a parcel.

parfait: a dessert mousse; also, a blend of chicken, duck, and/or goose liver.

parfum: flavor.

Parmentier: dish with potatoes.

> **Parmentier d'agneau limousin:** ground lamb topped with mashed potatoes.

passe-pierre: an edible seaweed.

pastis: anise-flavored alcohol that becomes cloudy when water is added; the most famous brands are Pernod and Ricard.

pâtes: pasta.

> **pâtes fraîches:** fresh pasta; noticeably drier than that cooked in Italy.

paupiette: slice of meat, usually veal, beaten thin and then rolled around a filling.

pavé: a thick slice of boned beef.

paysanne, à la: in peasant style; usually a dish made with vegetables and wine.

pêche: peach.

> **pêche melba:** poached peach with vanilla ice cream and raspberry sauce.

pêcheur: literally, "fisherman"; applied to various ways of preparing fish.

perche: freshwater perch.

perdreau: young partridge.

périgourdine, à la: in the style of Périgord; with a sauce containing truffles and foie gras.

persil: parsley.

petit-beurre: tea cookie made with butter.

petit déjeuner: breakfast.

petit four: tiny cake or pastry.

petit pois: small green pea.

pichet de vin: a pitcher of house wine; comes in liter, half-liter, and quarter-liter sizes.

pigeoneau: pigeon.

pilaf: rice sautéed with onion and simmered in broth.

pilchard: Atlantic sardine.

piment: hot chili pepper.

> **piment d'Espelette:** a hot pepper from Espelette, a village in the Basque region.

pimenté: hot, peppery, spicy.

pineau des Charentes: a sweet aperitif made from fortified wine from the Cognac region.

pintade: guinea fowl.

piquant: sharp or spicy tasting.

pissaladière: a white pizza (no tomatoes) or open-face tart, with sauteed onions, anchovies, and black olives; specialty of Nice.

pistache: pistachio nut.

pistou: sauce of basil, garlic, and olive oil, specialty of Provence; also a rich vegetable, bean, and pasta soup flavored with pistou sauce.

plaice: a small, flat ocean fish from the English Channel.

plat de légumes: a plate of vegetables.

plat du jour: today's special.

plateau: tray; platter of cheese, cold meats, or mixed desserts.

> **plateau de fruits de mer:** seafood platter combining raw and cooked shellfish.

poché: poached.

poêlé: pan-fried.

point, à: cooked medium rare; also, ripe, ready to eat.

poire: pear.

poire Williams: fruit brandy, or eau-de-vie, made from Williams pears.

poireau: leek.

pois: pea.

pois chiche: chickpea.

poisson: fish.

poisson de lac: lake fish.

poisson de mer: sea fish.

poisson fumé: smoked fish.

poitrine: breast of meat or poultry.

poivre: black pepper (from peppercorns).

poivron: pepper (the vegetable).

poivron doux: sweet pepper.

poivron rouge: red pepper.

poivron vert: green pepper.

pomme: apple.

pomme de terre: potato.

pomme de terre vapeur: steamed or boiled potato.

porc: pork.

carré de porc: pork loin.

côte de porc: pork chop.

porc rôti: roast pork.

porto, au: with port.

potage: thick soup of puréed vegetables.

potage Parmentier: potato soup.

pot-au-feu: literally, "pot on the fire"; beef simmered with vegetables, with the stock served first as a soup and the meat and vegetables as the main course.

poulet: chicken.

poulet de Bresse: high-quality chicken from Rhône-Alpes.

poulet fermier: free-range chicken.

poulet au pot: whole stuffed chicken stewed with vegetables; specialty of the city of Béarn in the southwest.

poulet rôti: roast chicken.

poulpe: octopus.

praline: caramelized almonds.

printanière: dish served with fresh spring vegetables.

prix fixe: literally, set price; a fixed-price menu.

prix net: service included.

profiterole: a classic French dessert; usually a puff of pastry filled with vanilla ice cream and topped with hot chocolate sauce.

provençale, à la: in the style of Provence; usually cooked with olive oil, garlic, tomatoes, and olives.

pruneau: prune.

quatre-épices: four-spice blend of ginger, nutmeg, white pepper, and cloves.

queue de boeuf: oxtail.

quiche: baked eggs and cream in a pastry shell.

quiche lorraine: quiche with bacon and cheese bits.

quiche aux poireaux: leek version of quiche lorraine.

quiche d'asperges: asparagus version of quiche lorraine.

raclette: cheese scraped from a block and melted in front of a grill, served with boiled potatoes, small pickles (*cornichons*), and onions; popular in Switzerland and Savoie; also the name of the cheese.

ragoût: meat-based stew; also the name of the sauce used to cover noodles in France.

raie: skate, or ray.

raisin: grape.

rascasse: scorpion fish; an indispensable ingredient of bouillabaisse.

ratatouille: specialty of Provence; a cooked dish of eggplant, zucchini, onions, tomatoes, peppers, garlic, and olive oil, served hot or cold, and without the film-star mouse.

raviole de Royans: miniature ravioli filled with goat cheese; from the Rhône-Alpes.

rémoulade: sauce of mayonnaise, mustard, capers, herbs, anchovies, and gherkins (*cornichons*).

repas: meal.

rhubarbe: rhubarb.

rhum: rum.

ris d'agneau (de veau): lamb (veal) sweetbread.

riz: rice.

riz blanc: white rice.

riz brun: brown rice.

riz sauvage: wild rice.

rognon: kidney.

romarin: rosemary.

roquette: rocket, or arugula, a spicy salad green.

rosbif: roast beef.

rôti: a roast; roasted.

rouget barbet: red mullet.

rouille: a sauce of olive oil, garlic, chili peppers, and breadcrumbs; usually served with fish and fish soups, such as bouillabaisse.

roulade: slice of meat or fish rolled around a stuffing; also, a rolled-up vegetable soufflé.

royale, à la: served with truffles and a cream sauce.

rumsteck: rump steak.

safran: saffron.

saignant(e): cooked rare; of meat, usually beef.

Saint-Hubert: a sauce of crushed peppercorns with chestnuts and bacon.

Saint-Pierre: John Dory, a mild white ocean fish; also called *poule de mer.*

salade: salad.

    salade composée: mixed salad.

    salade de crudités: salad of chopped raw vegetables.

    salade lyonnaise: green salad with frisée or endive lettuce, bacon, and poached egg; specialty of Lyon.

    salade niçoise: salad with tomatoes, green beans, anchovies, tuna, potatoes, black olives, capers, artichokes, and sliced hard-boiled egg.

    salade russe: mixed diced vegetables in strong-tasting mayonnaise.

    salade verte: green salad.

salé: salted.

sandre: perch-like river fish, found in the Saône and Rhine regions.

sang: blood.

sanglier: wild boar.

sanguine: blood orange.

saucisse: small fresh sausage.

    saucisse chaude: warm sausage.

    saucisse de Francfort: hot dog.

    saucisse de Toulouse: mild pork sausage.

saucisson: a large, dried sausage, such as salami, served cold.

    saucisson chaud: fresh hot sausage.

    saucisson à l'ail: garlic sausage, usually served warm.

    saucisson de Lyon: long, dried pork sausage flavored with garlic and pepper.

saumon: salmon.

sauté: browned in fat.

savoyarde: in the style of Savoy; usually flavored with Gruyère cheese.

sec (sèche): dry, or dried.

sel: salt.

    sel gris: unbleached sea salt.

    sel gros: coarse salt.

    sel marin: sea salt.

selon grosseur (S.G.): according to size or weight (menu term).

selon le marché: according to what is in season (menu term).

service compris: service included in the bill.

serviette: napkin.

sommelier: wine steward.

soufflé: light, fluffy baked dish made with egg yolks and whipped egg whites.

soupe: soup.

    soupe au pistou: vegetable soup with pesto, beans, and pasta.

spécialité de la région: regional specialty.

steak: beef steak.

    steak au poivre et pommes frites: pepper steak and french fries.

    steak-frites: classic dish of grilled steak served with french-fried potatoes.

    steak tartare: raw ground steak mixed with onion, raw egg, salt, pepper, parsley, and capers.

sucre: sugar.

suprême: a sauce based on a chicken velouté and thickened with cream.

table d'hôte: private home that serves fixed meals and often has guest rooms as well (*chambres d'hôte*).

tagine: spicy North African stew of veal, lamb, chicken, or pigeon, with vegetables.

tapenade: a blend of black olives, anchovies, capers, olive oil, and lemon juice, sometimes with rum or canned tuna added; specialty of Provence.

tartare: raw ground steak mixed with onion, raw egg, salt, pepper, parsley, and capers.

    tartare de poisson: a popular highly seasoned raw fish dish.

tarte Tatin: upside-down apple tart with caramelized apples.

terrine: meat, poultry, or fish, baked into a pâté in a casserole or earthenware dish and served cold.

    terrine de canard: duck pâté.

tête de veau: head of veal; more precisely, pieces of the calf's face; not for the faint-hearted.

thé: tea.

thon: tuna.

> **thon rouge:** bluefin tuna.

thym: thyme.

tomate: tomato.

> **tomates à la provençale:** baked tomato halves sprinkled with garlic and breadcrumbs.

tomme: a cheese from Provence and the Alps.

tournedos: thick slice of juicy beef.

> **tournedos Rossini:** sautéed tournedos with foie gras and truffles.

traiteur: caterer, delicatessen.

tranche (tranché): slice (sliced).

truffe (truffé): truffle (with truffles).

truite: trout.

> **truite aux amandes:** sautéed trout with crème fraîche and almond sauce.
>
> **truite meunière:** floured trout fried in butter.
>
> **truite saumonée:** salmon trout; a trout with pink flesh.

turbot: flatfish from the Atlantic and Mediterranean; a small turbot is called a *turbotin.*

vache: cow.

vanille: vanilla.

vapeur, à la: steamed.

varech: kelp.

veau: veal.

végétarianisme: vegetarianism.

velouté: a velvety sauce prepared with a light chicken, veal, or fish stock and thickened with a roux of butter and flour.

> **velouté d'huitres:** velouté of oysters.
>
> **velouté de volaille:** velouté of chicken.

verdure: green vegetables.

> **en verdure:** garnished with green vegetables.

viande: meat.

vichyssoise: cold, creamy leek and potato soup.

viennoise: coated in egg, breaded, and fried.

vin: wine.

> **vin blanc:** white wine.
>
> **vin doux:** sweet wine.
>
> **vin rouge:** red wine.
>
> **vin sec:** dry wine.
>
> **la carte des vins:** wine list.

vinaigre (vieux): vinegar (aged).

vinaigrette: oil and vinegar dressing.

volaille: poultry.

vol-au-vent: puff pastry shell.

waterzooi: literally, "watery mess" (in Dutch); Flemish soup, with eggs and vegetables to make the broth. It can be made with chicken (*waterzooi de poulet*) or fish (*waterzooi de poissons*). Variations include cooking in beer or wine.

yaourt: yogurt.

FRENCH CYCLING TERMS

Abandon: To quit the race.

Arc-en-ciel: Literally, "rainbow"; the rainbow jersey of the world champion.

Ardoisier: The chalkboard man on a motorcycle who conveys time splits to the riders; usually a passenger on the only bright yellow motorbike in the race.

Arrivée: The finish line.

Arrivée en altitude: Mountaintop finish.

À la danseuse: Literally, "like a dancer"; standing on the pedals when climbing.

Attaquer: To attack from the front of the race on an escape.

Autobus: The group of riders who stick together in the mountains so that they do not finish outside the time limit.

Benjamin du tour: The youngest rider in the race.

Bidon: Water bottle.

Bonification: Time bonus.

Caravane publicitaire: The publicity parade that precedes the race.

CG: See *Classement génerale*.

Chasseurs: Literally, "hunters"; the chasers in pursuit of a breakaway.

Chute: A crash.

Chute massif/collective: A crash of multiple cyclists that has probably blocked the road.

Classement générale: General classification; the overall standings in the race. Abbreviated as "CG" in results sheets.

CLM: Abbreviation for *contre-la-montre* (time trial).

Coéquipiers: Teammates.

Col: Mountain pass.

Commissaire: A race official who enforces the rules.

Contre-la-montre: Literally, "against the clock"; a time trial.

Contre-la-montre par équipes: Team time trial.

Costaud: A hard man; a tough, strong, sturdy rider.

Coureur: Rider.

Crevaison: Flat tire.

Décrocher: To fall off the back of the peloton or be left behind by stronger riders.

Départ: The start line.

Départ réel: The real start of a stage. In most cities and villages, the stage starts with a ceremonial procession to let the riders warm up and get safely outside the city limits. The real start is signified when the Tour director waves the white flag.

Défaillance: When a rider runs out of gas; the bonk. See also *fringale*.

Descendeur: A cyclist who specializes in descending fast.

Directeur sportif: The team's road manager.

Domestique: Literally, "domestic servant"; the teammates who ride in support of the team leader.

Dossard: Race number on a rider's jersey.

Doubler: To pass another rider.

Échappée: Escape, breakaway.

Équipe: Team.

Étape: Stage of the Tour.

Flahute: A tough Belgian bike racer (slang).

Flamme rouge: The red pennant that signifies one kilometer to go.

Fringale: Raging hunger. A rider suffering total collapse from lack of food is said to have had a *coup de fringale*.

Grimpeur: A good climber, one who does well in mountain stages.

Hors délais: Finishing outside the time limit.

Lacet: Switchback turn on a mountain.

La course en tête: To lead a race from start to finish.

Lâcher: To drop a rider from the group.

Lanterne rouge: Literally, "red lantern," as on the caboose of a train; the rider in last place in the general classification.

Maillot à pois: The polka-dot jersey worn by the leader of the mountain points competition.

Maillot blanc: The white jersey worn by the best young rider (under 25) in the general classification.

Maillot jaune: The yellow jersey worn by the overall leader.

Maillot vert: The green jersey worn by the leader of the points competition.

Mécanicien: Team mechanic.

Médecin: Race doctor; follows the race in the second car behind the peloton.

MT: *Même temps*, or same time; an abbreviation used in race results.

Musette: A shoulder bag containing food and drink, handed to the riders as they pass through the feed zone.

Palmarès: A rider's list of victories and significant results.

Parcours: The race course.

Patron: The boss of the peloton. Bernard Hinault was the modern prototype.

Pavé: Cobblestones.

Peloton: The main group of riders.

Poursuivants: A group in pursuit of a breakaway; see *chasseurs*.

Prix de combativité: "Most aggressive rider" competition; the leader wears a red race number.

Profil: The profile, or topography, of a stage.

Ravitaillement: Refueling; taking on food in the feed zone.

Remorqueur: Literally, "tugboat"; a rider who pulls at the front.

Rond-point: A roundabout or traffic circle.

Rouleur: A rider who is strong on the flats, turning over a big gear.

Routier: A road racer.

Soigneur: A team staff member who takes care of the riders with massage, food preparation, handing up musettes in the feed zone, handling baggage, and so on.

Souvenir Henri Desgrange: Prize given to the first rider over the highest summit of the Tour.

Suceur de roue: A wheelsucker.

Tête de la course: The head of the race; in the lead.

UCI: Union Cycliste Internationale, the international governing body of cycling.

Vainqueur: Winner.

Vélo: Bicycle.

Virage: A turn or bend in the road; also see *lacet*.

Voiture balai: The broom wagon that sweeps the rear of the course, picking up riders who have abandoned the race.

Voiture neutre: Neutral support car; in the Tour they are bright yellow, sponsored by Mavic.

Voiture pilote: The gendarmerie command vehicle that precedes the head of the race convoy.

Zone de ravitaillement: The feed zone.

INDEX

ABOUT THE AUTHOR

GRAHAM WATSON has devoted his celebrated career to the art of cycling photography. His renowned work has been published in magazines, books, newspapers, posters, calendars, journals, and Web sites on every continent, and his reputation is founded on 31 years' experience photographing the great cycling races of Europe, North America, Australia, and Asia. He has covered the Tour de France each year since first seeing it in 1977 as a tourist, traveling today both within the Tour press corps and on his own to scout the best vantage points for his unique photography.

An oenophile and gastronome, Graham has collected an extensive library of information on the best restaurants, hotels, bistros, brasseries, bars, and auberges of France, which he shares in this insider's guide to the world's greatest bicycle race. As the most experienced photographer still shooting the Tour, Graham dedicates a chapter to professional advice, providing unparalleled insight for camera enthusiasts aiming to capture the race in their own photographs.

On those rare days when he's not on location shooting a race, Graham makes his home in Hampton, England.